Up on
America

A Worldview and Investment Guide for Every American

By
Richard Catts

To America:

Let's all get on the same page…

Get the facts straight…

Acknowledge what we have achieved…

Remain proud of our heritage…

Know the challenges that lie ahead…

And then dream.

"I'd just like to say to the American people that I have every confidence that this economy will recover, and recover in a strong and sustained way. The American people are among the most productive in the world. We have the best technologies. We have great universities. We have entrepreneurs. I just have every confidence that as we get through this crisis, our economy will begin to grow again, and it will remain the most powerful and dynamic economy in the world."

—Ben Bernanke,
Chairman of the Federal Reserve Board of the U.S.
June 7, 2009, *60 Minutes* interview (CBS)

For my wife, Ann,
my two daughters,
Melanie and Madeline,
and my friends and family

Table of Contents

Education

Worldviews

Globalization

Acknowledgments

This book is about the new order of the world and how the United States is uniquely positioned to thrive and lead the global economy. The book is derived from a formulation of beliefs in my twenty-five years of investment management, in addition to twenty-five years of education, including degrees at the master's level and beyond, teaching at the MBA university level, committee meetings, and presenting to clients. Much of the research for this endeavor has pulled together information from various sources, including both public and private, constantly seeking the most updated thinking related to economics, investment markets, and the state of the world economy. Most of the information assembled here has been selected to make a point and there is obviously another side to every story. However, this is one side of the story that doesn't seem to be well known.

The genesis of this book was developed during the financial crisis of 2008, when after an investment presentation, I would challenge the audience to discuss the state of our country and our position in the world. Despite the overwhelming negative commentary of the media, we went on to un-cover many great aspects and attributes of our country. Many industry specialists in one business did not know of the great market position we had in another. It is from these interactions with business leaders that I uncovered many of our core strengths as an economy. After thousands of presentations, interacting and communicating with CEO's, CFO's and COO's of different industries, viewpoints and opinions, these themes became fully developed. A good idea will remain just a theoretical construct until it is communicated to another person to provide a structure for feedback and opinion.

It would be impossible to thank everyone who has shaped my worldview and investment beliefs during my life. I am an impressionable person and my imagination is both my best friend and my worst enemy. I must thank the many people who took the time to explain things to me, as that time has been returned many times over to others I have touched. First, to those with whom I have worked, including Jim Lyons of PIMCO, John Brummett of Julius Baer, Jim Durocher of Eaton Vance, and Stuart Shaw, world traveler. To the two most remarkable salespeople that I followed at Regent, Larry Sinsimer and Joe Staskiew. To Phil Sloan, who hired my firm in 1990 and has been a dear friend ever since. We have exchanged many an investment idea and worldview over the years.

To Chuck Widger and John Coyne at Brinker Capital for their friendship and job networking for me. For Wolf, Webb, Burk and, Campbell (R.I.P.) for hiring me in 1987 before the crash and teaching me that the true value of an investor is patience. For Steve Borowski of Met West, for finding a place for me at Pally-Needelman because of my sense of humor. For Bill Taylor of Regent, who desperately needed me to raise billions and billions of dollars and I complied. To the three CIOs at Regent who taught me the world of investments: Harold Stein, Gene Lancaric, and especially Catherine Wood—thank you! Mike Delfino, thanks for hiring me.

Every idea had to bubble up from somewhere and the advisors with whom I have worked over the years deserve much credit for helping me verbalize, correct, and expand the investment ideas that I have used. From Morgan Stanley Smith Barney, Mark Axelowitz and Todd Kauffman, Ron Vinder and Ken Gunsberger, and Tom Seiler, who always had time for my visits. From Merrill Lynch, the list is long but includes: Audrey Kurtzman, Janine Craane, Bill Thompson, Gersh Trimpol, Woody and Kelly Griffiths, Bruce Vivino, John Parisi, Paul DeRosa, Arnie Plonski, and Jeff Cave. From UBS, my good friends Jim Chin, Joe LaFerla, and all the former Paine Webber associates whom I have known over the years. Also from Raymond James, the legendary Arthur Rosenberg, and the hockey player turned advisor from his own firm, Dino Macaluso.

Writing a book is a task that I wouldn't wish on my best friend. Endless hours of writing and editing, without ever really being sure how the finished product will turn out. Getting it published, I wouldn't wish on my worst enemy. With minimum book orders needed BEFORE printing, you could end up doing more marketing for your book than the actual writing. To CreateSpace, the Amazon company, thank you for taking this project on and assisting me through the long and tedious process. To my brother Dave, for knowing the difference between a bitmap and a jpeg, and to Bob Deutsch of J.P. Morgan, thank you for reading the dreadful draft and harvesting some good ideas from mere seeds.

Lastly, thanks to my wife, Ann, whom I met at the copy machine at the Bryn Mawr Trust Company, and all of our friends there. She is a realist and brings my feet back to earth, making me a better, more grounded person. She was a fantastic investment trader and can still remember phone numbers from two decades ago. She went though each page of the draft, word by word, never changing the ideas, just the grammar. To my daughters, Melanie and Madeline, who show me what is really going on in the world. If you don't have teenagers at home, rent a few for the weekend. They could educate you how to multi-task, text message and put pictures on Facebook. Finally, to my dog, Rocky, who shows me what really matters...not much besides love, affection, food, a good afternoon nap and playtime.

Foreword

Everyone today has responsibility over their investments, either through a self-directed 401K, an IRA, or just advising other members of their family. People need to understand investing and how difficult it is to "pick stocks," as even the professionals make a great deal of mistakes. Instead, you can outperform the markets by paying attention to what is happening in the world, investing in overall trends, and making the right choices for broad asset classes, not chasing individual securities. This is where the individual investor may have an advantage over the institutional investor who may not have the flexibility to deviate from benchmarks within a long-term horizon.

This book will seek to make complex issues simpler and more understandable for the general reader. We have come through the largest financial crisis since the Great Depression and it is important to know what happened and what the repercussions are for our country. Ideally, it will help Americans feel better about the country in which we live and point us in a new direction.[1]

We are experiencing a rapidly changing world economy and an innovative thrust from faster calculation and information flows. America is well positioned to take advantage of these trends. In fact, we may be the best-positioned developed economy due to our highly responsive market-based system. We are the "information economy" and have adopted new technologies quickly in the past. The future will be even faster. The wealthy countries will continue to enjoy ever-higher living standards. We are and will be the "haves" of the world and need to strive to help the "have nots" because the chasm will get larger between us. The larger this difference becomes, the greater the chance of social unrest.

The United States is a world leader and will remain so for many decades, if not centuries, to come. We are an innovator in many key industries that are essential for global growth and prosperity, and we need to continue to provide the structure for constant innovation and technological change.

What is leadership? Does it mean being the biggest? The most dominant? The authoritarian ruler? No, not by a long stretch. Leadership is about creating a way for people to contribute to a common goal. According to Jules Masserman, an American psychoanalyst, leaders must fulfill three functions: provide for the well-being of the led, provide a social organization in which people feel relatively secure, and provide a set of beliefs.[2] There is nothing here about directing or ordering people, but that's usually what we think when we hear the term "leader."

Leadership is about listening as much as about talking. It is about understanding what everyone in the team has to do in order to direct the team toward goals and properly allocate resources. More importantly, though, a leader evaluates people and provides feedback about who they are and what they are capable of.[3] A leader then motivates people to do their best. A true leader can lead by example and actions. There are "born leaders," and those who have been thrust into leadership situations, but all of us have to work at it. It is not a science that we can download; it is an art of dealing with people and motivating them. Teddy Roosevelt once said, "The most important single ingredient in the formula of success is knowing how to get along with people."

So who defines who the leader is? It's in actions, not words. In sports, we have leaders, like Derek Jeter, Lebron James and Peyton Manning. If you looked up the statistics for these individuals, there may be many others who may surpass their paper achievements, but their team is substantially better because he or she is there. The quarterback is not the most physical, nimble, or necessarily smartest player on the field, but he is the most important in that he makes everything run. In every play, the quarterback touches the ball. The players look to him to lead and set the tone, execute plays, and determine strategies for winning. It is the makeup of a man or woman that determines their leadership qualities, not just the physical characteristics or their records of achievement. What sets these people apart is motivation and attitude. It can't be measured by tests or statistics. It can only be measured by judgment.

Who is the leader in business throughout the world? Things get a little bit more confusing when trying to compare and contrast companies in different countries, sectors, and industries. There are no clear leaders in the field of general business; however, there are many experts, outstanding in their own fields, who contribute to total business knowledge. This is an important point in that no one individual has all-encompassing knowledge about all things having to do with the world's businesses, and that's the point of market economies. But if you had to define leaders, you would come up with names like Warren Buffett of Berkshire Hathaway, Bill Gates of Microsoft, Jack Welch formerly of GE, Jamie Dimon of JP Morgan, and Alan Mulcahey of Ford. You would want to have individuals such as these lead by committee, to draw on each other's own individual experiences, rather than have one lead alone. The team would be better than any one individual. The way a team plays as a whole determines its success. "You may have the greatest bunch of individual stars in the world, but if they don't play together, the club won't be worth a dime," so said Babe Ruth. And he should know a little about it.

Is Coca-Cola a leader? How about Nike? Intel? Home Depot? Absolutely. These companies are thought of as leaders in their own particular industries. But are they the largest producers in their industries? Maybe not. So much of what a large company actually sells today is a joint venture of many companies coming together for a common purpose. It is the final sale that usually determines where the bulk of the profits will reside and who will get the headlines. As the manufacturer of the state-of-the-art Dream Liner 787 jet, Boeing draws from many manufacturers from different countries throughout the world, assembles the planes in the U.S., and reaps the majority of the profits. All the suppliers compete for these coveted orders and force their pricing to the bone in order to get the sale. This technological feat, unprecedented in its size and scope, has thrust Boeing to the forefront in aviation.

In energy, where large companies look bigger than countries, Royal Dutch Shell takes the gold medal for sales of $450 billion[4]. Exxon Mobil would take the top spot for profits of $45 billion. Petro China could take the top spot for market value, depending on the day, with upwards of $300 billion in market value. You see, it's a difficult exercise to determine who the leader is.

Just as in business, there are many ways to measure an economy. Country gross domestic product (GDP) measures are good for an estimate of final sales of goods and services, but not completely accurate in accounting. GDP doesn't measure things like barter transactions, cash payments, and the underground economy. It doesn't measure quality of life, freedom, and the ability to vote, either.

The United States has been an extraordinary world leader in an extraordinary time. From about the time Isaac Newton sat under an apple tree, America has been the world's rising power and a force with which to be reckoned. There have been other countries in world history with such a position, but not for a period of time like this. From the Industrial Revolution to the invention of the computer, the United States has dominated the world economy like no other. How have we done this? Through innovation, government initiatives, venture capital, our melting pot, small business, a "can do" work ethic, and many other facets of our free market-based society. It's been a wonderful ride. But it's not over. In fact, it may just be beginning.

The innovative spirit of the entrepreneur and markets is inherent in our culture and it may be what propels us faster through change than any other country in the world. Markets work how humans do. The small stuff of life works with each separate individual cell being somehow linked in to the happenings throughout the body. Each cell contributes and knows about the whole. The world should be structured the way life is. Yes, we have a brain and bloodstream, but it's the combination of all parts that make us function. Where would we be without eyelashes? Blind! Every part plays a part.

The only thing constant is change. The Internet has accelerated this. History as a guide isn't much use because, today, people and markets adjust so much faster than they ever did. Consider that only a decade ago, many of today's companies did not exist. Twenty-five years ago, there were few laptops and cell phones. Fifty years ago, we saw the launch of the personal computer, air conditioning, the jet, the microwave oven, and the robot. Fifty years! Humans have walked the earth for how many years? Two million? The last fifty years represents 0.0025 percent of man's history. It's the blink of an eye in a long day. What will happen in another blink? Don't expect a simple, straight trend line upward. Change is accelerating and bending the trend line upward.

Not only are we inventing faster, computers are taking over the functions of people: ATMs, 800-number phone calls, surveillance, automobile diagnostics, trading in financial markets, etc. Computers think a million times faster than people. With innovations in technology, rapid change will spread across all sectors of the economy, affecting every industry, every person, and every cell.

America is in a leadership role in adapting to change. Our market-based economy will enable disruptive innovative change to be identified, tested, prototyped, marketed, and serviced faster and more efficiently than government policies. America's markets have so dominated the world in the past 200 years that it is unprecedented in human history. Markets, however, need to be policed. We are moving at a high rate of speed and policy makers must watch the dials and windshield to avoid potential disasters. Some civilizations in the past have led the world for a longer time but, eventually, disruptive change led to their decline. It is going to be very important to learn from past mistakes quickly because policy failures today will have more widespread and rapid effects. However, we are humans and will make mistakes. We need to be prepared for them. We need to be proud of what our fathers and forefathers have achieved in the past, but understand how the world is changing and adapt.

Change is all around us! Letters are giving way to e-mails. The publishing business is rapidly transforming itself to the web. People will not pay big money to have an old-fashioned newspaper delivered to their door when they can get it for free on-line. Some magazines are closing down for good. Hard line phones are declining. People want mobility and phone companies no longer want to maintain the wires in the ground. These are just some of the changes today. What about those coming tomorrow? Biotechnology will expand lifetimes, computer chips will assist your memory, automobiles will drive themselves, and your refrigerator will not only choose your menu but prepare your food.

From the rise of Google, to Facebook, to Twitter, the Internet is pushing more information into the hands of more individuals than ever before. You can reach a million people instantly with a little ingenuity—a billion, if you're lucky enough to have the right video or say the right sound bite. We are responding positively to this new access. People want to creatively contribute and not be told exactly what to do. They want to be heard. Information flow is empowering people. It is making "bottom-up" decisions more efficient and effective as more people participate. It is threatening the "top-down" government directives, CEO letters, and expert opinions. You have to be careful what you say because one mistake and it's all over the Internet—tonight! This power is increasing. It's where we are going. It's who we want to be. Power to the people!

But what of the changes that we can't foresee? What about the changes that are not positive? How will humans react to challenges and conflicts? Those are known unknowns. Now more than ever, an individual on this planet has to be able to adapt. It is about change and how you can react. Education should be focused on change and how to respond to it. Traditional systems of support are essential to provide comfort and stability in our lives, but they need to change with the times, too. Yes, if we live in the past, we are doomed to repeat it.

What of the unknowns? There are many things that cannot be predicted but are life-altering. How will we cope with these? It depends on how we have prepared for the future: by digging into old ways of doing things, or by accepting what is inevitable and going with the flow.

We must completely understand the new order of the world to understand how to change. In fact, we must see what is coming and act accordingly. We need to be appreciative of how great a country this is. Many immigrants to the U.S. will tell you, if you just let them. The United States of America will continue to be a world leader in many key industries and shine like a beacon in many important ways for the world to follow. It's not about who is biggest or baddest; it's about who can direct intellect and energy to where it is needed and gain cooperation of the group toward a common goal. That's what we do best! We need to act like a leader in this new multi-polar world. We are not the center of the universe, just a leader of the world.

We should be proud of the history of our country, but be understanding of other views and people and realize that the world is changing—and that we need to invest in that change now.

∞ ∞ ∞

Introduction

A recent Pew Foundation poll found Americans quite depressed. 44% now say that China is the world's top economic power, whereas only 27% say it's the United States. (This is down from just two years ago, when 41% thought the United States was the number one economic power, and only 30% thought it was China).[5] Let's get the facts straight. The United States is the largest economy in the world by at least a factor of two, depending on currency adjustments. The United States leads the world in intellectual capital, value-added manufacturing, entrepreneurship, and technological innovation. The U.S. model of market-based systems is based on information and computation that have, in the past, and will, in the future, be superior to top-down decision-making in socialist-based economies. And the best is yet to come! The trend lines of growth in human knowledge are accelerating. Societies that are able to grasp and assimilate the changing information base will progress further and faster than those that choose to fight modernization. We want to change! Most Americans want to do better, want to push the envelope, and want to provide a better life for our families. We are in a unique position in history to lead.

By some measures, the United States will lose its leadership position in several areas, which is entirely expected considering our population, but this does not mean that we will lose our leadership in everything. In fact, there are many more industries in which America's leadership will continue for decades, if not centuries, to come. Granted, data can be tortured to say anything that you want, but the point of this book cannot be refuted. The developed world is moving from a physical world to a mental one. Since cavemen invented fire, most human challenges have been physical, whereas, today, the tipping point is changing this balance toward mental challenges and solutions to physical problems. Our computational and measurement abilities are the force behind this change and as we expand technological innovation, we also expand human knowledge.

What has changed in the world? The question really is: What hasn't changed? Picture yourself waking up in bed one morning. The alarm is ringing hours *before* your regular wakeup time. You look over at your partner and don't recognize who it is. You hurry to the bathroom and end up walking into a closet. You're lost! Your schedule was changed, you have a new partner, and the house in which you live is now foreign to you. You see, the world woke up on September 16, 2008, the day after Lehman Brothers failed, the largest bankruptcy in U.S. history, and the perilous rescue of Merrill Lynch and AIG. The world had a new schedule, partner, and structure. The world order was already changing before the cataclysmic turn of events. However, the perception of the economic system in which the world economy operates would be changed forever.

The markets would fail—not just become inefficient. They would fail, with various experts telling us, in quotes, "I told you so." Many of these experts had been calling for apocalyptic falls for years. What was unexpected was that the majority of experts got it so completely wrong. Many of the so-called "active" investment managers were fully invested throughout the decline. Our whole belief structure in how efficiently markets can allocate resources has been shaken. It makes sense that if markets are based on individual decisions, at times they will be inefficient. I mean we're talking about people!

So the world woke up to a new schedule. Asia and the Middle East woke up much earlier than Europe or the United States, and began to exert their newfound influence throughout the world. A new global partner was taking over as government actions and guarantees followed the financial turmoil. In the meantime, the framework of basic economics was being challenged. The movement toward more market-based economies around the world came to a screeching halt. Socialist policies were resurrected to save the day. The concept of efficient markets was not only questioned but ridiculed. But is this an ending or a beginning?

It is a fact that even though the United States is growing, it is becoming less of a percentage of the world economy. It is a fact that the U.S. dollar accounts for most of the transactions around the world, but will account for less as other currencies and currency baskets take more shares. These two trends, a decline in the U.S. share of the total world economy and the share of world transactions in dollars, are very long-term. They began when we were born, and will continue for our lifetimes and maybe our children's lifetimes. These trends simply mean the world is growing around us. No longer are we the dominant force that we were...and that might make us better. A little competition never hurt!

Let's say that you were the oldest child of what eventually would be a very large family. As the oldest child, you would have tremendous responsibility and leadership for the direction of your siblings. As life progressed in your family, some of your siblings grew up to be smarter or stronger or faster than you. Your leadership style may evolve to this new dynamic. Your management becomes more mental as problems and challenges become more difficult to solve and need

cooperation and Interaction. The United States is one of the siblings

cooperation and Interaction. The United States is one of the siblings
of the world, but certainly not the oldest. It surpassed the United
Kingdom many decades ago, which, before that, passed its other siblings: France, Germany, Holland, and Spain. This, in turn, took the
baton from Italy and Greece, who had taken the leadership role from
Egypt, who took it from China, Japan, Mesopotamia, or Iraq. You see,
there has been a great evolution of leadership in the world throughout human history. The fact that the United States may not be the
largest economy in the world at some point in the future does not
mean it will lose a leadership role. All former world leaders and their
countries are well worth listening to for their expertise, experience,
and point of view.

Too many people with whom I meet and too many news stories suggest that our country is in a state of decline—that Americans
are lazy, stupid, self-obsessed, and being overtaken by the rest of the
world. Most of us are not! If you look at the facts, the United States
is the world leader in many key industries. We can't be the best at
everything, but we are where it counts! We are a hotbed of creativity,
invention, research, innovation, and ingenuity. Just look around.

Consider:

- Education—The United States is the world leader in education. Seven of the top ten universities in the world are right
  here in the United States. Ever run into someone who came
  to America to be educated? I have. Although our primary education network does need evaluation, our higher education
  colleges and universities are well run, profitable, and world-

renowned. The professors at these educational institutions must "publish or perish," and in so doing, push the limits of their specialized fields further. Nobel Prize winners? Over 300 of them were American.

- Technology—When you say "technology," world investors look here. Dell, Microsoft, Google, Amazon, Qualcomm. We are the leader in technology! Nine of the top fifteen technology companies in the world are here in the U.S. We invented the personal computer and the Internet, and know how to use it. Just ask my two teenage daughters; actually, you'd better text them—they respond to that quicker than a call to our home phone.

- Health care—Much has been said about the state of health care in the U.S. How about drug discovery? Eleven of the top twenty-five drug companies are based in the U.S. We mapped out the human genome and are using that research to discover a plethora of new drugs every day. Ten of the top fifteen biotech companies are researching new drugs right here in the U.S. Amgen, Genentech… They are as big as Pfizer and Merck!

- Entertainment—That's something we know how to do! We entertain the world with movies, books, cable networks, music, and 100 different news channels, as well as Time Warner, Disney, Viacom, CBS, and GE. People in other countries of the world tune in for our daytime TV. Imagine that! And sports… we know sports. We invented a few of them, too!

- Agriculture—We feed the world. The U.S. leads the world in food exports: wheat, cotton, beans, etc. Ever take a drive across our plentiful country? There's lots of land for more planting, too. With the emerging consumer in the developing world upscaling their menus, this is a *growth* business!

- Consumer goods—Ever been to a mall on Saturday? It's our national pastime. Guess who wants to be like us? The rest of the world. We're exporting the Mall of America to Istanbul, Dubai, Red Square. Five of the top ten consumer companies in the world are here and many more want to be here! Shop 'til you drop!

- Venture capital—We have the largest pool of capital willing to be spent on risky, yet provocative, new ideas. Billions and billions of dollars. Not just from Gates and Buffett, either. No government in the world would think of spending money on some of these projects, but we have people here who are ready to reinvest their hard-earned wealth in America and create the American dream.

- Brands are recognized throughout the world as a value. Fifteen of the top twenty-five brands and fifty-two of the top 100 are American. From Coca-Cola to Microsoft, and IBM to General Electric, the United States dominates the creation of value through name awareness. Of the twenty-five largest companies in the world, half of them are in the United States, with Exxon Mobil, Wal-Mart, AT&T, and Procter & Gamble among the top ten.

- Space exploration—First on the Moon, first robot on Mars. Last time I checked, we are the only ones with a plane that can fly into space, too. What do we do it for? To boldly go where no man has gone before—and to make a profit from all the discoveries along the way: from telecommunications, barcoding, cordless tools, miniaturization, ceramics, and plastics to those fancy pens that write upside-down!

- Small business accounts for half the jobs in the country. Why? Because we know how to create businesses, look for profit opportunities, and work together as a team. We are not standing around waiting for instructions; we're making it up as we go. Just like the Olympic men's swimming four-by-100 free relay in Beijing, we pull together and bring out the best in one another. It's the American way.

Ingenuity, entrepreneurism, innovation, creativity…these are all American words. It's our lifeblood; it's in our DNA. America was born out of liberty, free speech, independent thinking, the right to assembly, and sheer determination. It's what created the light bulb, automobile, microwave, MP3 player, GPS, ATM, cell phone, and a few other things we don't make anymore because there's no profit in it.

Where else in the world would an aspiring singer named Michael Jackson rise to such power and fame? And where would a young man named Tiger Woods be able to make $1 billion playing a game? Success sometimes comes from failures and we have plenty of them, too. We are not afraid to fail; it's also part of the American way. But we pick ourselves off the mat and try again. No loss of pride. No shame. We love people who have turned their lives around. One was just president.

When I grew up in the 1960s, my family, like many others, had one TV in the house. Today, my house in the suburbs of Philadelphia has seven, not including the portable one. However, TVs will soon be irrelevant. The actual TV very well may become a thing of the past as computers and mobile broadband bring video just about everywhere. Why be fixed down to the anchor of a wire coming out of the wall when anyplace, anytime, you may, with your fingertips, access streaming video, or a three-dimensional hologram where you can not just watch, but see through the eyes of the batter as the pitcher delivers the ball? The family room will be the home theater room and once again homes will end up having but just one TV, although it will be like a movie screen. When was the last time you got a new cell phone or computer? It's probably every three years or less. To which kind of media will my children's children have access? I can only dream.

As long as our democracy is not radically altered, and tax rates remain low, we will continue to lead and be the most important economy in the world for decades to come. There is no real immediate alternative to America's leadership. Europe and the evolving European Union, which is still forming its government and policies, will be our strongest ally, but not the only global leader. Europe is still a collection of countries with different viewpoints, not unified states. Japan, most recently the second largest economy in the world, is struggling with its leadership position. It has been caught in a battle for status quo resulting in minimalist policies and incremental change. China, which recently surpassed Japan as the second largest economy in the world (more about that later), needs decades to open its economic, financial, and political systems so that they are transparent to the world. This is something that the Chinese culture will not do rapidly. Slow, steady, predictable, incremental change is more the mode of market evolution in China. America's leadership role will be somewhat offset by these other world powers and the rising leaders, but not eliminated.

Likewise, there is no alternative at this time to the U.S. dollar as the global currency. The Euro, the second largest currency in transactions across the world, is still in its infancy and is still including or excluding countries within European borders. Although the euro has made great progress from the diverse, complicated currencies of the many states of Europe, it is still under a period of great transition. Recently, the World Bank and the international monetary fund have begun work on a global combined currency. Called Special Drawing Rights, or SDRs, these units are a combination of all major currencies in the world and could one day be called a global currency. This baby was just born. It will be decades before governments of the world would have the confidence to place substantial assets in these units. So the United States will be "big brother" for a while longer, in fact about as far as the eye can see.

We have a leadership role in the world, which means we have to be less obsessed with what happens here and more understanding of what happens overseas. We can embrace this leadership role and show the world how to lead by incorporating multicultural viewpoints and listening to alternative suggestions. We cannot continue down our path of pro-American policies for all in the world, in a kind of "one-size-fits-all" structure. Every person in every country in the world stands in relation to others.

The Pew study found that about half of all Americans think the United States should "mind its own business internationally and leave it to other countries to fend for themselves" and that America should "go its own way in international matters, not worrying about whether other countries agree with us or not." [6] To the contrary, as a leader of the world, we need to understand other countries' and cultures' viewpoints and incorporate them within our worldview. We are the world's police force but need not involve ourselves in every minor conflict, and when we do get involved, we need a majority of world countries behind us. We should not go our own way because, in a sense, that would make us weaker. America needs to be as interconnected and coordinated with the world as any other country, maybe more so. We are the beacon of rights and freedom for people around the world, and the hope for the billions of impoverished.

There are several things that need to be done: We need to determine which products can be provided by the marketplace and which need to be driven by public policies. We need to understand housing, unemployment, and the interplay of securitization in the recent market bubbles. The future of capitalism rests on our analysis. We need new financial regulation that does not put together a patchwork of prior agencies where issuers of securities can choose who regulates them. We need to address our deficit—both of them: fiscal and trade. These are monumental challenges, but the history of the world is riding on them. Where should we start? Why not with our strengths? And they are many!

Capitalism is at a crossroad, where free markets have lost the confidence of people. Government regulation is on the rise. Computers, now trading faster than humans, can create daily price movements that are volatile, based on complex mathematical relationships and not what the daily news tells us. It's people who created this mess. In fact, it's the basic human tendencies of fear and greed that created the panic of 2008: The Great Recession. Economics is playing a more important role in the movement of capital than ever before. Experts are trying to predict the direction of markets after the Great Recession. But economics as we know it has changed. Alternate theories incorporating behavior and psychology are now defining market movements. Game theory, which takes into consideration random, unpredictable events, is probably more accurate in describing market actions than the magic of the "invisible hand." Governments and regulatory authorities will need to implement new rules that will change the way business is conducted. Financial tools need to be altered to better prevent the miscalculation of risk. It is, however, confidence and trust that need to be restored.

The world is in a highly unpredictable state, with large money flows distorting even the most liquid markets and the massive governmental monetary stimulus making up for the equally large loss of private activity. How governments choose to react to these events will be especially important in the coming decade. Because of the never-ending escalation of technological innovation that we have experienced, the *next decade* may feel like the last hundred years. One hundred years ago, you rode your horse to town and bartered with the corn grown on your property for the wheat you needed to make bread. Times have changed a lot in a hundred years.

Which type or combination of economic systems will be most adept at assimilating new information, creating new technologies, and fostering entrepreneurial activities to bring new ideas to market? Will it be those economies that are centrally planned? Will it be more market-based solutions? Or will it be a mixture of the two, but in what combination?

ᖇ ᖇ ᖇ

1. The American Dream

*"To think that a once scrawny boy from Austria could grow up to become
the governor of California and stand in Madison Square Garden to speak
on behalf of the president of the United States, that is an immigrant's
dream. It is the American dream."*

—Arnold Schwarzenegger[7]

The American dream, a term first coined by James Adams in 1931, is the idea that citizens feel they can achieve a "better, richer, and happier life" in America. The idea of the American dream is the ability to search for higher levels of social acceptance and wealth. The right is rooted in the Declaration of Independence, which states that "all men are created equal." It's up to you what you do with it. Citizens have certain "inalienable rights including life, liberty and the pursuit of happiness." The ideal is that anyone can rise to a level of power and prestige, like our current president.

The American dream is often is used synonymously with home ownership, as this is the first goal to which most people aspire in their lives. Homeownership was achieved by about forty-four percent of all families in 1940, and reached almost seventy percent in 2004.[8] The peak in homeownership was partially due to aggressive mortgage lending practices, but in the four decades before, it averaged around sixty-five percent.

The dream also includes the opportunity for one's children's to grow up and live a better life than their parents. Economic growth has resulted in rising incomes for most taxpayers. From 1996 to 2007, median incomes of all taxpayers increased by almost twenty-five per-cent, after adjusting for inflation.[9] The income mobility of individuals was considerable, with roughly half of the taxpayers who began in the bottom quintile moving up to a higher income group within ten years. The chart below shows the percentage change in median income for each income group, with the lowest being the poorest. That group saw close to a doubling of income.

Income Mobility in the U.S.

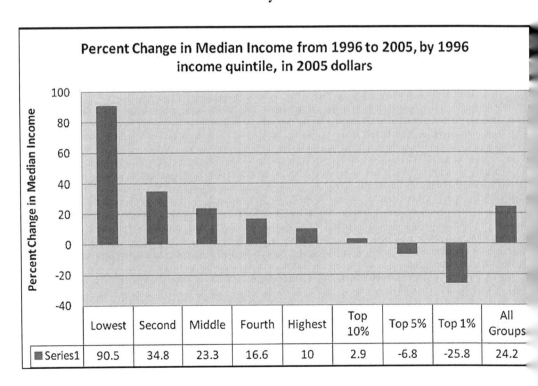

Percent Change in Median Income from 1996 to 2005, by 1996 income quintile, in 2005 dollars

	Lowest	Second	Middle	Fourth	Highest	Top 10%	Top 5%	Top 1%	All Groups
■ Series1	90.5	34.8	23.3	16.6	10	2.9	-6.8	-25.8	24.2

Report of Department of the U.S. Treasury, November 13, 2007
All income levels have benefited from U.S. economic growth,
but the lowest income group saw the most percentage increase.

—Source: Economistsview.com

෮ ෮ ෮

The American dream is about the opportunity to receive a solid education and make the most of subsequent career opportunities. Ideally, it is also the ability to achieve these benefits without restrictions of class, religion, race, or ethnic group. The United States has always regarded itself as a beacon of liberty and prosperity.[10] Our system of market capitalism relies greatly upon individual choice. It is common to measure economies of the world exclusively in measurable economic activity such as sales or transactions, since this is easier to measure. More difficult to measure is happiness or freedom, since these are subjective and based on moods, not hard facts. The American dream, though, ranks high in overall human ideals and aspirations.

Americans

She was born in Mississippi to unmarried teenage parents. Her mother was a maid and her father was a coal miner; they quickly broke up not long after her birth. She spent her first years living in poverty with her grandmother, who was so poor that she often wore dresses made of potatoes sacks. She was sexually molested beginning when she was nine years old and, as result, ran away from home at thirteen. At the age of fourteen, she became pregnant but her son died shortly after birth. She went on to become an honors student and was voted the most popular girl in her high school.[11]

He was born in Brooklyn and the hospital in which he was born serves as a homeless shelter today. Some critics say it is one of the worst areas in the city. After birth, his doctors kept him a few extra days in the hospital to clear his lungs of mucus. His father worked as an equipment supervisor at an electrical plant. His mother worked in banking. He was the fourth of five children. His family moved to North Carolina when he was small. He did not make his high school basketball team during his sophomore year because he was deemed too short to play at that level. He rounded out his high school career by playing baseball and football and, eventually, basketball.[12]

He was born in Bavaria to Jewish parents; his father was a school-teacher. In 1938, fleeing Nazi persecution, his family moved to New York, where he spent his high school years in upper Manhattan but never lost his heavy German accent. He suffered from childhood shyness, which made him hesitant to speak. He attended high school at night and worked at a shaving brush factory during the day. While attending the City College of New York, he was drafted into the U.S. Army, where he became a U.S. citizen. He became a German interpreter of the counter-intelligence division.[13]

He was born in Hawaii to a white mother and a black father. The two met in a Russian language class where his father was a foreign student on scholarship. They separated when he was young and his mother remarried an Indonesian student, who was quickly recalled home and the family moved to that island nation. When he was eleven years old, he returned to Hawaii to live with his maternal grandparents. Growing up, he was a witness to a variety of cultures in a climate of mutual respect, which became a critical part of his worldview.[14]

He was born in Moscow, Russia, where his family lived in a three-room, 350-square-foot apartment that they shared with his grandmother. His parents were highly educated and had already begun the long process of trying to exit the country, which was granted when he was six. They arrived in New York and settled in Maryland: "I know the hard times that my parents went through there, and am very thankful that I was brought to the States."[15] It was hard getting used to a new school, a new home, and a new language. He attended grade school and was a good student but was also taught mathematics by his father at home.

These are all great Americans who went on to become contributors to our society. Oprah Winfrey became the youngest and first black female news anchor on a national TV show. She moved to Baltimore to co-anchor the six o'clock news and began her talk show career in Chicago in 1978. Michael Jordan holds so many records in the NBA that it boggles the mind. He led in scoring for ten years, led his team to a championship six times, and, with each championship, was named the NBA finals' MVP. A two-time Olympic gold medalist, Jordan holds the record for twenty-eight game-winning shots at the buzzer! Henry Kissinger received his BS summa cum laude at Harvard College, where he eventually received his Ph.D. and went on to become a director of the Harvard defense studies program. He served as secretary of state and national security adviser under two presidents, Richard Nixon and Gerald Ford. Speaking of presidents, Barack Obama has one of the most unique backgrounds of any of our presidents, not only having interracial parents, but living in an Islamic country when he was young. He went on to become the editor of the Harvard Law review and graduated magna cum laude from Harvard Law School. Later, as a community organizer, he set up a job training program and college prep tutoring. Sergey Brin is the cofounder of Google, along with Larry Page, who summed up his company's motto with the thought of making information "universally accessible and useful."[16]

These stories are simply traditions of what is possible here, from Alex Rodriguez (born in New York by Dominican parents), Jerry Yang (the founder of Yahoo and born in Taiwan), Madeleine Albright (another secretary of state, who was born in Czechoslovakia), to Michael J. Fox (who is both a Canadian and a U.S. citizen). The United States offers opportunities like no other place in the world. It is certainly a gift to be born to the world, and certainly another gift to be born here—but if not, at least to be able to live here from being born in another country. As the book *The Millionaire Next Door* documents, more than eighty percent of American millionaires are self-made.[17] Most of the Americans on the Forbes 400 list got there through their own efforts.

In many other countries, one's future is almost preordained. Many cultures have layered social classes that are hard to breach and arranged marriages that violate the basic freedom of choice. By contrast, in America, you get to write your own autobiography. A rap music star can become a record producer. A part-time carpenter can become a major movie star. An actor can run for and become president. A college dropout can create a billion-dollar company. American parents say, "What do you want to be when you grow up?" and they really mean it because your destiny is not set; it's up to you!

It is important for people to keep an open mind. The future of society depends on it. The capitalist society is not the *end*, but it is the *means* to a better civilization. It is an important component of economic structures. This ideal of finding a vocation at which you can excel does not have to be fixed to the capitalist model. There are also socialist ideals that can be incorporated within it. The old socialist motto of "make according to your abilities and take according to your needs" is an ideal that capitalists can also follow. The American system of finding that occupation or profession that you love, and therefore doing it well, has an element of this ideal. In doing what they do best, human beings can strive to push the envelope rather than just going through the motions. A decentralized, bottom-up economy in which job choices are varied and widespread is the best structure for bringing out the best in a person.

The U.S. Economy

The United States is by far the largest national economy in the world. It is the largest in both nominal value and by an equivalent calculation, taking currencies into consideration, called "purchasing power parity." Its nominal gross domestic product (GDP) was $14 trillion in 2009, which is about three times the size of the next largest economies, Japan and China.[18] Currency exchange rates sometimes do not reflect actual value, especially in cases where the government closely regulates currency transactions. Taking valuations into consideration and translating them to a single monetary unit uses the idea of purchasing power. Trying to equate purchasing power, our GDP is almost twice that of the second largest economy, China.

Some people think that China has already passed us in GDP. It has not and will not for at least another decade or more, and that is assuming its continued high growth rate without interruption. The United States had many interruptions along the way to becoming a world power and we have seen Russia and Japan both suffer from growing pains. Market economies have corrections but avoid the larger mistakes from top-down socialist policies. As the world operates mostly in markets and China integrates more market systems, it will be more subject to market corrections. As the center of world trade, the U.S. enjoys leverage that no other country can claim.

Since the U.S. is the world's leading consumer, it is the number one market of countries all around the world. It is the top export market for more than fifty trading nations worldwide.[19] Since the U.S. is the world's top importer, U.S. dollars are used in these transactions all around the world. The stable and sound monetary policy of the United States has led to its dollars being legal tender for transactions and serving as the currency of most of the world's transactions. Some countries use the U.S. dollar as their currency, whereas others mark their currency to move with the dollar. Oil and gold are two commodities that are officially exchanged in dollars. As of today, the U.S. dollar remains the largest force in consumer and financial markets, and will probably remain so for many decades to come.

The U.S. economy begins and ends with the American consumer. Consumer spending makes up a large portion of economic activity in the United States, reaching seventy percent but averaging sixty to sixty-five percent over the past several decades.[20] The U.S. consumer is the envy of the world, as many American brand names are sold in far-off places and primitive settings. The Mall of America ideal has been exported to the rest of the world because it has been demanded by consumers there.

The United States has been one of the best performing developed economies, ranked high in competitiveness, income per worked hour, and productivity. We attract many of the world's population not only to our goods but to our shores. The U.S. attracts immigrants from all over the world and has one of the world's highest migration rates. Almost half of the people in the world are paid below two dollars per day for their labor, with unemployment rates estimated to be thirty percent or more in non-industrialized nations. The United States offers a possible escape from poverty. Many families in this country have a parent, grandparent, or relative who sailed through New York Harbor on the way to Ellis Island, passing by the Statue of Liberty. Each individual story is a rite of passage. It is part of the American dream.

America the Beautiful

The United States is rich in resources; it has a fertile farm belt, as well as some of the hottest deserts and coldest icescapes in the world. The United States is the world's third largest nation by total area, ranking behind Russia and China, and just ahead of Canada. The United Nations statistics measure the United States at 3,717,000 square miles.[21] Its unique size makes it one of the few countries in the world where the ecology could be considered "mega-diverse." The United States is home to the largest geographic and climate variety of any country in the world. Russia, the largest country in the world, has very limited area in a temperate zone, since literally all of the country is over the forty-degree parallel latitude, a line about equal with New York City and San Francisco. China, with more landmass in the temperate zone, reaches farther toward the equator, touching the Tropic of Cancer just above Hong Kong. The United States lies between these two extremes. On each side, you have the two largest oceans in the world, one gyrating northward in the East, one pushing southward in the West. The U.S. is the only major super-power with borders on **both** of the world's largest oceans. The East Coast is humid, and filled with older rolling hills and deciduous forests, whereas the west coast is drier, with treacherous mountains and a marine climate on the coast. Including Alaska and Hawaii, you experience both tropical and arctic extremes. In between the coasts, you have the bread basket of the world in the prairies and boreal forest of the Midwest. With the northern Canadian tundra and the southern Mojave Desert, the United States has a piece of everything.

The United States has 25,000 miles of waterways and 12,000 miles of coastline, putting it just behind Canada and Russia, except for island nations like Japan and Australia. There are fifty-eight national parks and hundreds of other federally and state managed parks, forests, and wilderness areas. Altogether, the government owns almost thirty percent of the country's land area.[22] Every American should be able to take a summer vacation and drive across this great land. Either top to bottom or side to side, it will take you 2,500 miles or about ten days driving 250 miles a day.

We have almost 6,000,000 miles of roadways, double that of India and triple what is currently in China.[23] We have 135,000 miles of railroad tracks, which is almost triple that of Russia and China and four times the size of India.[24] We have more major serviceable airports than any country by far with almost 15,000 or about 300 per state. Brazil, Mexico, Canada, Argentina, and Russia combined do not even have that many. China and the United Kingdom have each less than 500. With our roads and airports, we are the transportation and logistics leader of the world.

Private Sector

In 2009, the private sector is estimated to constitute about 79% of the economy, with the federal government and states accounting for 21%.[25] Whereas most individuals on the street would probably tell you that the private sector accounts for 90%+ of economic activity in this country, the truth is that almost a quarter of our country's activity is with the government. However, that is low by modern and developed market standards.

The service sector contributes about sixty-eight percent of GDP and the leading business field is trade, both wholesale and retail. The United States is the third largest producer of oil in the world, as well as its larger importer. It is the world's number one producer of electrical and nuclear energy, as well as liquid natural gas, sulfur, phosphates, and salt.[26] The U.S. is a leader in agriculture and is the world's largest exporter of food.[27]

The New York Stock Exchange is the world's largest stock exchange by dollar volume and combined market value of all domestic listed companies, totaling over $10 trillion at the end of 2009. The next largest are Britain, Japan, France, Canada, Australia, and Germany, in that order. China is ninth and Brazil is tenth. India is seventeenth and Russia is twentieth. The United States has half of the top twenty-five largest companies in the world measured by market capitalization, including Exxon, Wal-Mart, Microsoft, AT&T, Procter & Gamble, Johnson & Johnson, Berkshire Hathaway, IBM, and General Electric.[28]

Productive Americans
⊢————————————————⊣

The people of America are productive. Americans rank near the top in the percentage of the work force holding at least two-year college degrees. One hundred and forty million people were employed in the United States in 2010, of whom eighty percent have full-time jobs.[29] Most of these people are employed in the service sector, with about 15 million people employed in health care and social assistance, a leading field of employment. About twelve percent of the workers are unionized, compared to almost thirty percent in Western Europe.

The World Bank ranks the United States first in the ease of hiring and firing workers; labor mobility has been important to the growth of the American economy, as workers are able to adapt to changing conditions quickly. This makes the United States labor force of 150 million people the most flexible, adaptable, and dynamic work force in the world. In addition, over half of the work force is now women, making the percentage of working women among the highest in the world.[30]

The United States maintains one of the highest labor productivity rates, partly as a result of longer work hours throughout the year. According to the United States Census Bureau, the pre-tax median household income in 2007 was $50,000. The per capita income is not the highest in the world, but considering the diverse metropolitan cities and urban challenges, the rural population could be the wealthiest in the world.

There is considerable diversity among members of the middle class who, depending upon definitions, constitute anywhere from 25% to 66% of all households.[31] True, there are large inequalities of income and wealth in America. Europe, for example, is more equal.

Americans, though, may be more socially equal than any other people in the world. America offers more opportunity and more social mobility than any other country. Word has gotten around! The percentage of Americans who are foreign-born is 13% of our population, but nearly all Americans came from somewhere else in the past couple of centuries. America's foreign-born population of over 38 million people dwarfs the number in other countries; Russia has 12 million and Germany has 10 million.[32] China has only 4 million immigrants in a population of 1.3 billion people, which is less than a half of one percent. Japan, the second largest economy in the world, has but 2 million immigrants.[33]

Around the world, even the middle-class in some countries may lack basic infrastructure like water and sewage; public transportation may be overcrowded and unreliable, and telephone service is at times unobtainable. If you were a person who came from a poor area of an emerging country entering America, the first thing you would notice is the cleanliness of the roads, the accuracy of highway signs, the accessibility of public toilets, the reliability of telephones, and, when you bought something from a store and weren't satisfied, you could take it back! In comparison, even the poor in America have TV sets, automobiles, and microwave ovens. In America, we don't always work into old age. Seniors are incredibly vigorous in pursuing their pleasures and interests in retirement.

Globalization

The nation-state as an economic and political institution is slowly losing control over the international flows of people, goods, funds, and technology. Globalization and market-based forces have combined together to form a democratic world where buyers and sellers meet regardless of the country of origin. Capitalism has been on the rise since before America's War of Independence from Britain, and has accelerated sharply after the fall of the Berlin Wall in 1989. Of the 6 billion people in the world, most, if not all, would call themselves capitalists, except for a few rogue territories. The two competing economic systems of socialism and capitalism battled it out for many years following World War II, but it's obvious that the capitalist systems won the vote of the people. There are only a few truly socialist economies left, including North Korea and Cuba. Every day, Venezuela is moving closer toward this goal of socialism, but very few others are following.

We have socialist-capitalist economies like China, where most of the major resource allocation is made from top-down decision-making to regional planning. Japan has elements of socialist structures in its interlocking between businesses and political leaders to determine country direction and investment. Europe, for the most part, has a more market-based socialism, with government control and regulation being the norm. Among the more market-oriented societies, several countries such as Taiwan, South Korea, Australia, and Brazil have further embraced the capitalist ideal. Central governments are losing their stringent decision-making powers as more information is flowing to individual market participants to allocate resources. The interconnectivity of everyone in the world leads us to a market-based capitalist system as the most efficient, productive style of economy.

It is amazing that our country has held together through wars, famines, plagues, natural disasters, and its vast geography. This is especially true when so much of the world is breaking itself into smaller, regionalized pieces that defer to an ethnicity or culture. The diversity of world cultures is so vast with so many languages and written words; it is an example of human compassion that continues to bring the world together. While America, like all countries, has struggled with racism and cultural divisions, our country has gone further than any other society in establishing the equality of rights. Minorities in America have a higher standard of living and more freedom than many comparable people in their native countries.[34]

The United States has been a leading force in the development of the human race. We have been the "keystone" of the world economy for a century or more. Our country may not be the absolute first in one area or another, but that shouldn't cloud the fact that we are a leader in many areas of action, policies, structures, and thinking.

2.

The New Order of the World (NOW)

"No one pretends that democracy is perfect or all wise. Indeed, it has been said that democracy is the worst form of government except all those others that have been tried from time to time."

—Winston Churchill, House of Commons speech, November 11, 1947

Today there is much said about the new world order and the United States declining a leadership position. The globalization of the world has resulted in cross-border trade, in which every country does what it can do best and specializes to the benefit of its region and the world. In this new order of the world, border crossings have become less meaningful, tariffs have fallen, and the cost of communication is near zero. The costs of globalization are declining while the benefits have risen and world growth will benefit. Countries in this new order will be more successful with making friends than with the alternative of going it alone and seeing what they can achieve for themselves. The world has tried that, and it didn't work.

Did 2008 represent a turning point in global trade or just a brief step back? Global trade had increased every year from World War II. Will 2009 possibly represent the first year in which global trade has declined? Although the decline is not as severe as many experts expected from the global recession, it may the first step back from free market-led globalization. A re-analysis may be healthy in evaluating the intertwining, co-dependent markets and economies and the rules and regulations that govern them.

Globalization is affecting how economies work. Fixed assets have shifted away from the United States to their suppliers abroad. Low-cost producers around the world are, for the most part, partners in the supply chain, not competitors to U.S. multinationals. Making products is about partnering and finding the right inputs in a supply chain. It's not about vertical integration where companies try to do everything under one roof. It's "how" companies do something, not "what" they do, that will define them as old or new. Dell Computer's business model turns the old process of a vertically structured company that designs-builds-sells and turns it upside down with their sell-design-build model. First, they receive the money from a sale upfront then build a computer to specifications utilizing partner/suppliers, and then pay them afterwards. It is a collaboration of many companies working together to solve a problem for a price and profit. What a great model!

Globalization is a key driver of our economy; exports have tripled since the depths of the Great Depression, as measured by the percent of our economy. Imports have increased even more, increasing fivefold since bottoming in the 1940s. It is unmistakable that the more we interconnect and understand what everyone brings to the table, the better off we all will be. Every individual has his or her own strengths and weaknesses. Every country, area, or region does, too. As a result of free trade, profitability is returning quickly in both the developed and emerging economies. And that's the point. Globalization made the decline in 2008 worse due to the interconnectivity of failing financial systems, but it will also make the recovery quicker in the Internet age. Globalization did contract, but is in a long-term predictable trend line upward; in the short term, turbulence may be only one step back in a multiple series of steps forward.

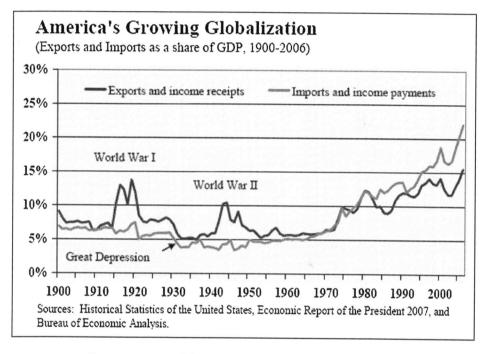

America's Growing Globalization
(Exports and Imports as a share of GDP, 1900-2006)

Sources: Historical Statistics of the United States, Economic Report of the President 2007, and Bureau of Economic Analysis.

Inter-country Trade Has Been on an Increasing Growth Trend since World War II.

(Source: CSA.com)

The stage has been set and the forces have been unleashed to further connect the globe. Once you have offered farmers, who used to live in shacks and work in fields, a clean dry, modern living space and all the conveniences of shopping malls, fast food, and entertainment, it will be very hard to reverse. Since the Berlin Wall fell in 1989, there have been waves upon waves of populated countries and regions that have been introduced to free democratic marketplaces. Three billion people have been brought into the global community from closed systems. The U.S. has benefited tremendously from low labor costs due to the flood of new global workers. From China, India, and the Eastern European bloc to Brazil and Russia, the progress of providing people basic living and feeding structures to their satisfaction has been greatly expanded.

Over the brief span of a few decades, the labor force in the free world has essentially doubled, providing low-cost human power for everyone and creating a backdrop of deflationary wage suppression. Very low wage inflation has been the result. With new consumers, raw materials have become more valuable. Commodity inflation has been the result. Economies that are more dependent on raw material imports will suffer. Even though the United States imports the majority of its oil, it has a wealth of raw materials with its large, highly skilled labor force.

There are two large forces moving in opposite directions. First, there is a spike in consumption in the emerging markets. Secondly, that is being partially offset with the declining ability to consume in the developed markets. The world economy is teetering on this delicate balance. It's hard to imagine anyone in the world who can forecast if emerging market demand is going to offset the developed markets' slower consumption. It will be a tug of war for the next five to ten years to determine this. Estimates are encouraging. It wasn't too long ago when a trip to Asia was followed by a comment about how many bikes were seen. Today, the comment is about cars. Chinese purchases of automobiles have recently eclipsed Americans', and many of those were initial automobile purchases, as opposed to the American replacements. There will be imbalances as demand shifts from developed to emerging economies. It will not be a smooth transition but a series of give-and-take over many years.

It is the United States that has embraced free trade from the beginning and is the market most coveted by export nations. In 2009, the United States was 25% of world GDP at $14.4 trillion.[35] The United States' economy will be the largest single country economy for at least the next two decades. Let's do the math. Japan, the second largest economy in the world at the end of 2009, had a GDP of $5.1 trillion. Growth rates in Japan have slowed and the population is aging with the ability for that country's growth to exceed the United States' greatly diminished growth. China, with $4.8 trillion in 2009 GDP, has by now eclipsed Japan as the second largest single economy in the world. China's growth has been breathtaking and unprecedented—and most likely unsustainable as it becomes larger. The larger the economy becomes, the more difficult it is to grow at a high rate.

China has grown at an above eight percent per year in GDP over most of the last three decades.[36] The United States, in the same period of time, has only grown at three percent. For the sake of calculation, let's suppose that China can continue this breakneck growth of eight percent for the next twenty years. That rate would result in a GDP of $21 trillion. Let's also suppose that the United States substantially slows its long-term average growth rate to only two percent per year. That would result in a GDP of $21 trillion at the end of twenty years. These are simple trend line calculations that assume a simple compounding and do not take into consideration many factors that may affect the eventual outcome. There will be challenges to this analysis, as China must slowly transform its economy from export-oriented to consumption and services. Japan and South Korea made these transitions over long periods of time and at slower rates of growth.[37] It won't be easy for China.

It would be doubtful that the United States will only be able to grow its economy at an added two percent rate for the next twenty years. We are undergoing one of the largest technological transformations of human civilization. Most all of the innovation, invention, research, and product development in the world happens right here. We are a quarter of the world economy, but probably even more when measuring thought. We are the value-added center of the universe. Even if, in twenty years, China surpasses the United States in a GDP calculation, it must tremendously change its export, sales-oriented, and inward-looking culture before it can be crowned as the leader of the world. Every country is a leader in something. From Brazil to India, Russia, and Indonesia, the world is full of leaders. At the top, a joint leadership role of China and the United States will come to be. It may be that "Chi-merica" will be the best of both worlds: market-based solutions with social direction.[38]

China

Of course, economic and financial numbers have to be converted into the same currency to compare the U.S. and China. Here, we are using U.S. dollars. That brings up a whole new problem of what China's artificially depressed currency is really worth. Well, it's worth more than the current exchange rate. How much more? Some experts estimate a range around thirty to forty percent undervalued. So that would mean that China's GDP is far more than what is being counted. A stronger or higher Chinese *yuan* would convert into more GDP. Let's measure each economy in something else that can be measured, say Big Macs. Instead of dollars, let's convert each economy into the famous McDonald's hamburger or the equivalent. The *Economist* magazine calculates this index measuring how much it would cost to purchase a Big Mac in each country due to its currency valuation.[39] In China, it costs less than two dollars; in the U.S., it is four dollars; and in parts of Europe, it's five dollars. Using Big Macs, China is already the largest economy in the world.

A country with over a billion people may be only half our economic output as measured by GDP statistics. Well, that is going to change eventually. The population of the U.S. is a fraction compared to that of China! The fact that we are still the leader of the world in many industries is a statement to our strength. It's a thankless task to be the world's economic and military leader. You can't please everyone.

What is China's philosophy of being a world leader? In the view of the late Deng Xiaoping, the leader of China who brought it out of the Maoist era: China should keep a low profile, not take the lead, watch developments patiently, and keep its capabilities hidden.[40] China has come a long way from the communist rule of Mao Zedong and collective farms, but the current political leaders are fearful of setbacks. It is doubtful that even if China surpasses the United States in several economic statistics that they will want to take a leadership role in the world. It is not in their best interest. China is in its growth mode and at the same time changing the mix of its economy. It must move its economy from export and infrastructure to consumption and service, the attributes of a developed economy. It is about halfway through its task of moving a half a billion people out of the fields and into the cities. That will take another ten to twenty years. It has a massive, historic challenge ahead of it, not behind it.

"Like older rising powers in past centuries, China is imbued with a remarkable sense of patriotism... People are proud of their country's economic miracle over the past thirty years."[41] China's newfound influence in the world and newfound wealth has also made it an acquirer of assets around the world. Chinese demand for copper represented almost forty percent of world demand in the first quarter of 2009, thirty-seven percent of aluminum demand, forty-three percent for nickel, forty-seven percent for crude steel, and seventy-five percent for iron ore. On average, China's share of the world's base metal demand represented about forty-five percent of global market share.[42] Oil demand is also rising. China's thirst for oil accounts for the largest force in demand. It is rapidly becoming the second largest consumer of oil.[43] The Chinese are going to spend a lot of their time finding resources to "feed the beast."

What is the chance that China can plan this massive change just right: build the right amount of infrastructure and housing just as people migrate out of agriculture into manufacturing and then into consumption and services, attributes of a developed economy? Before you answer that question, also know that China is not relying on a market mechanism to guide it; rather, it is planning the economic transition quite like Russia did from the "top down." Since political officials are the most powerful people in China, they are the ones that allocate resources and money. The job comes with many special interests intersecting with regional needs, let alone trying to make

good business decisions. There are stories of widespread misalloca-
tion of resources, bridges to nowhere, empty buildings, massive over-
capacity, and the like. Much of the "Chinese miracle" has come from
government spending on infrastructure. What if the infrastructure is
too large for a slowing world economy? It appears there is no market
mechanism to alert them to stop building. The Chinese economy may
be overbuilt for the new order of the world consumer. The amount
of consumption in the Chinese economy is about one-tenth of what
it is in America. Developed economies will slow consumption; they
have already. Then *what* are they building so rapidly for?

Technological innovation isn't likely to drive the Chinese expansion, either; it's simply brute force in manufacturing. Analysts suspect
that most, if not all, of China's glorious GDP rate is made up of government projects for fixed capital formation. Again, this is a socialist
economy that doesn't open its books to the rest of the world. Profit
is not the motive. Most of the investment is directed to industries
with the largest sales growth, whereas profits show little correlation with capital expenditures. It is all about sales, expanding market
share, and growing businesses. It may be that China is building itself
up for a continuation of globalization and migration trends of the past
ten years and may not be prepared for a slowdown. "Many countries
that relied heavily on exports as a growth strategy are now geared up
to provide goods and services to heavily indebted countries that no
longer have the will or the means to buy them."[44] China is dependent
on the U.S. economy to help it through this transition. Without our
markets, it is overbuilt and not yet self-sufficient.

Much of the Chinese growth strategy has been about importing
innovation. China's first commercial jet hits the market in 2010 but

experts say they're based on older McDonnell Douglas designs and that foreigners will supply the core systems. Once Chinese engineers and manufacturers start producing a world-class passenger jet, the question will then become: Can they innovate? Only a decade ago, Boeing looked invincible in its monopoly of passenger jets but a consortium of several European aeronautic giants formed Airbus to rival Boeing's greatness. Airbus has received substantial government funds and support to become a competitor. Although Airbus has won market share, Boeing seems to be able to be more innovative, as it is more profit-oriented. It remains to be seen whether government-funded initiatives without a profit motive can innovate or create just as quickly. That is the age-old question, which we think has already been answered. Market systems over time will work better. Why did we win the Cold War? Because we were good and they were evil? No! They went with central planning and we went with the market. The market won!

People easily mistake growth "rate" for "size." The fact that China is growing faster than us does not mean they are bigger. The per capita (per person) income in China is a tenth of that in the U.S. Unfortunately, China is still a poor country and only recently have they emerged with modern structures of social services, support, and assistance. Its legal system is just a few decades old, and, under communism, there was no legal structure. China is moving in the right direction, but it's certainly not to the point of leading the world, at least not yet. It has many more challenges ahead in human rights, news media suppression, basic property law, pollution control, creating consumer demand, and providing healthcare for over a billion people.

Most of the so-called passing of the torch between America and China has been caused by a currency. Keeping the Chinese *yuan* competitively devalued has made imported goods to America seem quite cheap. As the dollar decline has reached some momentum, the Chinese *yuan*, being pegged to the dollar, has actually depreciated the *yuan* in other developed countries. China continues to undercut its competitors in the global environment.

The U.S. trade deficit is indeed the largest financial imbalance in the history of the world, but it is caused by a governmental policy, not a market system. Our trade deficit is caused by an insatiable thirst for oil and a consumer need for low prices. Within this, there is a lack of market forces in appreciating the Chinese currency to reflect its stronger economic position. By keeping their currency undervalued, the Chinese have an economy that is much stronger today than it should be because it is stealing orders away from other countries with less advantaged and manipulated currencies. It is also providing goods to us at a lower cost than we, or anyone else, for that matter, could make them. Without this unfair advantage, America would not have benefited from extremely cheap goods. Our trade deficit would not be materially less, but it would be spread out amongst more of the developing nations, not concentrated. China, in order to become a world leader, must let market forces move its currency. It is unfairly reaping profits at the expense of other nations and our national debt is being highly concentrated in its hands due to this imbalance.

How long will we allow China to build up its economy artificially? Since they do own a lot of U.S. Treasury debt, the Chinese government feels they can dictate to us and tell us what to do. In a recent visit to China, Barack Obama was scolded for his expansive health care plan and how that would affect the dollar and interest rates. China does not have the power to dictate to us. If China sold its holding of treasury securities, the value of the bonds would go down and our interest rates would go up. First, China would harm itself by forcing lower prices for what it is selling and then the higher interest rates would attract other investors. U.S. Treasuries are the largest, safest, most liquid securities in the world. Without the U.S. consumer, the Chinese economic machine collapses and cannot be supported by demand from within, from its own consumers. China is a partner and, in a partnership, there are a few key points that may be argued, but partners come together in an agreed-upon strategy. In the new order of the world, we must be more understanding of other people's viewpoints, especially the people who are funding our national debt. We must not back down from our own policy initiatives that will benefit our country. We will obviously listen to our partners and welcome their input, but must make the decisions that direct our economy.

The challenges to China's growth are now far greater than they were at any time in its history. Not only does it have its own internal growth responsibilities, but, as the second largest economy in the world, it also has responsibility to others. It was much easier to centrally direct a small emerging economy to areas where it could be competitive using labor input as its primary cost advantage. As hundreds of millions of people moved from the farms to the cities and began brushing their teeth for the first time, using toilet paper, paper towels, utilizing makeup, and, of course, drinking a Coca-Cola and having a McDonald's hamburger, a large consumer buying trend was born and will continue. Have you ever told an American teenager to eat rice or beans instead of a cheeseburger? Try it. Not only have the emerging consumers had a hamburger, they have been to a disco, made a stock trade, bought a new car, and are looking to invest in property. Hundreds of millions of people won't go back. China must change its economy from export and manufacturing-oriented to consumer-oriented through this evolution, and quickly—more rapidly than any other civilization in world history. For them, there is no historical reference; they must invent the tools to use in such a massive transition.

China must transform its economy from production to consumption and it will need the market mechanism to accomplish that. More developed economies work more from the "pull" of demand from consumer spending. In the U.S., detailed knowledge networks detect a pair of jeans purchased at a specific outlet and suppliers are immediately notified to replace it. Consumer tastes are instantly recorded in shops and stores to find where the trends of demand are signaling movement. The buying and selling networks also signal feedback, positive and negative, in anonymous outlets, some within the very same company that produces the product. On the other hand, China is restricting or ignoring this information flow. It is still "pushing" out product and services, not listening carefully to the consumer, because they have so many of them. The economy is rushing to supply the vast developing Chinese population. As a result of its socialist direction in funding projects and extending loans, it will have too much of one thing and not enough of another. This in turn can create investment bubbles and shortages. This was a typical failure of the Soviet system in the past and can be seen in Venezuela today.

The price of a good or service will determine its demand and therefore, how it is used. Without prices, resources will be allocated inefficiently. Prices, however volatile, don't lie. It requires an agreement between a buyer and seller. People setting prices without this agreement are at best, just estimating. At worst, they're lying. Information is needed in pricing things and restricting the flow of market knowledge is like cutting off the oxygen in the economy.

Of course, we do know that market systems can also create bubbles, but over time they have re-balancing mechanisms that will bring more information to buyers and sellers. Eventually the population of China will make it a larger economy the United States. It is only a matter of time. In the meantime, it must change its economy using methods that have never been used in such a large, inter-connected and fast paced world.

Japan

Many of the state-run monopolies in the world measure their success by growth in sales, not in profits. This is similar to the way Japanese companies tackled the world in the 1970s and 1980s. Market share dominated Japanese management thinking. It wasn't long ago that Japan was the envy of the world. It seemed that every airport bookstore had Japanese-style management courses for sale to the American manager. Toyota, with its revolutionary just-in-time inventory, high quality, beautiful production techniques, and worker enthusiasm, was the example for all production companies. Except for Toyota, however, exports never amounted to much more than fifteen percent of Japan's GDP. Japan's focus tends to be very inward-looking and more based upon stability of the country as an independent unit of the world, not connected with other countries.

At one point in Japan's real estate bubble, the price of the land under the Emperor's Palace in Tokyo was valued at more than all the land in California. The Japanese stock market rose to a price earnings level of around eighty, about five times normal historical valuation measures. The EAFE index, composed of Europe, Australia, and the Far East, was sixty percent invested in Japan. The value of that market dominated others. The Japanese economy was the envy of the world, coupled with the country's low crime, excellent schools, good labor relations, and great managers with long-term horizons.[45]

The real estate market eventually collapsed and the financial sector was heavily exposed to it, resulting in a deflationary debt spiral. The Japanese had a severe and long recession caused by declining asset prices and debt that was extended for those assets: a balance sheet recession.[46] It was an economic contraction caused by too much debt and not enough economic activity to pay it off.

For two decades, the Japanese economy has never fully recovered and now it is fighting an aging of the population that will put increasing pressure on the system. A large impediment to growth was the small efforts over long periods of time at which the Japanese government addressed the banking problems. Private companies were also too slow to change. Japan is still one of the world's largest economies and despite its slow growth has remained competitive and is enjoying newfound political footing. The ruling party of the past two decades has recently been outvoted. Change is on the move!

There are many similarities in this experience with America today, but also a few major differences. Real estate prices never got to such lofty levels and the stock market, except for the tech boom, also never reached Japan's excessive heights. The U.S. government has acted quickly and decisively in the banking crisis of 2008. America has been able to change and adapt new methods of business. We have been the diplomatic leader of the world, the world's strongest military superpower, and the research and development capital of the world for many decades. A few decades down the line, the U.S. will not be the world's largest economy. It still may be the best place to start a business, have an idea, create a new product or simply live! China or Japan's economic size does not mean they will be equal in diplomacy, military strength, or innovation. Looking at the history of past empire declines and falls, we see a common element of overreaching or overextending a civilization's base. We must learn from history's lessons.

Written History

Written history only goes back to about 5000 B.C., but there have been many other civilizations where the written word has either been lost or destroyed. The Sumerians were in Mesopotamia or Iraq in 5000-2000 B.C. Since agriculture was the primary strength of the civilization, when droughts and temperatures changed the harvest of the region, the balance of power was toppled. It was in 3000 B.C. that ancient Egypt came to be a world power. Again, the civilization was agriculturally based and would rise or fall depending upon the flow of water down the Nile River. The written history of China begins around 500 B.C. The May Zhou Dynasty, beginning in 1000 B.C., provided the framework for modern Chinese writing. At one point in time, China had the world's largest army and navy, and was a world superpower. However, there was thought to be no need for outside influence and emperors essentially closed the country for hundreds of years.

The Roman Empire was the wealthiest, most powerful, most complex society the world had ever seen. Roman regions stretched from Scotland to the Sahara, from Spain to the Middle East. There are many reasons for the fall of the Roman Empire but to simplify things, it simply got too big. The Romans had a slogan, "imperium sine fine," which meant "empire without end."[47] The fall of Rome, like any major economic depression, was caused by not one or two crisis situations, but the **combination** of many. Military leaders began to mettle in political affairs. There was a huge gap between the rich and the poor. Economically poor harvests and disruption of trade led to decline and the fact that there were no more real enemies of the empire meant that there were no more treasures to be had. There became a crushing tax burden on the average citizen. Militarily, problems began with recruiting citizens, which turned into the hiring of mercenaries who did not have the same interests as Romans. "When Rome was sacked in A.D. 410, it was by the warrior-contractors who had once been in Rome's employ. That's as if Washington were one day to be sacked by Halliburton," says Cullen Murphy, author of *Are We Rome?: The Fall of an Empire and the Fate of America*.[48] Rome, too, was based on the ideals of democracy, free speech, and culture.

For three centuries, the Spanish Empire was the most important power in the world. During the Renaissance, it became the center of literature and fine arts. Its far-reaching empire touched Holland, Italy, France, and Germany, which led to ongoing conflicts with England and Sweden. Deficit spending also led to its decline. Within the turmoil of the French Revolution and the Napoleonic wars, Spain was destabilized and overextended.

The second half of the 1800s witnessed the expansion of the English Empire from Asia to Africa to America. The United Kingdom emerged from the Napoleonic wars as a renewed strength, industrialization progressed, and its citizens became more urban. It was said that the "sun never set on the English Empire." By the First World War, though, British military dominance began to wane; the Empire was overextended and became too difficult to manage.

Human civilizations sometimes reach the same crossroads time and time again. The overextension funded by debt is usually the largest component in the decline of these historical civilizations. In the words of Niall Ferguson, the Harvard economist, "excessive debt is usually a predictor of subsequent trouble." There are major similarities to the United States today in these other historical civilizations. Most likely, history will not repeat itself exactly. Our challenges will be much more complicated than in the past. The U.S. is at a crossroads in many areas, not the least of which are entitlements that threaten to balloon the budget for years to come. Our public debt, current and prospective, like many of these historical examples, is our largest challenge.

Speed and Size

Modern economies don't compare with ancient civilizations. There are two major differences in today's global environment. The first is **speed**. The speed at which information travels is unprecedented and therefore the speed at which mistakes can be magnified and profited from by others is also more rapid. As the United States was dealing with its subprime meltdown in 2008, the financial markets were moving much too rapidly for the politicians to keep up. The complexity and intricacy of these financial intermediary dealings was mindboggling even to the most expert among us. It was as if only a few people in the world could understand them completely, and they were certainly not the politicians. This new information age will not decelerate. We must be cognizant that humans are going to make mistakes but we must seek feedback immediately to determine if we are on the right path.

The second major difference in today's world is **size**. The amount of money about which we are talking is obviously a record, but the size of these flows around the world in proportion to the world economy is also large. This means that we don't have the tools at hand to properly evaluate the repercussions of saving and borrowing on a massive global scale. The present tools that we have were made for prior times. There are challenges ahead for which we have not yet done our analysis and preparation.

The American style of democracy has been more about consumer choice than voting at elections. The market based society that we live in lets consumers vote every day with their dollars of disposable income. From our beginnings as a democracy we have emphasized the freedom to choose who to represent us in government. There has been a shift in focus to investors and consumers.[49] Our economy has been more responsive to our needs as consumers than as citizens. The average American consumer today has the same information at his fingertips than a CFO of a major company had ten years ago. We are best at figuring out where the "best deals" are!

America does have a large national debt. The rates of interest that we are currently paying out on our debt are minimal, compared to the equity-like returns we could enjoy if we were investing that money into ownership opportunities. Our cost of capital is low; the opportunity to expand as owners throughout the world is vast. If we are borrowing just to consume, to pay back at some later date, we could find ourselves paying back debt with no dedicated funding source. We, as a country, must be using this opportunity to reinvest in ourselves and to create new businesses that far exceed our cost of capital. Outside of the United States there is opportunity. Even though we are the world's largest consumer, eighty percent of all the consumers in the world are now *outside* the United States. These are our new customers, our partners in business. We can't look inward anymore; we must look outward.

The U.S. is a world leader in manufacturing. It will be giving up the title to China as many manufactured goods here are produced overseas and then assembled here. The measure of the value that is added in the U.S. is a better indicator of what our nation does with its labor force and capital constraints. The manufacturing share of global manufacturing "value added" has barely budged from its 1980 level of twenty-two percent.[50] It is expected that, within the next decade, China will surpass U.S. manufacturing value added. The chart below documents the rise and then projects the next ten years. The U.S., Europe and Japan will all lose manufacturing market share to China, the line that is slanted upward to the right. The trend may not be as smooth as this line demonstrates since it will be difficult for China to continue this growth.

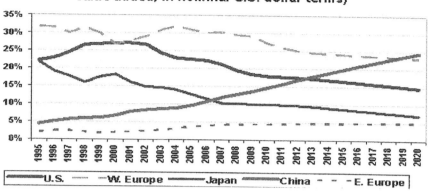

Regional Shares of World Manufacturing Output (Based on value added, in nominal U.S. dollar terms)

China Looks Set to Lead in Global Manufacturing.

(Source: ISH Global Insight)

∞ ∞ ∞

The United States is the world leader in manufacturing chemical products, transportation equipment, processed foods, beverages, computers, and electronics. Despite manufacturing representing less of the work force in United States, it provides high valued-added jobs, which spill over to other industries and smaller companies. Manufacturing is the largest sector of U.S. exports.[51] "We are losing the world market share relative to consumer goods, but we continue to have a fairly strong hold on the higher end products like machinery capital equipment, tractors and aircraft," says Thomas Runiewicz, an economist with IHS Global Insight. Because our economy is more market-based, in theory and in practice, we may be better able to allocate resources than a centrally planned economy.

That is the question of the day. Can we trust markets? What will be the economic structure of the future? What is the more perfect combination of market-based and central planning to move economic growth forward? A simple statement of future possibilities may very well be that the U.S. moves toward more regulation and more central planning with China moving more toward market deregulation and private enterprise. Quite a dichotomy!

Europe

Where does Europe fall into these calculations? The European Union accounts for over \$18 trillion in GDP. As a coordinated body of countries, it is certainly by far the largest economic force in the world. At thirty percent of world GDP, it is and should be a leader of the globe. Accounting for an increasing number of transactions, the euro, the currency for most of Europe, is now a secondary currency of choice. Europe also combines many diverse populations, cultures, history, and topographies, and, as such, is a microcosm of the total world economy.

For people who question how one of the largest economies in the world can overcome difficulties and change for the better, look no further than Germany. Sixty years ago, this country faced total annihilation and humiliation after the Allied defeat of the Nazi regime that altered world history forever. Germans reconstructed a partitioned country, divided into four parts initially, but eventually into East and West Germany for the better part of four decades. After the fall of the Berlin Wall, reunification brought responsibility to the West Germans to provide opportunity and assistance to assimilate the former socialists into a free democracy. Within this tremendous upheaval and change, Germany has survived and succeeded in becoming the world's largest exporter and a booming economic power. Germany's role as the conservative and stable center of economic and monetary policy in the new Europe is coalescing foreign countries into using the euro. The transition that this country has undertaken in the sixty years since World War II is amazing.

However, the "United States of Europe" is only united in name. The euro currency, although created twenty years ago, is still in its infancy as many countries are still waiting in line to be a member of the euro community. The United Kingdom has decided not to participate, for now. Some countries with particular countrywide problems may find the need to leave the European community, at least in respect to currency, to tackle and address their own regional issues. Then what happens? They come back to the euro? Investors do not like change, especially in paper currencies.

Eastern Europe provides its own challenges, as many economies extended far too much in the recent economic boom and will need to be assisted by the richer economies to the west. Will the Germans and French help out? Even small countries like Iceland are affecting the union. As bank policies leveraged depositors' money into poor investments, the Bank of Iceland has to make good on hundreds of billions of dollars of depositors' money. The nation has only 500,000 people, about the size of Cleveland, Ohio.[52] The problems do not end there for countries; as they try to adopt the currency of the euro, populations may become disenchanted with the overall goals of a continent that are required, as opposed to the immediate and specific needs of its own region.

Europe is both market-based and socialist. The strengths that have made parts of Europe relatively resilient in recession, the social safety nets, could emerge as weaknesses in the recovery. There's a price to pay for more social programs, security, and job protection. The "generous welfare states that preserves peoples income's tends to blunt incentives to take new work."[53] That becomes a drag on future growth as companies slowly respond to new technologies, innovation, and change. European market socialism has won the hearts of many. It feels good to have the government there in case the market fails. Some say people in Denmark are the happiest in the world. Why? Free education, free healthcare, and the ability of people to pursue a career of their choosing. At what cost? Tax rates of eighty percent!

India, Brazil and the Arab world

India has been in China's shadow for the past decade, but that country deserves some respect. It is the largest democracy in the world and the 1.1 billion people are growing at twice the rate of China's which will most likely make it the largest country within the next few decades. It is one of the fastest growing economies in the world and ranks fourth already when the purchasing power of their currency is adjusted for. India could also become the largest economy in the world at some point in the future given the right combination of public policy and private enterprise. Unfortunately, most of the population still lives in poverty and their per capita income (per person) is among the lowest in the world.

The Indian people have a special affection for Americans. They seem to identify with the "American dream" as most work hard in school and their careers to advance. The political system is modeled after England and English is the most common language as Hindi is not used completely throughout the country since there are so many other different dialects and languages used.[54] Economic reforms have boosted the growth of the economy far above the lower "Hindu rate of growth" that guided their public policy following independence in 1947.

Brazil may be an example of how quickly things can change in this new world. Coming from a true banana republic and ruled by military dictators until 1985, Brazil is now the largest economy in Latin America and tenth largest in the world. It has a truly modern and developed economic system and is a free, elected democracy. Exports are booming not only from its vast natural resources like coffee, orange juice, and beef, but also in higher valued-added goods like aircraft, electrical equipment, and textiles. Needing an IMF rescue package in 2002, the country and its economy quickly recovered and paid the debt back early. Brazil is an example of how quickly free markets can revitalize an economy and an example for countries around the world to globalize. It is also an example of the **speed** and **size** of the issues that we face today and how quickly forces can emerge.

The Arab world is at a crossroads, too. It is battling its religious laws and traditions against change in the modern world. The enormous flow of wealth has changed their economies but there is resistance in changing their culture. They're building new economic cities, pouring billions of dollars into commercial real estate projects that are not yet economically viable. They are shunning expert advice from outside the Middle East. How long will they be proficient and productive in this closed system without outside innovation? In many of these oil countries, including others outside the region like Mexico and Venezuela, there is a citizenry that either doesn't work or doesn't have the skills to work in the high-tech oil service. They hire foreign workers to manufacture and produce. These countries don't like

outside Influence even though that puts them at a disadvantage in a
fast moving information world. These natural resource based economies don't yet have the attitudes, the skills, or the training in order to
be part of an entrepreneurial economy.

Globalization Challenged

Globalization is being challenged. Trade tariffs and disputes are on
the rise. Protectionism, leading to nationalistic interests over global
competitiveness, is certainly brewing. However, the world has moved
in one direction for decades and even despite the past twelve months
and the financial and economic crisis throughout the world, it is still
anticipated that the globalization march will continue forward. It is
the most rational structure of the world economy as each country
emphasizes what it can exploit to a competitive advantage. It would
be difficult to move backward. Headwinds do persist. From some
Islamic economies that are reluctant change to more firmly established developing economies that don't want to be subject to factors
out of their control, some form of nationalistic prioritization will be
evident. People have simply lost confidence that markets always work
to the benefit of all instead of to the massive profitability of a few.

The United States has acted like an empire, with its roots in
over 800 military bases around the world. "We are an empire now,
and when we act, we create our own reality", as a high level U.S.
Government official once said.[55] Instead of annexing countries like
prior civilizations did by planting a flag and declaring that the region
is owned by the king or emperor, we instead provided security. We
do not and cannot represent the world with its diverse groups of
humanity. But just like the members of a jury, they all must appoint

a leader. Indeed, for the last hundred years at least, we have played that part.

If freedom is our inalienable right, then we have done our job by bringing freer societies to the world. There has been an explosion of democracies and individualistic rights, giving each person the perspective that they are indeed important. We cannot micromanage hundreds of millions of people for our own selfish goals. Just like the members of the jury, we must all reach agreement in some way or else. America's role going forward should be more of the spokesperson for global society rather than the decision-maker.

The United States' twin strengths are our **decentralization** combined with our **connectivity**. We allow people to take responsibility for themselves.[56] As a result, America could become a stronger leader to countries in the future from how we handle this current challenge. We need to reinvent ourselves and our labor force to our own competitive advantage.

In his latest book, *The Next Hundred Years*, George Friedman argues that America's power on the world stage will actually increase for three major reasons:

- The immense size of the U.S. economy. The current crisis is painful and America's deficits are shocking on an absolute basis, but are trivial relative to the country's net worth, which Friedman estimates is about $340 trillion.

- The unrivaled dominance of the U.S. Navy. Even in the digital age, control of the high seas is paramount to ensure geopolitics.

America sits on both the Atlantic and Pacific, whereas other world powers are on one or the other.

- The ability of the United States to absorb immigrants, both culturally and in terms of the nation's relatively low population density in proportion to land.

America must lead the world through this evolving time, identifying its own strengths and weaknesses within the new world order. "There is nothing wrong with America that can't be fixed by what is right with America", said former President Bill Clinton. Our society is dynamic; there is something inherent in not only our system of government but in the individuals who make up our citizenry that will allows us to make the changes we need to once again continue to assume our place in world history. America's self-perception, though, needs to change, to be brought back to earth, to be made more modest and more understanding of other viewpoints. Americans in a sense have to become better listeners in order for the world economy to function better. We need to think of ourselves in relative, not absolute, terms.

There is nothing here of which to be ashamed; we have been on a miraculous run. We have witnessed the most powerful rise a nation has ever experienced in the history of the world. It's been one big experiment. Yes, we are still in the laboratory figuring out the formula, the secret sauce, because capitalism didn't come with directions on the back cover. It is a trial and error procedure, an evolutionary process. What will not change is America as a leader; it's in our blood and we know it's our responsibility to the world.

The new order of the world depends on what you're measuring. Is it GDP or freedom? Is it consumer services or fresh water? The world economy is becoming more balanced with different leaders in many industrial sectors. The U.S. will not be dominant in every category but we will remain a world leader and our decisions will greatly affect the rest of the world. We must focus on skills in this knowledge-based, valued-added world in which we live. Skills are the critical ingredient for our success, not land, labor, and capital. These are available everywhere.[57]

Today, we can vote with our consumer dollars, identifying companies from countries with whom we want to align and favoring them instead of our adversaries. Yes, economics is a global war, which is won every day with the purchase of a product. You make your own choice: Do you fill up your car with gas at a station that's owned by the government of Venezuela? How about one from Russia? Did you know that Citgo gas stations are owned by the government of Venezuela? Did you know that Lukoil is owned by the government of Russia? Do you purchase products knowingly from China? Have you shopped around to see the cost advantage? Do you favor products made by friends and partners of the United States or enemies? When you go shopping, make sure you understand from where you're buying. An educated consumer is the best customer.

The U.S. economy today is seven times larger than it was during World War II when Harry Truman was president. The amount of raw material inputs needed for our level of GDP is only marginally larger. The growth of our economy has come from ideas, not physical inputs. The demand for conceptual products is also much less elastic than physical products. Water is almost free but in fancy, convenient plastic bottles, water becomes a product. The better the intellectual positioning through marketing and packaging, the better the sales and profit. The knowledge base of the average American is high. We are constantly exposed to media and information sources that teach us. Our ability to design and assemble products is strong. There is more pricing power in these intellectual goods and they are also not as subject to raw material price changes. We are moving into the mental phase of human civilization and America is a leader in thought.

3. Economists and Weathermen

"As far as the laws of mathematics refer to reality, they are not certain; and as far as they are certain, they do not refer to reality."

—Albert Einstein, "Geometry and Experience," January 27, 1921

America is the world leader in the study of economics, the social science about the production, distribution, and consumption of goods and services. The Nobel Prize in economics only began in the 1960s but, since then, forty-two of the sixty-two awards have gone to Americans. To say we are dominant in the economics profession is obvious, but it also began here. Economics, as a science, is thought to have begun with Adam Smith's book *Wealth of Nations*, in 1776. It was "the effective birth of economics as a separate discipline," so said the *Encyclopedia Britannica*.[58] Adam Smith identified land, labor, and capital as the three factors of production and the major contributors to a nation's wealth. In Smith's view, the ideal economy is a **self-regulating market system** that automatically satisfies the economic needs of the populace. In a market system, buyers and sellers both come together to pursue their own self-interest. They trade with each other in a mutually beneficial transaction. Each side of the trade perceives a value to the trade and as both perceive a benefit, society overall also benefits.

He described this market mechanism as an "invisible hand" that leads all individuals, in pursuit of their own self-interests, to produce the greatest benefit for society as a whole. Each individual, making his or her own decisions, allocates capital properly to the area of the most need from the pricing mechanism. The collective wisdom of a crowd is more accurate than any one individual. That's how markets work. The more participants in the group, the more accurate the market price. This is similar to the game show *Who Wants to be a Millionaire?*, when the participant gets a particularly difficult question and uses one of his lifelines to "ask the audience." The collective wisdom of the audience is usually right.

In order to understand the direction of the world, we must understand how markets work and also why they sometimes fail. Markets can be wrong, as prices reflected are not always right. We learned that! What really happened in Wall Street's "near death" experience in 2008? The resulting market decline will be the longest recession since the Great Depression of the 1930s. The longest two recessions, one beginning in 1973 and the other in 1981, both lasted sixteen months. We have had eleven recessions since the 1930s with the average length of each about twelve months. Recessions are part of the business cycles and part of functioning markets. They are a necessary part of capitalism, unfortunately.

Do you rely on weather forecasters, or do you bring an umbrella, just in case? We know it's not a perfect world. Much of economic theory, though, lies in a perfect world. Much of the economist profession gets involved in perfectly defined mathematical models, in which consumers always look rationally toward their own ultimate gain. Most of science has been trying to define the world in these perfect equations. Humans are, in reality, rarely perfect. Economists spent too much time on the science of their profession, not on the art. Economics is more a social science. It's a combination of fancy math equations mixed in with a frat party: Einstein meets *Animal House*.

The efficient market hypothesis is based upon a formula of individuals acting in their own self-interest rationally, fully discounting all information available and unemotionally determining a price for value. So much of economics is derived from mathematical formulas that former statistics professors can be superstars in this, the dismal science. Most economists deduce that if this is the way the world should work and if it doesn't work that way, the world must be wrong, not the formulas! The best new economists are empirically oriented in their work, rooted concretely in the observation of the real world.[59]

As we know from watching football games, players will usually do as they're told and as it appears in their playbook. But people are human and at times make mistakes, resulting in blown plays, roughing the passer penalties, and reversed calls. Yes, even the officials make mistakes. There's nothing wrong with that; we are human. Any NFL team can beat any other NFL team on any given day. It's the team's ability to execute a game plan and eliminate mistakes that leads a team to success. Each play in the game is dependent on everything that has happened before it. The plays drawn up in the locker room are theoretical, mathematical models of what should happen or what has happened in the past. Each time a specific play is used though, a different set of circumstances exists. The game itself unfolds as a story, a combination of the preparation, strategy, execution and the unpredictability of human behavior. It is not known before hand which of these elements will dominate the flow of the game and therefore, the outcome.

The football game itself is not easily predictable. The human element, the unexpected, is difficult to plan for. Each player will act on applying the coach's strategy to the real world. They bring the mathematical models and theories and put them into their own individual action. It is this application of what is known that requires us to play the games! The game is a combination of predictable outcomes and random material, unforecastable events. It is said that each team is only as strong as its weakest link, the person who covers the onside kick, the tackle behind the line, the blocked kick and the fumble! These are all turning points in a game that depend on individual actions for the benefit or detriment of the team.

Its people that make markets work, so instead of analyzing externalities, standard deviation, and optimization, we should be looking at people and what makes them tick. The more we understand people, the more we will understand markets.

The United States has been basing more decisions on people through the market mechanism than any other country in the world. The market system emphasizes what something can **sell** for rather than what it **cost** to produce. Classical economics focused on a price that covered the cost of production and a profit. Today's product manufacturers have expanded the profit portion by packaging it differently, creating a preferable brand or image and product placement. The price is what the market will bear.

Although there has been a lot of recent commentary on the United States' market moving toward socialism, we still are one of the freest-market societies in the world ranking 144th out of 160 countries for the percent of government spending of the economy.[60] Afghanistan, ironically, is ranked first, with only ten percent of government spending in proportion to the total economy. The United States comes in at a paltry twenty percent. The country with the most government expenditures in proportion to its economy is Iraq, with eighty-seven percent. Top on the list are Cuba, Romania, Hungary, and the Czech Republic, with over sixty percent. Interestingly, also high on the list are France, Sweden, Denmark, Belgium, the Netherlands, Italy, and Portugal. All of them enjoy fifty percent or more government spending as a percent of the total. That's a lot of socialism!

Market-based economies got too confident in their ability to predict events. Most of what economists used to forecast was boiled down to formulas that assume "perfect information," and, armed with that, people act rationally. First, there is no such thing as perfect information. A newspaper and a stock analyst report would organize information differently. Secondly, we all have biases that affect how we interpret data. Thirdly, have you ever been to a local sports event where people act rationally? Human nature is predictable most of the time, but when your team comes from behind in the last minute to win, irrationality is the norm. If you've ever been to a Phillies game, you will know what I'm talking about.

The economic forecasting industry grew confident by estimating the same amount of growth for next year about the same as we

experienced the year before, and usually they were right. What people didn't know was that these forecasts were seldom accurate and
mostly the best forecasters were either lucky or simply never changed
their opinion until they were finally right (the "clock is right two times
a day" strategy). What forecasting misses is change. It's hard to predict change. People think about trends continuing in straight lines.

A study was done on weather forecasts by TV news channels and
determined that the accuracy of their weather predictions over the
next three days was about the same as flipping a coin. Half the time
they were right and the other half, you guessed it, they were off by
some amount of clouds or rain or a "Storm of the Century" prediction that didn't happen. Weather forecasts use computer models to
try to predict something that is naturally unpredictable. Let's face it,
we are going to know where the clouds are and where they're going
to be the next day, but figuring out if they're actually going to drop
rain, now that's difficult! Sometimes those clouds can just evaporate,
too.

For economists, we know where the majority of transactions are
going to take place and we can pretty accurately predict the number
of transactions that will take place. What we don't know is when
it's going to rain—and when it not only rains, but pours, like when
somebody yells, "Fire!" and everyone runs for the exits, or someone
yells, "Bargain!" and shoppers fall over each other to get in the store.

Subprime

In 2008, the failure in one market, most notably the subprime mortgage market, did spread into other markets. Subprime is not a steak

dinner. It is the rating of the quality of a mortgage below investment grade. A prime mortgage is a standard of several different ratios of income to debt payments and assets to total debt. Subprime is below these ratios, or documentation is lacking to verify them. By itself, a subprime mortgage has no investors. Who would buy such a thing? Combined with other subprime mortgages, though, some of the risk can be diversified by type of mortgage, region of the country, and other characteristics. One bad apple does upset the whole apple cart sometimes and we will spend quite some time analyzing and trying to understand this failure and, more importantly, the psychological spread into other areas of the everyday economy.

Most of the market system is based on trust. When there is suspicion that all participants are acting differently than expected, the game changes. At a poker table, bluffing is the most important component of the game. When there are a million people at the table, one bluff will not change the game. When there are five people looking into each other's eyes, deception is everything. When markets are not liquid, the smartness of the collective group dissipates and gives way to the irrational individual.

The problem with our current thinking is we wait for something to happen, not look for the signs leading up to it. It is because it hasn't happened before that we have no data points. That doesn't mean it can't happen. Let's say the record for the triple jump is fifty feet. What is the probability that someone will exceed that? Using all the data from previous triple jumps, a statistician would compile a projection. Granted that the triple jumper was of Olympic caliber, one could predict with some precision a possible result. All the data would be formulated into distribution of expected outcomes from all things that happened in the past. The projection would be made with what has happened, not what could happen. If indeed the triple jump record was broken, a new data point was entered into the mathematics. The act of breaking a record is a result of many things lining up in favor of the athlete: training, previous attempts, weather, diet, and then extra, immeasurable factors like attitude and emotion. A broken record is the result of a confluence of events leading up to the competition. "All forecasting, economic forecasting, financial forecasting or, for that matter, weather forecasting, relies on precedent. No matter how sophisticated the mathematical model, forecasting boils down to this: in similar situations in the past, things have panned out a certain way, and from this, we predict what is going to happen this time around," says Dr. David Kelly of JP Morgan.[61]

In 1987, the stock market fell by 22.6 percent in one day, October 19. Prior to that day, that much of a drop had never occurred. Even during the Great Depression, stocks never fell by as much of a percentage on a single day. Does that mean it can't happen? Of course not. The predictability of standard deviation would have led one to believe that it was such an odd occurrence that there was one chance in a million that it could happen. Leading up to the correction, there was a great deal of speculation. The stock market was *up* forty percent by August. Portfolio insurance protected investors from a downturn, but was never fully tested in panic conditions. The quality of earnings was deteriorating for many quarters coming into the fall. There were many signs. Afterwards? The possible outcomes grew more varied. Since it happened, it can happen again.

Tail Events

Models are generally built around the idea of a normal distribution of outcomes. Most events are going to naturally occur in a range, a pretty close range, wherein some really odd circumstances can occur, but they do so rarely. These rare events are called "tail" events in that the normal distribution looks like a bulge in the middle and thin tails are on each end. In economics, these tail events are commonly thought of like a hundred-year flood. The problem with the hundred-year flood thesis is that these "abnormal" events have been occurring every three to five years, and the intensity has increased as well.

Our lives are usually remembered in light of these odd or seldom occurrences: a wedding, the birth of a child, the Challenger disaster, or 9/11. Humans react differently to these events. They are magnified by emotion. They draw people out of their everyday lives. Think of your own life. These big events are usually infrequent and cause or reflect a large change in your life's direction. The problem with evaluating "tail events" is that, in finance, these events seem to happen regularly. That is the nature of markets. What causes them? It is usually a sequence of many events leading up to the data point at which a "black swan" occurs. It is a string of several events that get connected to create the chaos and calamity.

But what about the 1930s? During the Great Depression, if you wanted to find out where your stocks closed for the day, you had to listen to the radio at 4 p.m. because, although TV was invented, it wasn't yet mass-produced. If you missed the stock market report, you would have to call your stockbroker, if you didn't have a ticker tape machine. Your friends certainly wouldn't know; they had their own jobs and, remember, the only phone that they owned was at home or in the office, fixed to a location and there was only one per family. Most likely, you would wait until the morning newspaper was delivered the next day and you would look up the high, low, and close for that particular stock. News traveled slowly, at a snail's pace. Today, not only would you be able to look up a stock quote on the Internet, but you could probably do it from the bottom of the Grand Canyon on your cell phone. The world today is completely and instantaneously interconnected with news media documenting the most minor occurrences in the most far-off places. We are in a brave new world and there is no historical precedent for our lives from this time forward.

The biggest difference between today and the 1930s is in human response.[62] How quickly governments have reacted in size and scope has never happened before. The amount of money in the United States stimulus has eclipsed all the other efforts to stabilize the economy in a crisis, combined! Experts are dusting off their history books and spouting off similarities with the Great Depression to give them predictive ability in this, the Great Recession. Good luck! We all should know that was a different time. It would be beneficial to review a little history here.

The Big One

When I teach students about the Great Depression, I always go to the blackboard and ask the question, "What caused the Great Depression?" Most of my students will remember the bank failures, the unemployment lines, and the stock market speculation of the 1920s. Others will say it wasn't until World War II, when the government had to spend money putting people to work, that the Great Depression finally ended. We will come up with ten or twelve things that happened that had an effect on the times. The actual causes of the Great Depression are many and varied, but it was the *combination* of multiple events that caused the economic collapse.

In the 1920s, there was great speculation and loose regulations that encouraged it. And, yes, the banks did fail as they operated under a fractional reserve system, just like today, when only a tenth of deposits are kept in cash on hand. When there is panic and more than that ten percent is demanded at the teller window... Houston, we have a problem. Remember there was no FDIC, the Federal Reserve had very limited power, and government intervention wasn't even a topic of conversation. The FDIC did not come along to guarantee bank deposits until 1934. It wasn't until Keynes came along, with his General Theory of Employment in 1936, that any government official truly thought he could save the day.[63] And even then, his ideas were not readily accepted.

We can now narrow the list down to three major events causing the greatest economic depression in recorded human history. There may have been other civilizations that failed this severely, but for some reason, the Mayans or people of Atlantis failed to document their fall. First, the U.S. government had a balanced budget and when tax receipts started falling, government spending had to fall also. Secondly, we were on the gold standard and, with the government spending gold, that meant currency in circulation had to contract. And, finally, tax rates were raised. Yes, raised! The highest income bracket was moved from 35% to 65%, a thought unimaginable today.[64] The Federal Reserve was simply an organizer of regional central banks that were

In turn trying to help monitor and manage independent commercial banks. It was very decentralized. You see, that's what we thought markets should be, independent and decentralized. Any semblance of central power was evil, or communist.

The truth is that the recovery in the four years after Franklin Roosevelt took office in 1933 was incredibly rapid.[65] However, that growth was halted by a second severe downturn in 1937 to 1938, when the government switched to contraction in fiscal and monetary policy. Tax rates were raised, Social Security taxes were collected for the first time, and the Fed went on an exit strategy from its aggressive expansion of credit in 1936. According to a classic study of the Depression by Milton Friedman, a withdrawal of money in the system was the central clause of the 1937-1938 recession. During Milton Friedman's eightieth birthday celebration, Ben Bernanke, then a governor of the Federal Reserve, said, "Milton, you were right. The Fed did cause the Great Depression. We won't do it again." He stuck to his word.[66]

In an article comparing macroeconomics with other sciences, Jacob Marschak noted that seismologists made progress in better instrumentation measuring possible earthquakes. In economics, the "earthquakes did most of the job."[67] The study of the Great Depression is a study of economics. Governments needed to step in where private enterprise had failed and created massive underemployment and low-capacity utilization. Keynes also observed how uncertainty leads to economic instability. He understood that free markets have an element of uncertainty that could not be predicted.

Joseph Schumpeter gave warning about a "quirk" in capitalism that could lead to its downfall. Entrepreneurism was the spirit of the capitalist economy in that "creative destruction" or innovation was brought to the market and unseeded more established players. Keynesians, working hand in hand with big business, would be able to stabilize the economy at periods of distress. The government would assist the economy. Schumpeter argued that that would kill the spirit of the entrepreneur. There is a tug of war between government intervention and market forces. The mix is important. Government needs to be injected where it can help and recede where markets work better. It is doubtful that we will ever get the mix just right, but in the rapid innovation surge that we are experiencing in the world today, market systems work best.

The Day the World Changed

On September 15, 2008, the day Lehman Brothers went bankrupt and Merrill Lynch and AIG were rescued, the loss of confidence was historic. It was building momentum throughout the year, but it was the quick combination of events that drained the brain-power that is normally available to solve cataclysmic problems. The world's financial system was overwhelmed with issues. The falling and failing Bear Stearns had been caught by J.P. Morgan in March, along with $30 billion of support from the Federal Reserve. This time, there was no arranged marriage or credit from the lender of last resort. Lehman was an investment bank and did not have a direct line to the discount window at the Fed. Neither did Bear Stearns, but its shotgun partner J.P. Morgan did. After Lehman failed, the thinking went that the next would be Merrill Lynch. Even though Merrill had done a better job at diversifying risky assets on their books, they were subject to a run on the bank. Eventually they would fail from a lack of confidence. AIG was another matter. With billions of dollars invested in mortgage securities and guaranteeing them too, AIG had cash flow troubles as well. Each of these three events was enough to send the market down. The combination could crush capitalism.

The Fed decided to not bail out Lehman, or even supply assistance, that is after the British authorities nixed a Barclay's investment at the last minute. The Fed most likely did not want to save every participant from failing, especially such a large one. It had to draw the line somewhere. The markets were hit with three 100 year floods at once! The dams and dykes wouldn't hold.

To some degree it was caused by the ignorance of rules and regulations. Even the regulators didn't believe in regulation, leading to bad loans everywhere. The Fed had to step in to restore liquidity, confidence, and business activity that had dried up. Since then, the Federal Reserve has been on a tear. It has expanded its balance sheet by trillions of dollars, buying paper in the economy in exchange for cash and injecting cash throughout the system. It also increased the money supply, the cash on hand, not only in this country, but around the world, where the U.S. dollar is legal tender for transactions. Everywhere! Well maybe not in Cuba and North Korea, but certainly from Paris to St. Kitts. Trust and confidence as central elements in the market mechanism are also being restored. The entire stimulus plan was needed to offset the lack of final demand in the marketplace, to restore confidence. The Fed has to walk the edge of a precipice where, if it withdraws this stimulus too soon, a double dip recession is a possibility and, if it withdraws stimulus too late, inflation is a possibility. The probability that they will get this exactly right, as Goldilocks said, will be extremely difficult. We are going to have to taste the porridge frequently.

John Maynard Keyes once said after a revision in his analysis, "When the facts change, I change my opinion. What do you do, sir?"[68] We have to pay attention to the facts, and, as they change, so should our policies. You may wonder why economists even have jobs at this point because most of them completely missed this event. Economists and weathermen forecast often, and are willing to change their opinion. So did the collective intelligence of millions upon millions of market participants. In early 2008, when two hedge funds at Bear Stearns were stressed, in hindsight, that was a warning sign that a financial heart attack was a possibility. What if it spread? It is only in retrospect that those soothsayers beating warnings about under-regulation and over-speculation for years became well-known for their accuracy in predicting the largest negative financial event in modern history. Lucky dart throwers. Most of them have been bearish since the last war to end all wars. Economists are not well known for their predictive ability. In fact, if you laid economists end to end around the world, they still wouldn't reach a conclusion. Anyone can be an economist; being an articulate one is another matter. As Yogi Berra said, making accurate forecasts is difficult, especially about the future.

Hyman Minsky

The economics profession will do some soul-searching and some finger-pointing before the final chapters are written in the new Economics 101 text books coming to your local university bookstore. One chapter that will be included is on financial instability and a little-known economist named Hyman Minsky. You see, Hyman Minsky made a huge contribution to macroeconomics under the label of his "financial instability" hypothesis. In essence, he said that capitalism is **destabilizing** because capitalists have a herding tendency to extrapolate stability into infinity.[69] What he did was provide a frame-work for how and why the invisible hand would sometimes break down. Minsky, who died in 1996, wasn't around to repeat his warning that economic stability leads to over-speculation in lending and then collapse and eventual disaster. In hindsight, that's exactly what happened.

The Minsky moment in this crisis happened when housing prices actually went down nationally. All the financial models that were created were based on the premise that it wouldn't happen. For years, only various regions of house values went down, not the whole country at the same time. American International Group had a part in the observation. AIG finally said "no" to the investment banks that supplied them mortgage-backed securities. It was one of the largest purchasers and guarantors of these, investing money from insurance premiums. After swallowing a half of a trillion dollars worth of securities and guaranteeing another half a trillion dollars worth, AIG finally grew suspicious of the assumptions baked into the lower quality of mortgages and said "no thanks". The extrapolation into the future of home prices increasing every year was called into question.

Home prices had never fallen, at least in the national average. The God-given right of someone's home value to go up every year was what the whole home lending industry was basing itself on. When taking the country as a whole, prices for homes never fell in any year since the Great Depression. Investment banks used securitization to spread corporate risk around the markets. It used the same fundamentals for consumer loans and home mortgages. New homebuyers were few, at least those who could qualify, so we found a few million that couldn't. Anyone could buy a house. No money down. Teaser interest-rate. No credit history. No questions asked. Psst, wanna buy a watch?

After creating securitization machines, taking everyday mortgages from banks and originators, combining them together to create securities, the banks had to begin eating their own cooking. One of the biggest buyers had enough. AIG used to buy only prime mortgages, but by 2007, almost ninety-five percent of the securities it was buying were in the subprime area.[70] The Minsky moment! The music had stopped and everyone had to look for a chair. There weren't any available! Too much stability created a lending frenzy, which created a crash. When AIG finally said, "No, we don't want any more," other participants looked around and said, "Me, neither." The value of all mortgage securities seized up, not just subprime. Very large buyers were supporting the market, and when they withdrew, word got around and the lack of other buyers forced prices to come down. Someone had stopped the music and everyone had to find a chair to sit in.

AIG was like an addict looking to stop its addiction, but it already was sick. Not only did AIG own a lot of this paper, they also guaranteed it. AIG sold credit default swaps, or CDS, on subprime mortgages. Credit default swaps are like selling insurance; if you write that insurance, you bring in a premium in telling the buyer that we will make you whole in a default. As the insurer has no immediate cost, the premium, after some percentage put away in reserve, is profit. This illusion about profit was what people paid themselves big bonuses on.[71] AIG had lost its coveted triple-A rating when its leader, Hank Greenberg, had to step down in 2005, as forced by Eliot Spitzer. When prices came down, AIG, now without its coveted triple-A rating, had to present collateral for its insurance guarantees against mortgage defaults. As the prospect of default rose, more collateral was needed. AIG had to sell or provide investment assets from all areas of its balance sheet, in turn affecting the price of all those other instruments, even high-grade bonds. Your local bank that was investing in mortgage-backed securities was affected. You were affected. We all were.

AIG was just a player. Everyone on Wall Street was involved. Citigroup Chief Executive Charles Prince said, "as long as the music is playing, you have to get up and dance".[72] Hedge funds leveraged and proprietary trading at banks were dancing. It all was a big party! Everyone was making money from nothing. Then someone yelled "fire".

Financial markets are supposed to reflect reality. Futures markets for oil should represent market participants' belief that the actual commodity will be delivered in a tank or barge at a certain date in the future. Bond prices reflect what market participants believe is the true value of name of the bond issuer with a coupon interest rate at a stated maturity date. Stock investors base more of their valuation metrics on future cash flows that will pay dividends, but are uncertain because they're based on earnings. Due to the variances of buyers and sellers, stock prices are set that may not reflect the underlying fundamentals, at least in the short term. These prices are based on opinions, emotions, and speculation. When the world's crystal ball becomes cloudy, stock investors grow nervous. As the expected cash flows are not nailed down in any contract, any decline in economic activity may have an adverse effect on the future steam of earnings, the future dividends, and the current price of the security. "A bird in the hand is worth more than two in the bush," stated Benjamin Franklin. In an uncertain world, optimism is valued less.

When economists around the world noticed a sudden stop in business activity, the central banks around the world were quick to respond.[73] Given the strong medication that was being administered by governments, most thought it was highly likely that the global economy would get up off the floor. It would take a period of time of confidence-building for people to trust the market again. So, it's been one year plus and, yes, confidence and trust has been restored to the marketplace.

The Creation of Money

Credit creation is a good thing. If a depositor places $100 in a bank, according to the fractional reserve banking system, the bank can keep ten dollars and lend out ninety. As it has lent that money out to a commercial enterprise, that company will deposit the ninety dollars in its local bank before it writes checks. That bank will take the ninety dollars, keep nine, and lend out eighty. And, yes, that eighty dollars is lent out to another commercial enterprise, deposited in another local bank, which will then in turn lend out the majority of the funds. If the Fed made the first deposit of $100, it's just created $170 more! The Fed has created money out of thin air but it all depends upon how quickly banks will lend. If banks do not lend, money is not created and the Fed has to work extra hard to make sure there is enough liquidity in the system to support transactions. That's the problem. Credit creation is a good thing but when it drastically slows, it takes a money pusher to make sure the economy does not falter. The Fed is the money pusher.

In the crisis of 2008, no bank was willing to lend money, not even to each other. If Lehman Brothers went under and Merrill Lynch could, too, what about Citibank? UBS? Bank of America? GMAC? Who would you trust as a banker? Only your mother and the Fed. Credit creation not only determines the money supply but credit increases the rate of growth in an economy. Credit allows businesses and people to buy things they cannot yet afford to pay for in cash. An increase in credit is directly helping the economy. Americans saw their homes as ATM cards and withdrew equity, took on debt, and spent the money. The average American consumer will need to pay off of this debt and deleverage, diverting money to that cause instead of consumption. American consumers are suffering from a balance sheet problem and will not be able to increase consumption until all their finances are back in order.[74] Banks are not lending because we are in a recession, and no one wants to borrow. The banks don't want to lend because they need to rebuild their balance sheet.

This is important because money cannot be created and therefore liquidity in the system is being withdrawn. This is like the oil in an engine that provides the lubrication between moving steel parts. In fact, credit creation is only one factor of liquidity, with many other factors working against the Federal Reserve Bank. This is like paddling a canoe up stream, as fast as you can but the current of the stream is faster than your top speed. The strength of the current counter-acting the Fed's injection of liquidity has been the equivalent of paddling against a rip tide. Despite the massive money injections, money growth is stagnating, even declining by some measures. As evidenced by the illustration below, we entered a liquidity trap where even the most robust monetary stimulus may not be enough to offset the enormous forces slowing transactions and the speed of money exchanging hands.

REAL ECONOMY LIQUIDITY TRAP

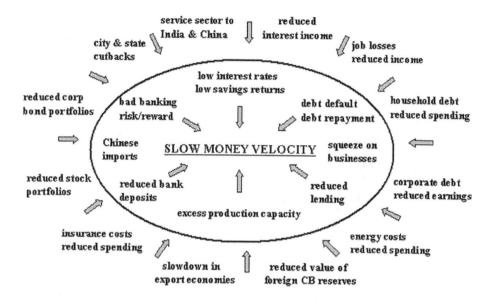

There Are Many Forces That Slowed the Speed of Money Flows.
(Source: FinancialSense.com)

Velocity is the speed of money exchanging hands in the economy. If the speed of money slows, then it is reflecting a slower business environment, less business transactions, and the economy slows. Think of this regarding yourself. When times are good, you are spending more and more often. Conversely, when times are tight, you pull back, spend less, and save money. Your household velocity of money expands and contracts with your income and net worth. So does the whole economy. Velocity slows when income can't cover expenses and you pay debts late or don't pay at all. You are a microcosm of the U.S. economy, just multiply by 300 million!

Gross National Product is a function of velocity. GDP is composed of three components: consumer, business and government spending. The faster people spend their money, more transactions are created and the more total exchanges that are recorded. In theory, money supply times its velocity equals GDP. Velocity can determine economic activity. If velocity falls, it must be offset by an increase in money supply or the economy will contract. When velocity fell, the Fed stepped in and provided liquidity. Lots of liquidity. The size of these huge offsetting forces is unprecedented and it will be very difficult for the Fed to manage this injection and eventual withdraw as economic activity returns. The so called "exit strategy".

Globalization is also based on credit. If not actual borrowing, it's based on trust and confidence. Letters of credit are used in international trade as collateral should products not be delivered on time. Most of these are only pieces of paper unless something adverse should happen at delivery, at which time they become loans. Remember, banks didn't want to lend money so they became much more cautious about signing documents that could eventually lead to lending money. That stops the whole system. A Taiwanese businessman shipping computer motherboards to Savannah, Georgia, may not be able to get the necessary collateral agreement in order to make his purchaser confident in delivery. That will slow globalization, hopefully only temporarily.

Credit creation and securitization go hand in hand. Securitization takes regular loans and makes them securities, sellable on the open market. If a bank has loans, it can securitize them, take the proceeds from the sale of securities, and then go out and make new loans. Securitization allows credit creation to grow. So it is an important component of the credit creation/economic growth machine. So what broke down? Well, in effect, everything, or at least everybody. There are a lot of participants in the securitization business, but everyone got lax on standards and the incentives to do improper or even unethical things got too enticing. The perpetrators are many, from the originators who offered fancy payouts for mortgage officers, to back offices that rubber stamped approval and stretched underwriting or loan quality, and law firms and rating agencies that took big fees to give favorable due diligence reports to regulators who failed to regulate, everyone is to blame. There was no interconnection. No one really knew what happened after the paper left their own hands. No one person overseeing the whole process. It was the "shadow banking system," not the more regulated official bank network.

The Many Participants in the Securitization Business

The Many Participants in the Securitization Business

(Source: JP Morgan, Private Bank)

Why and how did we lose our statement of ethics? Or was it just ignorance from the rules and spirit of regulation? There were few ethical concerns among participants, and the "golden rule"—treat others as you would want to be treated—was not practiced. Individuals became enchanted with their own piece of the security jigsaw puzzle and detached from the total picture.

Alan Greenspan

When Alan Greenspan first came to office in 1987, he was witness to one of the largest stock market corrections in American history. The S&L crisis that followed was also an era of deregulation, which led to speculation, this time in real estate. Banks had made a lot of loans that were never going to be paid back. As a result, many S&Ls had to be closed down and many banks badly needed capital. At the time, Greenspan and the Fed created the "3-6-3 rule": borrow from the Fed at the Fed funds rate, then three percent; lend that money out at the prime rate, then six percent. This difference or spread of three percent would certainly cover the costs of running a bank and allow them to replenish their capital. All it took was time, and bankers could make profits to replace those bad loans. So, borrow at three percent, lend at six percent, and be on the golf course every day by 3 p.m. The "3-6-3 rule"! Today, we have the "0-4-noon rule." Banks can borrow from the Fed at zero percent interest and lend that out at a prime rate of four percent. This will re-liquefy the banks. All it will take is time, and bankers who enjoy this four percent spread can now be on the golf course by noon!

Alan Greenspan, a formal economist in private life, had difficulty forecasting, too. He believed in the free market's ability to allocate.

He thought that it was his job as the chairman of the Fed to act swiftly only after a crisis. He did this after the 1987 stock market crash, the 1998 implosion of long-term capital, the Russian default, and in the aftermath of 9/11. He relied upon financial institutions' collective wisdom and hoped that if they looked out for themselves, the financial system as a whole would take care of itself. An "invisible hand" of sorts. An unregulated market system. Innovation comes easier to free markets. New products and services are tried in the marketplace, where they are accepted or rejected based upon dollar votes. Human progress can be entirely attributed to this quest for something better. Yet markets do fail at times, and in some cases the results can be catastrophic. In America's history during the 1800s, there were no less than a dozen banking panics, with a cataclysmic failure in 1907 resulting in the establishment of the Federal Reserve system. Innovation creates massive positive change for society, but it comes in fits and starts. Greenspan wanted to let the market innovate and self-police, and he stood by at the ready in case some incident arose that required the large resources of the government.

Unfortunately, the financial firms put too much faith in themselves and too much emphasis in their own self-dealings that it prevented them from helping society as a whole. They assumed that they would always be able to borrow in the open market to finance their assets. So the more they borrowed, the more they purchased, and the more they made for the company and, through bonuses, for themselves. The assumption of the "invisible hand" working both for the benefit of individuals and society as a whole was incorrect. It was only working for its own self-interest.

Leverage was built upon leverage and the world's balance sheet became tightly interlocked and woefully undercapitalized. After having led the Federal Reserve for two decades, stepping down in 2007 and witnessing the financial turmoil that rose in his wake, Greenspan had an uneasy feeling. He recognized there was a fundamental flaw in his overall worldview. His view was that regulation needed to be minimized to allow markets to grow most effectively. Control in the markets would come from the self-interest of each individual participant acting on his or her own behalf, but would result in common wealth for society. The fundamental flaw may be in human nature. A powerful individual like the CEO of a company may more be interested in his own riches than those of his company. "I made a mistake in presuming that the self-interests of organizations, specifically banks and others, were such as that they were best capable of protecting their own shareholders and their equity in the firms," Mr. Greenspan said.[75]

Financial economists formalize theories of the efficiency of markets in some sort of equilibrium that they would always regulate themselves, and financial innovation was always beneficial. Greenspan was in a state of shocked disbelief because his whole intellectual edifice had collapsed. The dynamics of the world economy was not as he imagined. Some regulation may be a good thing after all. "Waiter, there's a fly in my soup!" Now, if you or I made that miscalculation, we would harm the balance sheet of our family. When the **most powerful person in the world** makes this blunder, with everyone else following his lead, the consequences are magnified many times over. It was a failure of epic proportions.

Dr. Alan Greenspan is human and is subject to the same tendencies that we all have. He was extremely studious in his analysis and had a great reputation for thoroughness even before his ascension to the chairman of the Federal Reserve Board. The science of economics was his domain. Our interest-rate policies are imported by countries around the world, whereas not all our fiscal policies and government actions are followed in parallel. Interest-rate policy has a global impact. As evidenced by interest rates just in the last five years, though, there's been tremendous volatility. This makes it difficult for businesses to plan ahead. They use capitalization rates that serve as measuring bars to determine whether a new business venture goes ahead or is scrapped. Financing rates determine the cost of capital and if profitability cannot be projected over that cost, the hurdle rate cannot be overcome and the project becomes unviable.

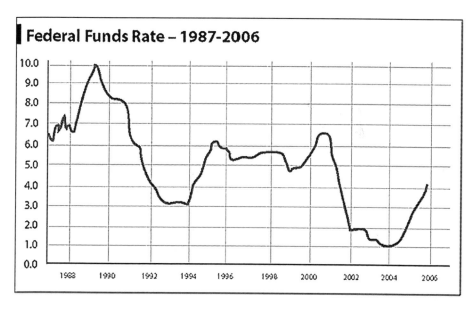

The Short-Term Fed Funds Rate Was
Volatile in Greenspan's Tenure.

(Source: InvestmentU.com)

Looking at what Alan Greenspan and the board of governors could control (the Fed funds rate), we see enormous volatility in interest rates in his tenure as chairman. Instead of pegging interest rates and controlling money supply like the Fed did in the 1980s, the Fed decided that with credit and debit cards substituting for money, it would be easier to control the economy through interest rates. The amount of money in the system was becoming less important. There were so many alternatives for cash. People were using credit cards to pay for their morning coffee! You know who you are!

From the chart, we see Alan Greenspan's main task of keeping interest rates stable was not achieved, especially in the most volatile time following the tech bubble. Short rates moved from six to ten percent, then to three up to six percent again and then to one percent before going back up again to four. How is a CFO supposed to plan in this environment?

What economists have become especially critical about is the lowering of interest rates in response to the 9/11 crisis and the fallout of the Y2K tech bubble. Keeping interest rates low too long was certainly a primary cause of the housing bubble. Ben Bernanke recently spoke out on the subject and said that it wasn't interest rates that caused the housing boom. Well, if it wasn't interest rates, then it was regulation or the lack thereof. So if the Fed didn't actually pull the trigger, at least they supplied the guns and the ammunition.

In softening the blow from one bubble, did the Federal Reserve's policies create another? Alan Greenspan believed that people could not foresee bubbles and therefore could not prevent them; then the process of cleaning them up largely fell to the federal government. This is another element of thinking that is certainly being challenged today. Even if bubbles cannot be predicted, at least we ought to be on the lookout.

2008

The current crisis has been the scarlet letter of market-based governments like the United States. We are the poster-child for the crisis. Those that followed us in the deregulation model have also suffered. We have to get back to the time when regulators believed in regulation. As the recovery develops, market-based systems should work better in allocating resources, which should lead to a quicker recovery. Granted, in the developed economies, there are headwinds in putting the massive number of unemployed back to work. This won't be easy, but innovation and information is our friend. The ascent of money has been a catalyst for the growth of civilization.[76] The innovation of securitization and financial intermediation has been a boon to the world. The financial system is the brain of the economy and, with renewed regulation, the market systems will work in correcting these excesses. Of course, it won't hurt to see a few people behind bars, too.

Most of the credit problems have dissipated but that does not mean we can't go through this type of panic again. Some areas of the credit markets will never be the same. It will be up to the economists and regulators to figure out some safety measures to make sure this domino effect from subprime mortgages on down to the shipment of Taiwanese motherboards should not take place again. However, we aren't going to get a universal law of economics. We're going to have to deal with the reality that sometimes humans are not predictable.

The government will continue to stimulate the economy until it recovers, looking for realistic signs of stabilization and growth. Without the government's artificial stimulus, the economy would continue down the path of debt destruction: lower prices on assets financed with high debts, forcing even more sales. If you owed a lot of money, would you want inflation or deflation? Let's say you owed $1 trillion. If you have inflation, eventually when you pay back your debt, you pay back in cheaper dollars. With deflation, those dollars that you're paying back are actually more powerful. Deflation creates more purchasing power. A dollar today is worth **more** than yesterday.

Let me ask you again: If you owed a lot of money, would you want inflation or deflation? There is no question that the United States government needs inflation, but at an acceptable rate with which the rest of the world will agree. Foreigners will continue to buy our IOUs. Even with inflation, we need growth in the economy. We have some real debt challenges but we must lean to the side of growth and inflation. With the massive stimulus we have unleashed, this will be the most likely result.

A growing consensus predicts a weak rebound from the recession, but that would go against a trend dating back to the Great Depression that recoveries always surprise on the upside. The debate is unfolding today. The rate of change of human civilization continues to accelerate. Innovation is rapidly increasing, putting America in a possible higher growth track. We will have to see. Time will tell.

Capitalists are people working in their own interest. Socialists are people who work for the common good. Both are right! Capitalist systems do get information out to participants, whereas socialist systems do not. The more information that's available, the better off is the informed decision-maker. Do you think the spread of the Internet, enabling even the poorest peasants in the world to own cell phones and to be able to text into a social network, is going to favor capitalist or socialistic systems? That's right, capitalism will win, and, in fact, it already has. "In essence, capitalist systems are a mechanism to which economies may generate growth in knowledge."[77] The Internet era has changed us. If governments make decisions, information flow will trickle down to the general public, who will then applaud or criticize the actions of the day. The information flow should be available to all. Let the market dictate who makes the decisions. The most informed can make the best decision. The madness of crowds is usually better than a madman! In this ever-changing information flow that makes markets work, governments won't be able to keep up.

Imagine a storeowner who has an "idea" one day. That one person standing in the middle of Nowhere, USA, has more information than any bureaucrat in an ivory tower. Not even the person standing next to him may envision the same idea, certainly not someone outside the man's line of work. The capitalist system gives ideas such as these opportunities to compete to be developed and be adopted in the marketplace. That "discovery" makes it far more innovative than a top-down system of socialism. These bureaucratic systems are unlikely to take such small pieces of information from far below and make accurate decisions as to what will be successful and what will not. It's kind of like the government deciding who will win and who will lose a football game. You have to play the game.

Yes, the U.S. is doing that today, playing the game. It does it every day with 300 million decision makers. Unfortunately, there is not a wide understanding of these benefits of market systems, but people use information mechanisms like cell phones or pagers or Blackberries every day. The person who makes a discovery broadcasts it over a social network such as Twitter and it is on the news tonight! The Internet and the rise of social media will alter the balance of power between governments and citizens. The market performs its own trial and error analysis. People want this color or that style. All the time, a feedback loop is created with the sale or purchase: "Hey, that works! Someone bought it. There, it happened again." Technology will provide this "Internet generation" with the largest increase in expressive ability in human history.

Economic theory should look at humanistic, game theory, and empirical evidence of what consumers actually do. The problem was not being able to incorporate conflicts of interests and self-dealing into our mathematical models. A long held belief in a school of economics is that markets are dynamic and individuals cannot be accurately assigned a probability of acting a certain way. Once the sporting event starts, it is very difficult to predict each movement as they will feed from the prior actions. Everything is connected. Markets are spontaneous and work in real time. Predicting human behavior is unrealistic. It was a selective reading of the literature on economic theory. "The consumers of economic theory tended to pick and choose those elements that best supported their self-serving actions", said Barry Eichengren in his book "The Last Temptation of Risk".[78] The top young economists are increasingly empirically oriented, so that their work is grounded in observation of the real world.

As hard as it is to see in this difficult environment, the U.S. must remain among the world's leaders in banking and finance. We need to push the science of economics further. It is a matter of national security. The principles that have been discovered thus far on risk management, option pricing, auction design, and the rest are all extremely important for the progress of the world. We need to spend some time working on separating risk from uncertainty. Just because something hasn't happened doesn't mean it won't. Risk managers have to be reined in. Private sector experts should be called upon and, at times, made to serve the public purpose.

The Nobel Prize was awarded this past year to Elinor Ostrom, the first woman to win the Nobel Prize in economics. Along with Oliver Williamson, she was awarded for research into the limits of markets. Surprisingly, her doctorate was in political science. She investigated how informal groups that used resources could better manage them than governments or corporations. My brother is an example of such an organization. He lives outside Mill Valley, California, where there is a large expanse of land that is too hilly to build on. With the dense undergrowth, it is subject to a natural fire time and again, and fire roads need to be maintained to make sure engines can quickly get to the point of the blaze. His loose organization of people who use these trails for exercise is much better informed to maintain and to correct problems in the trail network. Elinor Ostrom said people should have the capacity and power beyond the bureaucracies that govern them. The economists need to get out of their ivory towers and meet with the finance operators, the social scientists, the hot dog vendor, and the trail runners. We may have to turn away from mathematics for the time being.

～ ～ ～

Margin Call

"The bank is a place that will lend you an umbrella in fair weather and ask for it back when it begins to rain."

—Robert Frost, American poet (1874 to 1963)

Have you ever experienced a "margin call"? It is not a pleasant experience. Your banker calls at 3 p.m. and says, "We need to sell something to pay off part of your loan…the collateral value has dropped below what is required as security." The 2008 correction was a combination of many failures and margin calls. It was a "tail event" of many proportions. Risk is concentrated in these rare, hard-to-predict, extreme market events.[79] Did you notice that there were some days in 2008 when the stock market was up 200 points with an hour before the close but it sold off quickly in the last hours of trading? That's investors settling positions by the selling of assets to meet margin calls. De-leveraging is usually forced. Lenders require more collateral or funds to pay down debt. If the borrower does not provide these, the lender has the right to sell the collateral to pay off the loan.

We witnessed a margin call in the markets, the **largest margin call in human history**. Not just in stocks but in bonds, commodities, ETFs, closed end funds, anything that is liquid and sellable. Anything with a price must be sold! It must be sold! By midnight tonight! In a de-leveraging, assets that are not liquid cannot be sold. Those include private capital, hedge funds, partnerships, and over-the-counter securities (credit default swaps), but these assets cannot be sold quickly. As a result, the prices of liquid assets fall more to provide cash because of the illiquidity in other assets.

Bear Stearns was perfectly compliant with regulations of its liquidity on the eve of its bankruptcy. It had followed international standards of capital and even held billions in excess reserves. That capital must be immediately liquid but can be invested in assets like stocks or bonds, according to the regulations. This presents a problem if there is a "rush to the exits," or if there are too many sellers. In the panic, there was no market for the securities that Bear Sterns held. No one could or wanted to purchase them. The regulations for liquidity and capital proved to be too loose and not effective. On top of this was an equity cushion that was far too small. Bear Stearns' leverage ratio was over 40 to one. The top ten U.S. banks had leverage ratios of 35 to one. At Citigroup, at the end of 2008, it was 64 to one.[80]

The Pyramid Scheme

Hedge funds, which typically operate in a leveraged environment, magnify the prospect of gains for their clients but they also charge for it. Hedge funds typically receive 2/20, or two percent of the total assets under management, and twenty percent of the profits. Their strategies also magnify the potential losses. Operating on a five-to-one leverage, a fund would own $1 trillion in securities with only $200 million in ownership equity. A decline in the value of those securities of 20% would completely wipe out its capital and the hedge fund would have to be immediately liquidated. Should the hedge fund be on a ten-to-one leverage, only a 10% decline would be required. Hedge funds invested in these fixed income securities, too, because with the yields that were offered, although they were only incremental over treasuries, when multiplied by five or ten times leverage, an investor could enjoy a stock returns with bond-like risk. On paper.

All financial models attempt to simplify and explain a reality that is increasingly complex. A large assumption in most models is the ability to liquidate or sell something. "These simplifying assumptions are generally true most of the time. The problem is that they are not always true."[81] Markets are not infinitely liquid. Even if the securities are for sale and the buyer's cash is available, people are emotional and, at times, act irrationally.

Hedge funds, too, in the massive markdown, needed to provide collateral and liquidate not only their subprime investments, but any other investment on their balance sheet. Since nobody wanted to own subprime securities, there were no prices. They couldn't sell that. So what happens if you're leveraged ten to one and ten percent of your portfolio is in subprime? You end up keeping the junk and selling everything else. How about forty to one? Where were the regulators?

Securitization also had a hand in this. Until this crisis, banks would diversify risk by selling mortgages from their own local environment and purchasing a pool of mortgages from many regions across the country. This diversified their exposure to the local market. The conventional wisdom was that this diversification from many uncorrelated regions would experience the timing and depth of business cycles differently. This was so powerful that rating agencies caught on to this aspect and began to rank these diversified mortgage securities highly. Rating agencies are paid by the companies that create the securities, kind of like the lemonade stand you had when you were young that was frequented by neighbors and friends, not actual customers. The way that rating agencies ranked securities was also deciphered by the big security firms, so that they almost knew beforehand what the ratings would be. There were only twelve companies in January 2008 that attained the highest ranking of creditworthiness. Only twelve! However, the rating agencies had by that time rated 64,000 structured financial securities with that same AAA rating. Most of these had underlying mortgages. Some were also leveraged. These AAA-rated securities found themselves in high-quality portfolios. The buyer did not beware![82]

There was also, for several years before, an infatuation with private capital, venture capital, physical commodity, and real plant and equipment investments, which, over time, in part because of their illiquidity, could offer higher returns than the public markets. Due to their illiquidity, though, prices are difficult to come up with, as each transaction is unique and there is no "market" for these investments where buyers and sellers meet and exchange information. Yale and Harvard aggressively put these alternative investments in their endowments and claimed fame when their returns were above everyone else's. Every endowment, pension plan, and individual wanted those returns. These were illiquid investments. There was no market and, therefore, no price. The wisdom of crowds turned into the madness of the mob.

Our banking system was taking on leverage and illiquid investments. In fact, banks started looking more like hedge funds than banks. When the margin call came, President Bush's "No Child Left Behind" program was turned into "No Bank Left Behind." Since the elimination of the Glass Steagall Act in 1999, which separated banking from investments, banks took on more leverage and risk. Your typical money-center bank was trading, issuing securities, and making markets, in addition to providing loans, checking accounts, and taking deposits. The banking system needs to be just that, a banking system, not a hedge fund! The fear was that banks making investments in one little specialized area of the market could affect the whole economy by weakening their ability to make good on transactions on behalf of their depositors. That is exactly what happened. As a result, working people and small business are shouldering a large burden from a problem that they did not cause. It happened before in the 1930s and we fixed it. The fix was repealed by political pressure and contributions by anxious bankers eager to keep up with the less regulated foreign banks. There are a lot of risks in the world. When several or many of those risks come to a head at the same time, the combination can prove devastating.

Thomas Jefferson summed up the general reluctance to trust banks, stating, "I believe that banking institutions are more dangerous to our liberties than standing armies." Since the Depression, many shock-absorbing policies have been put in place, such as Social Security, FDIC insurance, and unemployment compensation, along with a strong Federal Reserve and deficit spending in the U.S. Treasury.

What is different about this credit crisis is the speed at which it happened and the global connectivity that has made this truly the first coordinated global recession. The momentum of the decline in stocks was similar to the previous bear markets of 1973-'74 and

2001-'02 —until September 15, the day that Lehman declared bankruptcy. That day credit froze all over the world as bankers and corporations alike did not know who was next to default and which investment values would be impaired. That's when stock market momentum
accelerated on the downside. The global economy was connected to
the credit markets.

The Great De-Leveraging

When we recover from the recent market events and a chart of
the stock market is displayed, what will the arrow pointing to this
period be labeled? What will we associate with this period? It will
not be called "The Great Depression"; most forecast a long and deep
recession, maybe the longest in the post-war period, but not a depression. Most likely, it will be called "The Great Recession," but
what follows will be "The Great De-Leveraging." There was a massive
amount of debt being extended and taken on by financial institutions,
hedge funds, and homeowners for several years that needs to be paid
off. Assets that were purchased on credit lost value, wiping out equity
and leaving the obligation. Homeowners now underwater know this
all too well. Governments are now shouldering a large amount of
new debt to stabilize markets to fill in for the lack of economic activity from the private sector.

We saw a lot of de-leveraging by the end of 2008 from the
corporate side:

1. $4 trillion in money market mutual funds
2. $1 trillion in Total Bank Reserves (above the $50 billion
   required)

3. Many prime brokers increased collateral requirements from 15% to 30%

4. Hedge funds increased their cash to nearly one-third of assets, a record level.

5. Banks reduced leverage as Morgan Stanley's ratio went from 25 to 12 in one year.

The household side, however, has a way to go. Leverage will need to be slowly reduced and home prices will suffer. Many houses are selling today for less than the mortgage that was made. These underwater properties will have occupants drowning from payments that they cannot afford. What is the incentive to continue to pay for a house that has no equity? Many homeowners will be forced with the decision to walk away. Banks have been reluctant to put foreclosed homes on the market; they don't want to flood the market with excess supply. There are several more months of homes yet to be available for sale in this "shadow inventory." With unemployment still high, pressure will build on Congress to continue to act and help.

There is a simple cause and effect, a chain of events that will work to stop the downward spiral. The corporate side, as mentioned, has already de-leveraged. In fact, corporations are beginning to ramp up leverage again. Households, though, are just beginning. Homeowners can't move as fast as corporations, especially when jobs are being lost. Most of the leverage in households is in the home itself. Policies that will stabilize employment will in turn support home prices, which in turn will improve the pricing of mortgage securities, which will help banks investments in mortgages. Putting people into jobs will help the real estate market, which will help banks and investors. Employment is a lagging indicator and will not turn until after the economy has bottomed, but it is the key here for this recovery. Government forces have to provide an early boost!

The U.S. is a very transient economy with many citizens picking up from one part of the country and moving quickly to another where there is an employment opportunity. The amount of initial claims for unemployment insurance from laid-off workers is the highest in all developed society. Throughout this crisis, 500,000 people were regularly laid off EACH WEEK! This is a function of our society's structure based on free markets. The number is vastly larger than all of Europe. More socialist economies, like those in Europe, have "work for life" norms or large and extended benefits for the unemployed. The U.S. is more dynamic and flexible. The forces are in place to move, motivate, and train our workforce into new directions. Some autoworkers in Detroit who were laid off are retraining themselves to become metal workers, service providers, or other value-added laborers. Retraining individuals is imperative since there are so many industries that simply won't be hiring at the rate that they once were. That's where government help is needed most. Some of those newly employed will be from initiatives by government mandates. That will serve to stimulate the market mechanism until demand recovers.

The Great De-Leveraging will take years of adjustment. The average consumer has spent far too much money in the past without much regard for the size of the debt. Many individuals took advantage of easy credit, purchasing homes and houses for investment. Mortgage debt outstanding since 2000 almost doubled (as shown by the chart below) through 2007, and there was an acceleration right after 2001.

**Consumers Took on Increasing Amounts
of Debt with Low Interest Rates.**

(Source: Prudent Bear)

Many mortgages were designed for interest-only payments because the principal would be based on a presumably ever-higher home market value. Mortgages could then be refinanced. This siren song has caught millions of people. Twenty-five percent of the homeowners in the United States now owe more to their banks than the worth of their home.[83] Credit cards have become a way of life for some individuals and, with high double-digit interest rates, have also become an endless merry-go-round of interest-only payments. Gerry Cuddy, CEO of Beneficial Mutual Bancorp in Philadelphia, says, "Credit cards...we won't touch them. We think they're destroying the economy. They're obsolete." Cheap money became a drug that led to a hangover the next morning.

For any student of finance, the credit economy was bound to run in trouble; it was just a matter of time. With over $2 trillion in consumer credit and card debt, the U.S. consumer will remain constrained from further exorbitant purchases. This will be a slow and steady challenge to our economy going forward. The margin call for credit card investors was where they could not make the minimum payment. The collection agency calls began. As many consumers started to realize, collection agencies will take less than the principal outstanding because, in a sense, that money has been already written off as a bad debt. High interest rates, especially favoring good borrowers, funded these charge-offs. Consumption that was paid for by credit cards and mortgage equity withdrawals hit an all-time high. Though consumption reached over its long-term average of around sixty-five percent of GDP to seventy percent, it should now be slowly reverting back for years to come. In order for the U.S. economy to grow, it must revitalize its export industries, reinvent its competitiveness, and remain the world leader in services.

Future Dangers

The Great De-Leveraging is already over in the corporate sector; in fact, the pendulum may have already swung too far. Too much cash is on the sidelines, enough cash and short-term investments to buy the entire market value of the S&P500. The storm in corporations is about over. The damage is already done. Now comes the rebuilding of confidence in the economy. We witnessed a time when stock values were cheaper than buying businesses in the real economy. If an investor were to buy stock in a company and then sell all the parts for more than the investment, that would attract private capital. Takeovers are already beginning to happen as companies are evaluating investments not only here, but abroad. Already this year, several mergers and acquisitions have been announced. The market appears to be recovering from the trauma of this margin call.

The financial meltdown led to a large surge in the ownership of dollars around the world and an equal increase in the trading value of the dollar versus other currencies. The crisis, as it is starting to fade, has now taken the dollar to a new low. This would mean the large foreign holders of dollars would see a depreciation of their investment. The worst may be yet to come but it is up to us as a country to determine what the future will bring.

Even though the combination of the United States consumer spending and Chinese low labor costs propelled both countries to new economic levels, the partnership is becoming strained. Should the United States not import from China, prices on all manufactured goods would rise drastically, creating an inflationary recession, as the same income would now buy fewer goods. Should the Chinese not export to the United States, economic growth would stall. Exports to the U.S. accounted for almost eight percent of their GDP in 2008.[84] To be sure, China is still buying dollar-denominated treasury bonds. However, since the world has slowed, their buildup of reserves has also been reduced. In 2008, Chinese reserves were built up by over $400 billion. In 2009, predictions have estimated the Chinese reserves will rise by only $100 billion. In the face of a deficit approaching

$2 trillion, there needs to be other buyers for U.S. Treasuries around the world or interest rates must rise to entice new investors.[85] Why interest rates haven't risen already is a puzzle.

As the U.S. is looking for investors for its debt and is being shunned by its large foreign holders, it may need to look no further than the mirror. As U.S. households reduce leverage and the savings rate increases, domestic investment in treasury securities could increase tremendously. After all, savings is the source of all capital. As the shock of the illiquidity from "the endowment model" of investing (where large allocations of assets are invested in private equity, hedge funds, emerging markets, and commercial real estate) wears off, these fund flows could easily move back into better liquidity trades like U.S. Treasuries. The greed of searching for higher returns with assets that may be needed quickly is one of the basic mistakes of all of investing. Many banks have learned from not matching their assets and liabilities. By lending long-term but borrowing in the short-term, assets that are needed in the short term should be invested in highly predictable cash equivalents. Harvard can afford to invest its endowment this way. It is impractical to invest teachers' salaries, lunch subsidies, and electric bills in illiquid long-term investments. U.S. Treasury securities don't appear to be as bad an investment as they used to. They provide immediate liquidity.

The United States government's reaction to the crisis has been to increase its own leverage to offset the de-leveraging in other parts of the economy. Once again, a large shift in assets from one direction has to offset a large shift in assets from another. Any expert would be merely guessing if these two huge forces of the world were going to be exactly equal and balanced out. Most likely, there's going to need to be a lot of tinkering and modifications to the Fed's strategy. The United States will have the largest debt ever incurred, not just in dollar terms, but among the largest in the size of its debt to the overall economy. The interest on the debt alone could easily amount to twenty percent of the annual budget of the United States government. Interest on this debt and the level of interest rates that we pay is going to be key.

More importantly though, is the fact that our system is already indebted and cannot afford another wave of financial panics. The action taken on financial reform is moving slowly and being watered down by special interests as it gets close to being law. There were incentives for financial firms to "beat the system" by creating opportunities for themselves in illiquid and misunderstood markets. Banks will slowly replenish their capital. However, the largest margin call in the history of the world has left American consumers substantially weaker. We must act quickly to repair the damage in the financial system to prevent another 100 year flood from spilling over into the real economy.

 Paradigm Shift

"Scientific advancement is not evolutionary, but it is a series of peaceful interludes punctuated by intelligently violent revolutions, and in those revolutions one conceptual worldview is replaced by another."

—Thomas Kuhn, *The Structure of Scientific Revolutions*, University of Chicago Press

A paradigm shift is what happens when normal science runs into two answers to the same question. The worldview enters a crisis: accept the new one or rely on the old model. Welcoming in the new view leads to a scientific change, a revolution of sorts.

What is a paradigm? A paradigm is a worldview or way of explaining how the world works. A paradigm could also be about your own worldview. As a child, everything is large and you feel powerless, except for the ability to cry and try to get what you want. As a teenager, the world becomes more manageable as you dramatically enhance reality through emotion. As a college student, we start controlling the world with intensive, innovative studying techniques and beverage consumption. As an adult, you feel more in control of your life and act accordingly

To follow the history of changes in the worldview, we only need to look at science. Aristotle's views dominated explanations for the heavens and earth for thousands of years. As he lived in 300 B.C., it was easy to say something and not be refuted because calculations were really just rough estimates. This paradigm of the earth, at the center of the universe, was made up of only four components: earth, water, air, and fire. This was a generally accepted worldview. When Galileo fashioned a telescope from glass lenses and a piece of lead pipe, he used it to change humanity's perception of its place in the universe. When Galileo pointed a telescope at the moon, he jotted down what he saw. For centuries before, the worldview was that Aristotle was correct. A better explanation for the movement of the planets and the sun was that the sun was at the center and the earth was merely one of the planets revolving around it. By changing this worldview, the scientists changed the focus of God and the world. If earth was not at the center of the universe, then it was not God's sole focus. Obviously the Roman Catholic Church did not immediately accept these new conclusions. Galileo proposed to get rid of errors of the Aristotelian paradigm and, as a reward, was subjected to house arrest for the rest of his life. Even though he died in 1642, his book was listed among the Index of Prohibited Books by the church until 1835, almost 200 years later. Astronomy moved from a medieval astrological **art** to a mathematical **science.**

There were many changes in worldviews throughout the next thousand years, but most of them involved religion and God's place as a totally controlling and universally intelligent being. Many more worldviews challenged this new paradigm from Galileo, and the introduction of mathematics and calculations gave evidence to support these theories. The Dutch became important in this regard as they had been a very tolerant people of other opinions; scientists were able to do their research and publish without dire repercussions from the Church. The search for truth came forward with Descartes, a French philosopher and mathematician living in Holland, who was not in a battle with the Church but simply on a search for the truth. A good scientist doubts everything. He said famously, "I think, therefore I am." Following that was the rise of Isaac Newton, with his 1685 publication on the principles of mathematics. This new paradigm used math to explain observations and led to the belief that earth was just a small planet inside a vast universe. Three hundred years ago, the ability to observe, calculate, record, and distribute findings was extremely limited. Three hundred years represents maybe ten generations. Today, a fifth grader with an iPhone has better calculating abilities than a world-renowned scientist did in the 1600s.[86]

Paradigms die a slow death and more likely are folded into new worldviews. Old paradigms sometimes prove to be useful, certainly to the people who are reluctant to change as they cling to their old beliefs. But even the new paradigms contain elements of the old. A paradigm that has really proven useful is hardly ever scrapped. Instead, the old paradigm is included in a more widespread developed theory with a broader application, even if the two views may not be totally compatible.

Quantum Physics

Take, for example, elementary atomic physics or quantum mechanics. When I went to grade school, it was simple. Matter was made up of atoms. Atoms were made up of atomic particles like neutrons, protons, and electrons, which behaved predictably and things were orderly. It was a very clean, certain view of the world of basic building blocks. We drew little diagrams of atoms and everything was neatly in its place. Since the particles were so predictable and orderly, this explained how objects were, too.

There has been some advancement since then with regard to this worldview. Scientists have identified even smaller elements than these with less predictability and order. In fact, one word can describe the depths into which we have been able to delve in subatomic physics, and that word is "chaos." The particles of the world are not orderly—that is, if you can observe them. Quarks are smaller than neutrons, protons, and electrons. Quarks actually compose them and are quite elusive. They're constantly moving, banging into each other, changing into other versions of themselves, and creating havoc. There is no predictability or explanation for the violent and chaotic nature of elementary particles. In a sense, shit happens.

Scientists have also discovered that the simple act of measuring something in the world changes what you are measuring. How you measure it depends on your point of view. The act of measuring is based on tools that are human creations. From a moving train, it is easy to look out and see things passing by, knowing the train is doing all the moving. From a boat, looking to another boat moving in the opposite direction, the answer is not as easy. How much is current? How much is our boat moving and how much is from another boat's power? Measuring nature depends on a viewpoint. Perceptions of boat speeds will be different from the shore than on the boat. Nature's laws may be more elusive that we originally thought.

Let's make it easier to understand these dynamics. Dating. There are many different characteristics that can connect two people together, from common interests to similar values and tastes. What really does determine if two people are compatible? Is it the science of compatibility or the art of human behavior? Some things are predicable but then some things are not. I am a Leo (lion) and I married a Taurus (bull). On paper, that is a match of two leaders who want to control things. Usually not good, but we've been happily married for twenty-two years. So, the science part of the equation was overcome by the art. Matchmaking is both art and science; although the dating services I see advertised on TV sell compatibility matches, you never know what is going to happen on that first date!

Why is this so important in a book about world change? Most of the world is defined by physics and mathematical equations that define how space, time, and gravity work. These equations come from Einstein's General Theory of Relativity. These two worldviews, quantum mechanics and relativity, are **incompatible**. The two paradigms that define the world today do not co-exist. In larger things, it's all about mathematical rules that are followed. In the study of small things, order is almost nonexistent and the rule is: There are no rules.

In a sense, there are two worldviews, one orderly and one not. We have a theory of big things, like gravity and planets, which is almost the polar opposite of our theory of little microscopic things. These two paradigms may explain how things interact, but what about life itself?

The more that we are able to understand ourselves, the universe, elementary particles, and the meaning of life, the more we will be able to build economic systems that are compatible with life itself. There is a recent shift in thinking that human behavior is more unpredictable than previously thought. But with what we know now about atom composition and behavior of elementary particles, that the essential building blocks of life are quite unpredictable, it shouldn't have surprised us or alarmed us that people can act this way too. The school of thought in economics has been dominated by the efficiency of markets and mathematical formulas. After 2008, the crowd chaos theorists will probably tug at this standard view. Hopefully, it will give way to a new thought process of how human beings act in a marketplace.

One economist leading this effort to combine new theories is Andrew Lo of MIT, who has created an "adaptive markets" hypothesis, which supposes that humans are neither fully rational nor psychologically unhinged. Instead, they work by making guesses by trial and error. If one strategy fails, they try another. If it works, they stick with it. He borrows heavily from evolutionary science and survival of the fittest in that he sees that markets are fiercely competitive. Because the world changes over time, people can make mistakes using old worldviews. The old strategies become obsolete and new ones are introduced and accepted.[87]

As human beings advance the civilization and discover more truths, previous worldviews may be shattered. Should God one day show himself to the world, all religions that do not conform to that worldview could perish. Yet, some could survive even in the face of an opposite truth. Human religious history usually does not change so suddenly. It's a gradual acceptance of a new worldview while still embracing the old. Some older paradigms are usually combined with new ones, despite being mutually exclusive.

Since the world is made up of both predictable, mathematical precision and randomly chaotic events, then the proper view to describe how the world works must also incorporate both. Since the first scientists began to measure things, that is what was emphasized. We became better and better at measuring and calculating. The more elusive mystical and unpredictable side of the world has become overlooked. Humans like certainty and conversely don't like what we cannot measure and predict. In our current paradigm, we have been working hard to advance the science but have left a lot to be discovered on the artistic side. We really have been using one side of the brain when we should have been using both.

Old Worldview

The old worldview consisted of a "free-market ideal" ideology that somehow kept in check the morality of each individual decision. Knowing human nature as we do, this would be a foolish assumption. Leading the markets to have free reign was none other than the most powerful man in the world, the chairman of the Federal Reserve Board, Alan Greenspan. Since this person dictates interest-rate policies and manages the largest economy in the world, he also affects just about every country in the world. That cannot be said for the president of the United States. Greenspan was the most powerful man in the world. The Greenspan "put" was used frequently to describe the ability of the U.S. government to bail out the markets should they fail. The "put" in financial terms is an option to buy at a lower price. Knowing Greenspan would support the markets in failure allowed participants to take on more risk without consequences. This is the issue of "moral hazard," where market participants know the government will bail them out so they take on risk without regard to failure. Greenspan himself said the Fed could not predict bubbles this is after his historic "irrational exuberance" speech in December 1995, saying that the stock market was wrong to think the economy was strengthening. That was just before one of the strongest economic moves in world history with the technology boom. It is also ironic in that most economists believe that the Fed created not just one bubble, but several. Greenspan believed the Fed couldn't either predict or deflate bubbles, but would be there to pick up the pieces when they burst.

The turning point of the old paradigm seems to be in 2008, whereas in the decades before that, risk in the world, as measured by volatility, was decreasing. Risk in the investment field is measured by volatility. Standard deviation. This is the average difference that the return will be from the mean. Risk is really the uncertainty of a value. Volatility can work both ways, good and bad. In the minds of most individuals, however, risk usually means one way, bad or down. Volatility in economic growth, the booms and busts of business cycles, was decreasing around the world for years. Measured in GDP, the boom-bust volatile swings of economic growth lessened considerably into the new millennium. At least the calculations suggest it. No country had it quite so good as the United States and, in the past twenty years, we experienced an enviable record of steady growth with low inflation combined with high employment. The Greenspan "put" looked like it was working. The Asian financial crisis and the Russian default that torpedoed Long Term Capital in 1998 was a crisis that the market quickly recovered from. The world after the Y2K tech bubble in 2001 seemed riskier, but volatility in markets fell. Even after 9/11, an Iraqi conflict, Enron, WorldCom, and Tyco, the recovery of the economy and the financial markets led participants to believe that the risk of investing had lessened. Most economies around the world followed suit. Americans became connected with free markets around the world, which encouraged globalization.

Corporate buyers, private equity investors, and fixed-income lenders appeared to be operating as if the world had changed. The drop in **volatility** was a sign that **risk** was also falling. These two terms are used almost synonymously in investments. Investors then made a wager that since risk is lower, the more leverage could be safely employed. What caused this decline in volatility? Several things— most importantly, the massive savings glut from Asian country export surpluses was invested in U.S. Treasury securities. As the emerging economies began saving to prevent another shock, their capital had to be invested. The easiest investment was U.S. Treasuries. As the most liquid market in the world, even these massive funds flows made a difference, keeping rates low and stable. Trade within the rest of the world created massive funds flows, offsetting countervailing influences of business cycle peaks and valleys from occurring. Around the world, the global consumers began to invest in housing, durable goods, and other nonessential products. Inventory management became a science, with just-in-time practices alleviating bottlenecks and surpluses left on the shelf.

These sources collectively accounted for a massive and historical decline in volatility. And it was a decline that looked durable. The world had changed into a less risky place and investors held on to this low-risk "siren song." In 2006, the aggregate level of mergers and acquisitions completed reached a record $3 trillion. This is triple the level just three years before. An incredible $2 trillion of that total was funded with cash. In the first quarter of 2007, the value of M&A deals announced rose another fifty percent to a $5 trillion-annual rate. But the largest leverage source came from the deregulation of the U.S. system.

Deregulation led to wide availability of credit and, along with the anchor of low treasury rates, lowered interest rates for all the shades of quality. This process had been reinforced in recent years by securitization. This allowed many new participants into the marketplace apart from the traditional banks. The so-called "shadow banking system,"[88] composed of lenders and borrowers that were not banking institutions, became as important to the overall workings of the economy as the banks themselves. Maybe even more so. These new players did not follow the same banking rules.

Securitization

Credit default swaps (really just default insurance) serve to transfer risk from a narrow sector or industry, spreading it throughout the system. Financial innovation contributed to a sharp decline in the cost of capital and its availability. For example, you went to a bank to get a mortgage to purchase your dream house. Your bank, being small, could not make your loan if it could not sell the loan in the open marketplace afterward. Otherwise, it was all lent out! All the money that it had to lend was already extended. As a result of securitization, it was able to sell your loan into the marketplace, take the proceeds, and lend again. Knowing that it was going to sell your mortgage, it paid close attention to the interest rate that it was going to offer you. It needed to be a competitive interest rate that was then prevailing in the marketplace; otherwise, if they offered you a lower rate, they would not receive the same proceeds for your mortgage when they went to resell it. Too high a rate and they may not get the business from you. So securitization performs two valuable services. You get your mortgage money and pay a competitive interest rate. On the other side, the bank not only makes a profit on this arrangement, but keeps a satisfied customer, which helps the community and is able to adjust its risk exposure. Securitization is one of the financial innovations that have benefited millions, if not billions, of people. In seeking a profit motive, banks were able to help society overall. However, one flavor of securitization was related to subprime mortgages, and in that regard, this one sector brought the whole house of cards down.

Commercial banks, in their effort to keep up with the other banks, also built leverage into their balance sheets, and off in separate vehicles with their own balance sheets, calling them "structured investment vehicles." They could exist on their own with their own funding through the commercial paper market. But in practice, after a crisis, the debts of this small company would have to be realized by the commercial bank. So an off-balance sheet investment became an "on" balance sheet one.

"What makes today's turmoil so disturbing is that one of the mechanisms which help to stabilize growth has suddenly become a threat to it. Financial innovation is central to the great moderation, but its most recent creations allow credit to be extended on easy terms."[89] With the Greenspan "put" in effect, financial companies leveraged up. This was part of the worldview. Debt, for better word, was good, to paraphrase Gordon Gecko, the Wall Street baron played by Oscar-winning actor Michael Douglas in the 1980 movie *Wall Street.* Greed was also good, as we learned, but it was debt that made greed pay.

The world now is pointing its figure at America and saying the self-indulgence of capitalism has led to human indignity, which cannot be accepted. "Man is an end and not a means. The state is a means and not an end."[90] The new prime minister of Japan, Ichiro Hatoyama, of the Democratic Party of Japan, has stated that each human being

> has boundless diverse and avowed individuality and that each human life is irreplaceable. That is why we believe in the principle of self-independence through which each individual has the right to decide upon their own destiny and the obligation to take responsibility for the results of their choices. At the same time, we also stress the importance of the principle of coexistence with others under which people respect each other's mutual independence and differences.

This may be the new world order for which we are searching, a combination of individual profit-seeking motives and a sense of unity to the total. A combination of the mathematical models and emotion.

It certainly makes sense and is in unison with that worldview of elementary particles, where each small particle will act on its own, but somehow knows it's a part of the whole. The latter is what we've been lacking. Americans should understand they have a moral obligation to look out for their fellow man. "Fraternity can be described as a principle that aims to adjust the excesses of the current globalized brand of capitalism."[91]

America's Worldview

There is a shift in the worldview of most people today regarding the position of the United States and the world. "About Superman and Batman: the former is how America views itself, the latter, darker character is how the rest of the world views America."[92] The new worldview must also realize that other countries around the world are vital participants in economic growth. Instead of a single super-power model, we must realize that it is a multi-polar world today and everything will have several different vantage points. The United States is not the center of the universe.

The new worldview paradigm must incorporate human behavior in the midst of a free global society. Economists must get back to the drawing table and come up with new ideas to explain how markets work. Politicians must also do their homework, understanding markets and where they failed, leading to government intervention. Market participants must seek profits, but at this time, at the same time, look out for their fellow man. Just like the little molecules of our bodies that seem to know what everything else is doing in order to contribute to the whole being, we must build our own ability to be responsible for one another. As we understand more about the meaning of life and how all living beings are connected in structure, we will be able to further our knowledge in structuring society toward these natural laws. In the meantime, we do need a few laws and regulations to punish the bad behavior. In the long term, we need to build our ethics.

A paradigm shift occurs when the scientific evidence starts supporting an alternative worldview. Many worldviews are being altered: America's place in the world, man's self-interest within the context of society, how markets work and don't work. It's not that our current world view is wrong, it is simply incomplete. It's a **combination** of forces; the individual and society, or of math and chaos. How will these two worldviews evolve? The two are contradictory, but are they? Will a combined new worldview encompass both ideas? There is a yin and yang to life that we need weigh and combine together.

6. Currency Conundrum

"Hey, Mister, you got change for a cow?"

—A History of Currency Trading: Sailing the Seas of Money, ahistoryof.net

What would the world be like without currencies? The better question is: What *was* the world like? Obviously, before currency, people bartered with shells or beads or cows. "I'll trade you three cows for your daughter." It still takes place in some regions. When someone had a surplus of things that could be traded, they would barter for things they needed. Over time, currency was invented because it was much easier to take a stack of papers with you to the market instead of a stack of cows. But what, really, is money? Pull a dollar out of your wallet and then take a look at it. What value does it really have? It's just a piece of paper, an IOU from the U.S. government, but it is also readily acceptable, "legal tender" for transactions around the world. Currency provides three functions: First, it's a **standard** of value, and a generally agreed upon measure. Secondly, it's a **store** of value, as someone could place it under a mattress for many years and it still retains its value, depending on inflation. Finally, it's a **medium** of exchange, which is easily transferred from one person to another in exchange for goods or services.

Man has been roaming the earth for thousands of years. How come it took him so long to invent a currency? The entire 5,000-year span of written history is only equal to about one half of one percent of the duration of human life on this planet. People had plenty of time to trade before they learned to write. It didn't take long to find out who had the most sheckles and, therefore, who was the richest man in town. A sheckle was an ancient unit of weight and currency and the first usage of the term came from Mesopotamia in 3000 B.C. It referred to a specific weight of barley, which really is a receipt for a barter transaction. A "barley/sheckle" was originally both a unit of currency and a unit of weight. Barley was a commodity currency. Sometimes a commodity currency was perishable, which meant it lost value or had very little value outside the region. Other examples of currency included pieces of leather, cloth, and tree bark that were blessed by the authorities with some insignia and offered some standardized value.

Interest Rates

Interest rates preceded currency by over a thousand years. Hammurabi was a king of the first dynasty in ancient Babylonian and set policies for the maximum rate of interest that could be charged. The best-preserved ancient interest rate was within the "Code of Hammurabi." The maximum rate was thirty-three percent per year for grain, re-payable in kind, and twenty percent per year for loans of silver by weight. Today those interest rates would seem quite unit onerous! The Romans also had a body of laws regulating credit. The famous "Twelve Tables," dating from around 450 B.C., dealt with credit with limitations on interest rates to no more than eight percent per year.

A transaction that was discovered to be higher than this legal interest was penalized by fourfold damages.

The progress of history of human civilization can be closely linked to the ability to trade. Innovations in finance parallel human progress. In Niall Ferguson's book *The Ascent of Money*, one can find a case that financial innovation propels humans to greater economic insights and wealth. However, there are always temporary setbacks in this long-term overall upward trend, as people need to adjust periodically to new methods.[93]

In 640 B.C., the king of Libya had a great idea! He began stamping ingots with an imperial coat of arms, representing the wealth of the kingdom, and attached a special value to them. Coinage became widely accepted in Greece as silver discoveries made the founding country rich. The concept of standard coinage was introduced since coins were pre-weighed, contained a certain amount of metal and were typically minted by governments in a highly controlled process then stamped with an emblem that guaranteed the weight and value of the medal. Although gold and silver were the most commonly used medals to mint coins, other metals were used depending upon the availability to each country. Gold typically traded at a higher value than silver, which typically traded at a higher value than copper and other metals. Just like today.

Precious metals served as the world's currency for many years. Spain's political supremacy on the world stage in the seventeenth and eighteenth centuries set up the first widely accepted currency. The "pieces of eight" spread from the Spanish territories to the Americas, westward to Asia and all through Europe. The pieces of eight symbolize how coins were chopped into pieces for smaller bits of value. International trade was denominated in terms of currencies that represented weights of gold. Most currencies at the time were really just different ways of measuring gold, which was truly the world's first global currency.

It was China that first came up with the idea of paper money...well, at least wood. They used tree bark stamped with imperial markings as a form of currency. The penalty for forgery was death. Europe also issued currency made from leather. It was the gold traders who really created paper money by handing out receipts to people who stored gold with them. Customers who had these gold receipts could trade them for goods and services. Stability came into the system when national banks guaranteed to change money into gold or silver. The British pound was originally a unit denominating a one-pound mass of silver. The pound sterling was the result. The term "backed by gold" became the driving force of the world's economies, known as the gold standard.[94]

Dollar

The term "dollar" had its roots in Bohemia, where coinage in 1519 became popular. After the United States' independence in 1776, a medium of monetary exchange was necessary and, in 1792, the dollar was created as the fundamental monetary unit. The value was set to the value of the Spanish dollar. The amount of equivalent gold per dollar continued to be adjusted as conditions warranted until the 1920s, when exchange rates began to fluctuate wildly and the international gold standard broke down. Many countries found it impossible to continue converting into gold, especially if the government was spending and printing more money than was available in gold reserves.

In the United States, the dollar continued to be redeemed in gold until the passage of the Gold Reserve Act of 1934, prohibiting the coinage of gold. This began the abandonment of gold as a standard value for change. The U.S. set the value of the dollar at a single unchanging level of one ounce of gold to be equal to thirty-five dollars. During World War II, the creation of the International Monetary Fund, or the IMF, conceived a new system and was adopted at the historical conference held at Bretton Woods, New Hampshire, in 1944. The system attempted to provide stability and international trade by pegging currencies to the dollar.

The U.S. government guaranteed the exchange of gold for dollars on demand, and other countries defined their currencies in terms of dollars, making the American dollar the international currency. The power and wealth of the United States at the end of World War II enabled the country to set the rules for the rest of the world. The golden rule can sometimes be known as "those who own the gold, rule." Since the United States owned roughly three-quarters of the world's gold reserves, it made the rules.[95] Once again, the real world of economics made this system fragile. Eventually, the U.S. could no longer pretend that the dollar was worth as much as it had been and officially reduced the value so that the one ounce of gold was now worth seventy dollars. And, finally, in 1971, we got off the gold standard altogether. This marked the beginning of a new structure of currency and transactions called "fiat" money.

Fiat Money

Fiat money refers to the money that's not backed by reserves of a commodity, where the money itself is given value by the government.

"Fiat" means "let it be done" in Latin, or by decree enforcing legal tender laws. Governments through history had often switched to this form of non-metal-based money in times of war, famine, or other calamity by suspending the exchange of money and printing what they needed. Periods of inflation usually followed and bankruptcy followed soon thereafter as many European countries went through this cycle many times over.

In 1970, foreign nations held almost $47 billion in U.S. currency and the U.S. had to face the fact that it no longer had the necessary gold reserves to back this up. The U.S. finally switched to fiat money and since many of the other countries of the world were affixed to the dollar, this meant that much of the world's currencies also became non-commodity-based. This can also be known as the "floating rate" system, under which prevailing currency exchange rates would fluctuate according to supply and demand. It also gave countries the ability to spend what they had in the bank and essentially turned paper money into IOUs.

Technology also aided in economic transactions as banks, which were accustomed to moving huge piles of gold from one bank to another, started to record activities on large storage devices. At the end of the day, these devices could tally up the pluses and minuses to equal a single figure of transfer, which, before long, took place in the form of book entry instead of physical movement. Transporting huge sums of commodities or cash from bank to bank had effectively become a thing of the past.

While the floating currency system allowed market participants to judge the economic stability of countries and to vote by holding or not holding their currencies, it also allowed market dynamics to be more powerful than the governments themselves. The value of the currency would be no different than any other tradable commodity since supply and demand would determine prices. Generally, today, countries with mature stable economic systems use floating rates and let the market decide. A policy of excessive spending or lax controls would not attract investors. Should policies be weak, it is reflected in a weak currency, and so forth. A weak currency, in turn, makes imports more expensive and exports more attractive overseas, thus giving the country the ability to correct its excesses through greater exports and lower levels of imports.

Where emerging countries feel they need more government control, they may "peg" their currency to a stable exchange rate. In a pegged system, a national bank must hold large reserves of foreign currency to mitigate changes in supply and demand. A black market may spring up where the currency traded is not at the official government exchange rate. When traveling to a new country, Jim Rogers, the famous international investor, would always check out how close the black market rate was from the official rate to determine how safe the country was to invest in. If the citizens of a country have no faith in the value of their currency, they will always seek to convert into other currencies and further depress their country's finances. This is another example of the market mechanism.

In January 2000, the euro became the single currency of the twelve-member nation-states of the European Union, making it the second-largest currency in the world. This was the **largest currency event in the history of the world**. Sixteen national currencies have now been replaced by the euro roughly equivalent to the size of the United States economy. The euro currency would increase trade across borders, provide price transparency, and eliminate exchange rate fluctuations, fees, and expenses across country lines. With a single currency, it would also be less cumbersome for people to cross into the next country to work and allow for more flexible cross-border transactions. When I traveled in Europe recently with my family, we took the Chunnel from London to Paris. As we pulled into the Paris Metro station, I told my family to be prepared for custom lines and baggage checks. There were none. Today, once you are in Europe, there are no customs, tariffs, or border charges to incur. You are in the euro-zone.

Dollar Today

According to the Bank of International Settlements, the average daily transaction amount in the foreign exchange market is $4 trillion dollars.[96] This market began in the 1970s, when countries switched to the floating exchange rate format. More recently there has been a call for a new international standard currency as the dollar has come under severe criticism for U.S. fiscal and trade policies. Large government deficits and large trade deficits mean an inflation of dollars around the world that would debase the value of the dollar holders. A super currency was believed to be the DEY, an acronym for "dollar, euro, yen," but that idea quickly became moot with the rise of emerging markets. The IMF has introduced the idea of a world currency through their existing Special Drawing Rights. SDRs would be made up of a basket of currencies representative of the amount of transactions around the world. Possible flexibility to this could be annual adjusting and rebalancing the mixture of currencies. The SDRs could calibrate the size of reserves accumulations and trade deficits thus aid in re-balancing excesses in the world economic system. This could further global stability.

Today, the U.S. dollar still accounts for over half of all financial transactions around the world. This is down considerably from a decade ago, when approximately two-thirds of the world's transactions were in dollars. The dollar will still remain a large, if not the largest, component of an SDR for decades to come. The fact that gold and oil are both priced in dollars will continue the dollar's importance. Until these commodities are moved to be valued on a basket of currencies, that will be the case.

There has to be a high level of trust between different countries before a true world currency could be created. As part of their religion, some Islamic countries are against the idea of paying interest for loans, and they will also have an important say in the matter. India recently has purchased a large amount of gold reserves to help create more balance in their foreign currency investments. China, with its very large reserves, has also recently purchased gold but holds most of its reserves with its largest trading partner, the U.S.

The Yuan

China has the largest currency reserves in the world. How did this come to be? China pegs its currency to the U.S. dollar. For a developing country, that's commonplace. As a world superpower, that's ridiculous. China officially delinked its currency, the *renminbi* or *yuan*, from the U.S. dollar in July 2005, resulting in an initial devaluation of 2.1 percent. Since then, it has been unofficially pegged. In the beginning of 2009, the dollar hit a high against most currencies amid fears of the credit crisis and worldwide recession. The dollar could be exchanged for eighty euros. It could also be exchanged to the Chinese *renminbi* at 6.82. At the end of the year, the dollar declined to sixty-five euros. The Chinese *renminbi*? It was still worth $6.82! China has pegged their currency at, what some experts believe to be, twenty, thirty or forty percent under its market value. Emerging economies do to this to stimulate export demand, making their goods cheap overseas.

As the United States took advantage of low-cost Chinese goods, China could not take the proceeds and convert them back into the country. The money had to remain outside China otherwise the Chinese currency would appreciate. For the most part, these funds went to purchase U.S. Treasury securities. Since China is a strong exporting country, letting the currency appreciate would make its exports more expensive, erasing its competitive advantage. Also, with a stronger *yuan*, imported goods would become cheaper to Chinese consumers and would increase consumption. China has to move its economy from emphasizing exports and infrastructure into consumption and services and the currency exchange rate will have a large effect on the transition.

The Chinese have taken part in the largest **financial imbalance in the history of the world:** the U.S. trade deficit and the under-valuation of the Chinese *yuan*. This imbalance could lead to a crisis.

The rise of Chinese economic power should also be reflected in their currency. The artificial "peg" to the dollar has benefited the Chinese as much as it has benefited the U.S. with low-priced goods and low interest rates. The Chinese export economy has really been unchecked without a free currency exchange and will remain so for many years until government pressure can increase against them. There was a time early in the current presidency when Tim Geithner and President Obama considered bringing charges at the World Trade Organization against China as a "currency manipulator," but it's difficult to be sounding off against a country that owns so much of our debt. China has been critical of the United States for its fiscal and trade imbalances without mentioning that some of those imbalances have been brought on by Chinese currency policy. By making prices so low, we certainly have consumed more. Economics 101 would tell you that demand increases with lower prices. The Chinese are fighting against an appreciation of their currency. By criticizing our own domestic policies, they are diverting attention away from themselves. It is the U.S. that should be criticizing China's export and currency policies, but we seem to be timid in confronting this issue. Yet it is the most important current topic for international finance.

Trade Deficit

The United States trade deficit reached $800 billion in the year 2008. Half of that is related to energy; the other half is related to consumer goods. Granted, many of these trade numbers do not take into consideration many goods that are imported to the United States and assembled here for value-added sales throughout the world. But they are the best measures we have. The partnership between the U.S. and China has been dubbed "Chi-merica" in that it has benefited both countries. Because the United States is such a wealthy nation, its minimum wage is far in excess of that of emerging economies. We will never be competitive in manufacturing basic goods unless transportation costs rise dramatically. Our value added comes from our

Ingenuity, intelligent design, and technical capabilities. We are a value-added manufacturer.

More recently, China has begun to issue *renminbi*-based debt outside the country. It wants to exert its influence in international transactions. If China wants to have a say in world finances, it must begin to consider to float its currency more in line with market rates. The government is delaying this flexibility because it is taking full advantage of the situation that makes the country richer. A flexible exchange rate with the Chinese *renminbi* would make their labor costs seem higher than many of the emerging countries surrounding it. It remains to be seen how long China will continue this game of cat and mouse.

The Group of Seven, the leaders of the seven developed economies, has something to say about this: "We welcome China's continued commitment to a more flexible exchange rate, which should lead to continued appreciation of the *renminbi* in effective terms and help promote a more balanced growth in China and the world economy."[97] There needs to be some type of central bank intervention in currency markets to be able to uncover unfair trade practices and make a system that is equitable for all.

China is stealing exports from other countries, just like it did in 1998 before the Asian contagion. Production had been built up too fast in the Asian community and without increased demand; a domino effect of devalued currencies toppled the countries and their growth prospects. It took a while for this area to recover. Could we be setting up for a crisis again? It certainly looks like it. China is ramping up production and spending that cannot be totally supported by its internal growth of consumption or renewed consumption from the overly leveraged developed world consumer.

There may be an announcement that the Chinese have adjusted the Yuan upward. Do not let this change your focus. Most likely the adjustment will be small and the effect will be minimal. There is a long path ahead to correcting this imbalance and it is not only the United States that will benefit; it will affect all exporting nations.

Dollar and Debt

The dollar standard has allowed the United States to finance incredibly large deficits throughout the world. By taking on this debt, the United States has had the ability to invest these monies elsewhere, possibly earning a higher return than the interest that's paid. The interest that we are paying today is minimal. If we take the majority of this money that's borrowed at a fixed rate and invest it into business equity with the potential to grow, we are borrowing to fund growth. By encouraging U.S. companies to invest and expand overseas, we could be creating a stream of tax revenue to pay the interest cost and the debt back. Equity growth rates over time will be higher than fixed income rates. We can borrow "short" from countries that need a safe, liquid asset and invest in "long" and more rewarding assets. The U.S. had $6.6 trillion of foreign equity shares and direct investments at the end of 2008, with foreigners holding $4.1 trillion worth of American stocks—a net difference of $2.5 trillion. It is with this in mind that we have been described as the "world's venture capitalist"![98]

If we are using these funds to pay out entitlements, that is not an investment; it's a payment that has little long-lasting value in the form of future tax revenue. By re-allocating human capital to industries that are creating jobs, we are creating future tax revenues. We should be using these low interest rates to invest in equity, maybe not directly, like the Social Security system buying stocks, but that is not such a bad idea, either. Many other social security systems of the world invest in equities. Just by investing, we can grow our way out of this debt burden.

The United States is acting as banker of the world. We are assisting China's development with the currency peg, much like foreign aid. Because of our world power, we have dictated that this arrangement be accepted by other nations. China would not want a substantial decline in the dollar; they own too many of them. By appreciating their currency, they would, in effect, be leaving money on the table. An appreciation of five percent would immediately lose them five percent in their dollar investment. I don't care if you are worth $50,000 or $5 trillion—no one likes to leave money on the table. It would be like leaving the heat up and water on in your house and then leaving on a long vacation.

If they continue to peg the currency and the dollar declines, they don't lose money and they win more export business. It is a win-win situation for China. Americans need to be as aware of this situation as they were in avoiding "French fries" to protest the French not strongly assisting us in the Iraq conflict. It is an issue of national security. Other countries, especially export countries like Germany, should be vocal that China is stealing business from them through unfair currency manipulation.

A growing number are concerned that a "day of fiscal reckoning" is imminent in the United States. Our balance sheet and its indebted citizens have been throwing a party and consuming like it's 1999! The welfare state, universal health insurance, Social Security, and entitlements are the largest portion of the United States budget, and have to be managed better. In the meantime, the role of the dollar in the world has to be redefined. It will be a very slow transition because, right now, there are no real present-day alternatives.

7. Demographics—Plain and Simple

"I choose America as my home because I value freedom and democracy, civil liberties in an open society."

—George Soros

The forecast of the population in the world is the most powerful, predictable, and investable trend that investors can utilize. It's easy to understand that population trends seldom change very much from year to year, yet over a decade or two, new regulations, conflicts, and security measures may have an impact on immigration and overall populations. If one can look into the future and see population trends clearly, one will have a competitive advantage in today's markets. These trends are not going to be pleasant for the developed world. In fact, the developed world is decreasing in size, not just relatively, but in absolute terms. The emerging world is *rapidly* increasing in size, and the world as we know it will never be the same.

Population trends are quite consistent. Over a ten-year period, fertility rates, death rates, and immigration or emigration don't change much. David Kay, professor of economics at the University of Toronto, says, "That's why I like demographics as the foundation for economic analysis."[99] What they tell us today is that the world will be much different in the future. The "haves" in the developed world don't want large families, while the "have nots" in the emerging world have no choice. The result is an ever-larger and increasing gap in the world between these two income groups.

When we look at world population growth through history, we see an amazing explosion in the growth of human beings in the world at about the time of the appearance of modern society structures, as we know them today. Looking more closely, at about the time of the Declaration of Independence, population growth rates began accelerating rapidly.

Past World Population growth

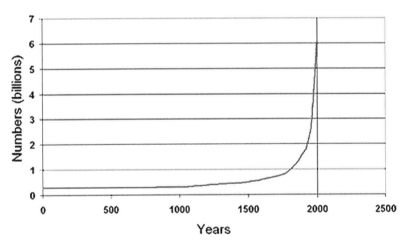

(Source: www.learner.org)

∽ ∽ ∽

The rate of change of growth was accelerating until just recently; the growth rate is still increasing, but now at a declining rate. This leads one to believe that eventually growth rates will start declining, although that still means growth. What is not expected is some disease, famine, or other step backward that would actually mean population declines. That is not in the cards, or it simply cannot be predicted. Even the

Black Plague in the Middle Ages put a mere dimple on the population charts.

Demographic trends tell us a lot about what will be spent in the world. As people move from college-age to young professional, they're buying their first car, their first house, or splurging on vacations and making babies. As they move from young professional to middle-aged professional, they're buying bigger houses, bigger cars, and more creature comforts. As you grow older, you generally spend more money every year until you reach the age of forty-five. At that point (middle-age), you have your largest house, you have all the toys that you've ever imagined, with two cars in the driveway, and you're in the middle of putting your kids through college. You begin to save for retirement, or at least that's what the demographic trend would dictate. If life begins at fifty, at least it is cheaper!

The world's most effective birth control device is affluence. As society creates a middle-class, women move into the workforce, family lifestyle decisions begin to emerge, and birth rates drop. Having large families is viewed as incompatible with being middle-class except in some religions. Better birth control education is also at play. The fact is that the rich are having fewer kids and the poor are having more.

U.S.

Let's analyze the population of the United States as of the last census survey estimate of 2008. With 304 million people in the United States, it stands today as the third largest country in the world behind India and China. White people make up almost eighty percent of the population, black over twelve percent, Asians almost 5%, Native Americans about 1%. Foreign-born amounted to thirteen percent of the total population.[100] How about the percent that had a foreign-born parent? Over 20%.[101] So roughly a quarter of our country is made up of the first-generation from immigrants. That's 70 million people—a population larger than France, England, or Italy. The United States' immigration level is higher than that of almost all developed countries. That will help America grow. And these are the official numbers; the total illegal immigrant population may be 10 to 20 million more.[102]

We are an education society. As far as education, of those over twenty-five years old in the U.S., eighty percent are high school graduates. Those who attended college and attained a bachelor's degree or higher make up over twenty-five percent of the population.[103] Although there are some countries with much higher rates, this is an extremely diverse and large country with many different rural and urban living environments. Those are numbers that are higher than most people would have guessed.

Demographic trends in the coming years present challenges for American businesses in employee recruitment and retention. The baby boom generation comprises about 80 million Americans born between 1946 and 1964. The first wave of this group has already begun to retire, a process that will accelerate over the next decade. There is a baby boomer turning sixty-five every seven seconds. Can you hear them? They're screaming that they haven't saved enough to retire! These retirements pose two problems. First, retirees will put an obvious burden on the health systems and services, falling mostly on the federal government. That's a given. Secondly, firms will see a mass exodus of proprietary knowledge that will be hard to replace. Many businesses will have to entice many of these possible retirees to delay their departure, if possible, as their retirements will pose challenges for firms to effectively train others to step into these roles. The departure of this large generation from the work force could lead to labor shortages in some industries, particularly in technological and health occupations. Labor shortages mean that firms may need to compete for skilled workers, and wages for those positions should reflect that through increases. Businesses also hire talented foreign workers, and immigration is an important component of our demographic trend.[104]

The 80 million U.S. baby boomers have had 76 million echo kids, and with the higher death rate for boomers, the echo kids will eventually be a bigger percentage. U.S. boomers have not exactly been replacing themselves. They've been having 2.1 children per family. This is the number of children that exactly perpetuates the population; in fact, at 2.1 children per family, population growth is zero. Why is it 2.1? Well, if two people get married and have two kids then it's easy to do the math; there's no population growth. But then statisticians have to point out that there are some women who don't have children, or some people who don't get married. That's where the 0.1 comes into play. So at 2.1 children per family, population growth is zero.

In Canada, people are having 1.5 children per family but with their immigration of 250,000 people per year, a much higher immigration **rate** versus its population than in the United States, Canada is still growing. But that's the exception. In Europe, the average is less than 1.4 children. In Italy, Spain, Germany, and Greece, it's around 1.2. At that rate, the working age population declines by thirty percent in twenty years. This has a huge impact on the economy. There are essentially no young people in these countries. There is a lifestyle decision that's made by married people. European workers get 400 more hours of vacation time per year than Americans. In August, the economies of Europe basically shut down when everyone goes on vacation. There is a real talent for living well and lifestyle decisions are important. These smaller working age populations will have to support more and more retirees in social programs. The solution is either higher taxes or lower benefits, and it looks like Europeans will have to experience both. These countries will have major challenges funding their pensions and health care systems, which will put pressure on the European community. Each individual country may want to solve its own individual problems and not be tied to the continent as a whole.

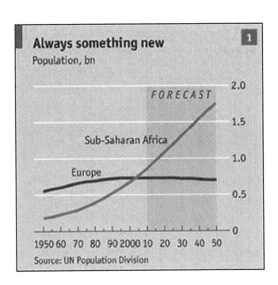

Europe's Population Will Contract while Africa's Will Soar.

(Source: *The Economist*)

Contrast that with Africa, which will continue its explosive population growth. In the chart above, Africa's population is already larger than Europe's and will be twice as big in twenty years. There is going to be an increased lack of "haves" and a preponderance of "have nots."

Japan

Compare this with the second largest economy of the world, Japan, and you see a challenge. The fertility rate in Japan is 1.3. Japan is probably the most rapidly aging population in the world and its population has been declining for five years. It's a power of the past, but not of the future. The latest United Nations median forecast estimates that while the United States' population will grow to over 400 million people by the year 2050, helped by immigration, the population in Japan will decline from the current 127 million to just about 100 million. Even worse, the number of Japanese working age people, which totaled 83 million in 2007, is likely to tumble to 49 million in the year 2050, a decline of forty percent. Japan has already closed 2,000 schools and is continuing to close them down at the rate of about 300 per year. By 2020, one out of every five Japanese will be at least seventy years old and nobody knows how to run an economy with those demographics, let alone a large, developed one. Europe and Japan, which comprise two of the world's major economic engines, aren't merely in a recession; they're slowly *shutting down*.

In Japan, this is primarily the result of society's norms. There is an emphasis on work and long hours spent building relationships away from home. It is also the result of government planning, as Japan always knew it had limited natural resources to provide for its population. It is an island and, by world standards, it is a small amount of land mass for its population. Japan could solve its problems by an aggressive immigration solution, yet today most foreign workers are issued only temporary visas and single males are preferred. Citizenship remains a high barrier of entry for foreigners.[105]

The population of Russia today is 140 million and has been declining for over a decade. The birthrate in Russia is so low that by 2050, the population is projected to be smaller than in Vietnam, Ethiopia, or the Philippines.[106] Russia has one-sixth of the earth's land surface and much of its energy resources, but you can't control or capitalize on that with a very small population. Immediately to the south, you have China, with 70 million unmarried men who need natural resources like water, energy, and something to do. It is cause for concern.

China and India

"Chindia," the combined power of China and India, is staggering. Together they are 40% of the world's population! What is interesting about the two most-populated countries is that China, for the most part, has a one-child policy. China's fertility rate is 1.6. Its population is declining. So with the fear of most Americans that China is quickly going to overtake the United States, China will have its own speed bumps. In fact, it may very well get old as a country before it gets rich. In India, the fertility rate is 2.8 children per family, but there are lots of young people and not enough jobs. In China and India, both societies prefer boys and with medical techniques able to determine that, populations between males and females are manipulated. When left alone, nature produces 103 boys for every hundred girls. In some cases in these countries, that ratio is as high as 130 boys. That will not perpetuate the population, either.

So, today, among the world's largest populated countries, stands China, with over 1.4 billion people. India is second with 1.1 billion people, and the United States is third with a large gap down to 300 million people. This is followed by Indonesia, Brazil, Pakistan, Bangladesh, Nigeria, Russia, and Japan, rounding out the top ten. In the year 2050, according to the United Nations' population estimates, the country with the largest population in the world will be India, with 1.6 billion people. China will be second, with 1.5 billion, followed again by the United States, with almost 400 million people. After that it's Pakistan, Indonesia, Nigeria, Bangladesh, Brazil, Congo, and Ethiopia. Asia will dominate and Africa will also become meaningful in its numbers, whereas the developed world will fall into the minority.

In 2050, Japan will become the sixteenth largest country in population. Russia is projected to be the seventeenth largest, Germany the twenty-fifth largest, and France the twenty-eighth. The United Kingdom, with almost 60 million people in 2050, will rank about thirtieth. For those of you who wish to have a larger say in the country in which you live, consider moving to Pitcairn. This is the island nation that was formed from the crew of the HMS Bounty after having mutinied and finding a place to live out their lives. The population of Pitcairn was sixty-eight in 2000, and it is estimated to remain constant until 2050. It is the 227th largest country in population, measured by the United Nations, and therefore the smallest.[107]

This dilemma between the developed world and the emerging world is best illustrated by looking at Europe and the faster growing populations of the Arab world. In Afghanistan, Iraq, and Pakistan, fertility rates are over four children per couple. These are countries where women are generally less educated, less able to work at a job, and have a social role to provide offspring. The youth explosion in the Arab world means that young people must find jobs in order to keep economies stable. Putting young people to work isn't the most critical thing in Europe, but it is in the Arab areas. The population of the Arab world is expected to grow some forty percent over the next two decades; that is almost 150 million people. "That amounts to the equivalent of two new Egypts," says *The Economist*.[108] Arab countries already have some of the highest unemployment rates in the world, with about one in five young people out of work. The median age in the three most populous Arab countries, Egypt, Algeria, and Morocco, is about twenty-five years old. Arab governments are going to need to address their current economic requirements, converting the flow of oil and petrodollars into self-sustaining structures of employment. It certainly can be done, but there need to be joint ventures with multi-nationals to spur innovation.

Population can be examined on a pyramid that displays how the numbers are distributed among certain ages. What we are witnessing in some of the emerging economies is a "youth bulge," as described by Gunnar Heinsohn. He foresaw that an excess of young males in emerging countries could lead to social unrest, war, and terrorism. The third and fourth sons find no jobs in their existing societies and bear their frustrations out in violent ways.

Raven/Berg, Environment, 3/e
Figure 8.14

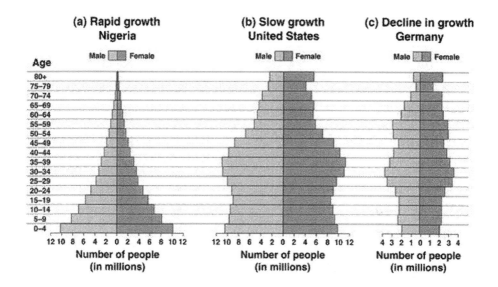

Harcourt, Inc.

Demographics of Emerging, Developed, and Senior Economies

(Source: United Nations, World Population
Prospects, the 2006 revision,
Population Reference Bureau, prb.org)

The Middle East and North Africa are currently experiencing such a youth bulge. It's estimated that around sixty-five percent of the regional population is under the age of thirty. In the northern African country of Niger, the largest section of the population is the youngest, those children under five, with the next highest being from five to ten, and the next from ten to fifteen. In Germany, the largest section of the population is between thirty to thirty four years old but there is a large cross section between fifty and sixty. The number of men and women over sixty-five continues to grow and will become a large cross-section of the population. The number of young people in Germany will not provide a worker base to fill the economy's engine all by itself.

In the U.S., the echo boomers will be crucial to the economic foundation of our country and to the large payments of Social Security, Medicaid, and Medicare that will go to their parents, the baby boomers. Immigration will provide a good growth engine. This is a healthier structure of replacement than all the other large developed countries, except for Canada. Immigration is a part of our national heritage, so in general we have a flexible and tolerable attitude toward it. People come here and can find little communities of their walk of life, and still be within the context of the larger country. Immigration may be the long-term ingredient in our mix that helps America grow.

These age trends will put enormous pressures on the developed countries' treasuries and health care systems, but it will be creating businesses for aging populations. The demographic trend does not bode well for four-bedroom McMansions. There is a chance that within each of those McMansions, there will be a small nursing home, with a nuclear family. A husband and wife may be raising their children along with two or three retired people, providing them a home in comfort in exchange for the ability to afford a nice place to live. In fact, condos in Florida look like a good investment again, demographically speaking.

Economic growth over time has generally exceeded population growth. In the year 2050, we can expect that world GDP will be substantially larger than it is today per person. But will that income be equally distributed? Instead, the well-off are contracting and the not-so-well-off are expanding rapidly. There has been an income gap, especially in the United States, created by the profiteering market mechanism, which has grown excessive executive compensation. In combination with the world population, this income gap has the similarity to the kings and queens of Europe. If not checked, who knows what it will lead to?

Technological innovation is available to the rich. It is not so accessible to the not-so-well-off, and certainly not accessible to the poor. We can't just go around the world and dictate to countries that they need to control their population growth. It is what it is. The United States has a leadership role to show the consequences of exponential population growth, but we can't lay down the law to other countries. The gap between the rich and poor will get worse. The United States must exhibit its leadership role in the world by bringing excessive executive compensation more in line with the rest of the world. In some parts of the world, executive compensation is voted on as part of stockholder rights in an annual meeting by proxy vote. This is a welcome idea to combat the exorbitant salaries of high-level executives and traders within diversified financial companies, and to actually vote on their value added. Now, this is not a market mechanism. It is a social goal that, as the tide rises, all boats will rise with it. Obviously, some boats are going to be bigger, but they don't need to swamp the people in the inner tubes.

Wealth and Population Growth

You'll understand why this is so important when you look at population growth and see that poverty is the fastest-growing characteristic in the world. Most demographic findings would conclude that the largest families in the world come from the most impoverished countries. There are several reasons for this, number one being that higher mortality rates encourage families to have more children. Then there is also the case of labor and the creation of workers by having children, and then there's the case of old age. With the lack of medical facilities, more children bring more possibilities for assistance in older life. Larger families also tend to have less educational opportunities. It's a result of larger families typically being in more rural areas, where educational options aren't available.[109]

The nature of the relationship between demographics and wealth has been debated for centuries. Economic growth has always been thought of as a way out of poverty. Healthcare, a primary determinant of population growth, tends to be better in more developed countries, and as a country becomes more developed, longevity typically grows. In this day of the Internet, population growth will most likely increase the flow of information and exchange between people. It will connect everyone. This type of exchange should result in more innovation. From increased innovation, we can assume that growth of the overall economy will benefit, which will lead to increased resources for all. It is a positive feedback loop.

World Population Growth 1750–2150

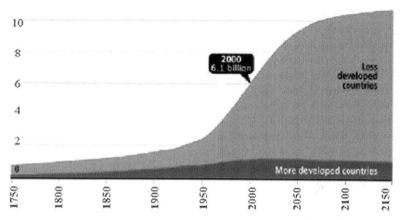

Population (in billions)

Source: United Nations, *World Population Prospects, The 1998 Revision*; and estimates by the Population Reference Bureau

World Population Projections:
Emerging Countries Will Outnumber the Developed.

(Source: Practical Action)

∾ ∾ ∾

We can simply say that the trends that are in place today will remain so. Secondly, we can envision some type of negative social change occurring with the two-tiered wealth structure. With it, there will also be some type of positive social change.[110] The Internet is certainly part of a positive social change, and empowering individuals with information is good. There are changes in health care with bio-genetics and the cost of existing medical technologies dropping. There is a lot of aid that is given to these emerging frontier nations.

Urban migration is also contributing to the population explosion. A million people every week flock to the cities, a rate of growth that far exceeds the pace at which housing can be built and sewage systems installed. This is evident in some of the largest cities in the world. In China, 20 million people per year have made this migration recently. That's a city the size of Philadelphia every four months. Cities have become an important ingredient in furthering civilization as the mass of population on top of one another forces innovative solutions to urban problems. The mixing together of people with different backgrounds tends to create a creative soup of innovative ideas.

What we do know is that we have a challenge to feed the people of the world and somehow raise the impoverished out of misery. This is a necessity for civilization because it would prevent the possible scenarios of conflict, war, or famine that could create social unrest. We have a necessity to manage and provide for an expansion of the human race.

Free markets and rapid economic growth may be the catalyst for future growth, but they can't do everything. Capitalism cannot make long-term social investments like education, infrastructure, and research, at least the capitalism that we know today, which is short-sighted beyond the next earnings report. A mixture of capitalism and socialism is needed. A change in the trend today can have enormous implications in the future.

America is growing. That cannot be said for the majority of the developed world. In fact, the developed world is shrinking and the *developing* worlds are growing. The *emerging* worlds are exploding. The United States is in a very unique position in regard to demographics. Without immigration we are just like the other developed areas with an older population moving into years of retirement and social support. Our immigration is what changes these dynamics.

It is what makes us unique. It is what gives us a chance. There is a combination here that people around the world want to be a part of. The American Dream. The freedom to choose. We are the largest developed economy in the world but people still want to come here. They realize our country offers improvement to their lives. This is the key. Without immigration, this country has large, maybe insurmountable problems.

8. Religion and Politics

*"When I do good, I feel good; when I do bad,
I feel bad. That's my religion."*

—Abraham Lincoln

There are two things that you should never bring up at a cocktail party: religion and politics. Now I know why! Explaining them requires a position, a reference point, and that's where things get distorted. Both are inter-twined with demographics and, as you will see, important in the new order of the world. I will do my best to explain each religion, how they all are similar and how that relates to national politics.

Religion plays a large role in the interests of people—and with any discussion of demographics, we must evaluate not only the economic state of the population, but also its interests. Someone's faith is a daily guide in life. In some countries, religion is not just a faith, but a lifestyle. In others, it is the rule of the land. In many of the developed countries, there has been a separation of church and state. In many of the developing countries, this separation has not taken place. In some of the emerging countries, neither really exists.

It is important to monitor the evolution of the Arab world into the modern age. Population demographics will lead to an explosion of growth in this region and, in particular, in the Muslim religion. It may come as quite a shock to many Americans, but once again that's the nature of the new order of the world, with prior paradigms at risk.

Today, Christians make up the largest religious group in the world, with over 2 billion followers, amounting to thirty-three percent of the world's population. Muslims make up the second largest population of almost 1.5 billion followers and twenty-one percent of world population. Hindus, making up just less than a billion, amount to 13% and Buddhists, with about 500 million followers, make up 6%. Judaism is considered one of the five main religions.

The Muslim world is rising. Within the next several decades, the Muslim population will be close to 2 billion, whereas Christians will just exceed 2.5 billion. Again predictions are hard to make, but it's conceivable in the year 2050 to consider almost a similar population of Christians and Muslims. Muslims could very well make up almost thirty percent of the world population.

Most religions in the world are actually quite similar. Most are monotheistic religions, which believe that only one God exists. In fact, many of the major religions involve the same people in history, but with different interpretations of events. When we look at religions as an outsider, we generally see differences. It is important to realize the commonality that all the major religions do have. A basic code of behavior is common to all. "It is this common denominator which binds us together in humanity and has helped us continue to grow and survive."[111]

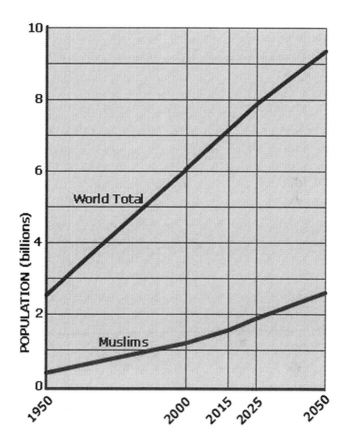

World Muslim Population Will Continue its Rapid Growth
(Source: United Nations Population Fund)

When we review other religions, we must remain open-minded. The easiest way to do that would be to view our own religion in relation to another. What are the guiding principles that support each belief? It is important to the future of the world that people get along with one another, not necessarily that they believe in the same things, but that they respect different viewpoints.

Understanding another religion would be like a foreigner in another country trying to speak the native language. There may be a myriad of misunderstanding until the "eureka" moment when both people understand what is being said. It is that common ground that creates the binding that moves understanding forward. Without the common ground, the relationship is unproductive and two people will part on their separate ways.

Let's first analyze the basic principles of each religion and then try to form some common ties. Many religions are identified with particular regions of the world and represent a race and culture. I apologize to the reader for the simplicity of these observations, but again we're looking for common ground, not making a case for right or wrong.[112]

Christianity

Christianity is the largest religion in the world today and probably will remain so for decades, if not centuries, to come. No religion in the world is more widespread. Christianity had its beginnings among a small group of individuals, led by a remarkable Jewish prophet named Jesus. Christians believe him to be the long-awaited Messiah, the son of God.

Christians accept their life as a test and they are offered choices as they select from alternatives. Faith becomes a major source of energy and decision-making. They're compelled to become what they can and ought to be, for, in a sense, they bear the image of God within them. We are human and make mistakes, but the forgiveness of sins provides a structure for self-improvement.

Islam

Islam was founded in Mecca by Mohammad in the seventh century. Islam is the religion that God gave to the Prophet Muhammad and is documented in the Koran. Muslims are the people who follow the religion "Islam," meaning "one who submits to God." Muslims regard their religion as the completed and universal faith revealed many times and places before, including, notably, in the prophets Abraham, Moses, and Jesus.

Mohammed insisted that each person was responsible for the manner in which he or she lived his or her life. The five pillars of Islam describe the five duties incumbent upon each Muslim. These duties are the profession of faith, prayer, the giving of alms, fasting during Ramadan, and a pilgrimage to Mecca. Muslims believe that humans are created with free will to obey and serve God.

Judaism

Judaism is the oldest surviving monotheistic religion. The texts, traditions, and values have inspired and influenced other religions, including Christianity and Islam. Over half of the people of the world practice a religion that has been influenced by Judaism. It had its origins more than 3000 years ago among the people called Hebrews, who followed writings from the Hebrew Bible also known as the Tanakh and to Christians as the Old Testament.

God revealed his commandments to Moses on Mount Sinai. There are 13 main Articles of Faith that are core beliefs but 613 other commandments which are principals of law and ethics. Jews believe the long awaited messiah, who will bring peace and provide judgment, has yet to come to earth. Actions are the most important aspect of life. Jews believe that they are responsible to build a society that helps "repair the world".

Buddhism

Buddhism is centered on the central teachings of the Buddha, who questioned the purpose of pain and sickness, old age and death. Buddhism does not center on an almighty God, yet around an amazing philosopher commonly known as the Buddha, from the fifth century B.C. Historically, the roots of Buddhism began in ancient India but have spread to other parts of Asia, including China. The foundation of all Buddhist thought is ethical conduct and altruism.

Meditation and wisdom through the study of the scriptures leads to enlightenment in this life or in a subsequent rebirth. Rebirth is seen as a transition from one state of mind to another in a dynamic progression. In Buddhism, karma is that mental act of intent that is more meaningful than the action. Every time a person acts, there is some inward, subconscious intent that will lead to the outward action. The four noble truths of Buddhism are, first: Life as we know it leads to suffering. Secondly, suffering is caused by attachment to worldly things. Thirdly, suffering ends when the attachment to things ends. And, lastly, by eliminating all delusion, you reach enlightenment. The Buddhist way is a solitary one and inner-directed.

Hinduism

Hinduism is the predominant religion of the Indian culture and is often stated to be the world's oldest religion. Hinduism is actually a multitude of religions and is a very diverse collection of ideas depending upon each tradition and philosophy. It is sometimes referred to as henotheistic since it involves devotion to a single God, yet acknowledges the existence of others. Sacred scriptures make up the basis for modern Hindu ethics and these are found in the Bhagavad Gita, which translates to "Song of God." One of the oldest scriptures of the Hindu faith is Mahabharata, which states that the sum of all righteousness is so that "a man obtains a proper rule of action by looking at his neighbor as himself."[113]

People should not hate any living creature, being friendly and compassionate to all. People should be free from attachment, and be content with whatever one receives. You must act as you think best. True happiness lies in the lack of all emotions. Salvation is selected by a contemplative life of meditation.

Confucianism

Confucianism is a philosophy based upon a man, not a god. Confucius was born in China about the time of Buddha in India, approximately 550 B.C. He is often referred to as the greatest teacher in Chinese history and gave his life to the training of the world's moral character. His teachings were recorded by his disciples into four major works and often referred to as the "Shu," or the four classics. His concerns were with stimulating individuals to have the courage to be themselves and gain the wisdom to be an active part of society.

Seeking knowledge strengthens the mind and results in the continual cultivation of society. Confucius said, "Everything has its beauty but not everyone sees it," "Our greatest glory is not in ever failing, but in getting up when we do," and, finally, "Respect yourself, and others will respect you."[114] The religion develops "Jen," a perfect harmony, which is made up of self-respect, faith, loyalty, and diligence.

Common Ground

It can be observed that all the major religions have some common ground. Most importantly, they all tend to deal with ethical conduct and with acting toward others as you would have others act toward you. The "golden rule" of Christianity preaches just that. Most religions realize that humans are imperfect and strive to resist negative human tendencies through principles and guidelines. **All religions seek to improve people and society**. All provide a framework to grow the spiritual life through thought, actions, and interactions with other people. All religions seek knowledge either from discovery or from application of basic laws and traditions.

Most religions are so grounded in a long history that it is difficult sometimes to translate them literally into the modern-day world. Some religions have developed more dynamic elements to deal with change. Some have not. Some versions of the same religion have changed with the world dynamics. Some also, have not. Thanks to TV and the Internet, the average eighteen-year-old is very savvy about what's going on in other places of the world, other religious views, and other types of governments. There's a huge global consciousness in young people and they want to be connected to the world.

America's Religion

In America, we do have a separation between church and state. The framers of the Constitution were largely devout Protestants whose parents left England in bitter opposition to the existing Church. The Church and state in England was not separate but combined, as kings and queens were earthly gods and had almost unlimited rights. To prevent this kind of establishment monopoly, the group that gathered in Philadelphia in 1776 separated religion from politics. In 1791, the first amendment was added, directing Congress to do nothing to favor or promote a particular religion, nor, indeed, to obstruct or penalize one. "In other words, public officials were expected to simply leave religion alone."[115] This allows each to grow and change as people evolve.

The U.S. Constitution brings to all citizens the power and freedom to practice religion of any type, provided it does not infringe upon others' rights as citizens. In a 2002 study, fifty-nine percent of Americans said that religion played a "very important role in their lives," a far higher figure than that of any other wealthy nation.[116] According to a 2007 survey, seventy-eight percent of adults identified themselves as Christian, down from eighty-six percent in 1990. The population of non-followers of a major religion could be as high as 30 million, representing upwards of 15% of the country. [117]

Total non-Christian religions make up only five percent of the faith of the population of our country. Those leading were Judaism at two percent, Buddhism at less than one percent, and Islam and Hinduism at about half of 1%. The majority numbers do not leave the typical American citizen with the feeling that other religions are valid, and supports a worldview that may not be complete. There is a lot of common ground, though, among all religions.

Despite being made up from many diverse immigrants of varied backgrounds, America's makeup is actually very similar and predominantly Christian. It is only when we experience other viewpoints that we can become understanding of alternate views and be compassionate with them. Americans must embrace this; in fact, we need to understand how and why other religions make people act the way they do. If we are going to remain a leader of the world, immigration is going to be a large part of that. How we integrate other people into our society will determine how attractive our country is to immigrants. We are a melting pot and people feel comfortable coming here and staying. We need to make sure, with history as our guide, that this remains so.

John Templeton, the famous investor, spent a good part of his life (and devoted a good part of his foundation after his death) to pursuing the scientific existence of God. The Templeton Foundation is to "serve as a philanthropic catalyst in areas engaging in the life's biggest questions." One funded experiment was using high-tech brain scans to examine how personal belief physically affects our brains—in a sense, how faith changes how we think and thus how we act. In 2001, the Templeton Foundation embarked on a new initiative in unlimited love: "Unlimited love means constant love for all people with no exceptions." I personally feel better about myself and others just thinking about that. Templeton, through his foundation, is trying to connect science with religion and is searching for that universal truth or set of laws that others have sought.

It seems that many of our scientific fields of study are disconnected with behavioral fields. In fact, most of the fields of intellectual curiosity in physics and nature of the universe seek to find a common explanation for all, that universal principle or a source of all knowledge. The highest ideal is some type of human perfection, some spiritual level in which the human transcends his earthly body. Body, mind, spirit: religion often invokes these three terms, or their equivalents, to describe the human condition. "Spirit is the life. Mind is the builder. Physical is the result."[118]

Universal Consciousness

In most religions, there is the quest for a universal consciousness, be it a god or some supreme being. An all-knowing, all-seeing force. An Internet library of sorts that has no physical existence, yet is accessible to one's spirit. A universal, timeless source of ultimate knowledge. It has an explanation for everything. Man continues to try to connect everything in the universe with some unified theory. We are always attempting to find this universal consciousness.

In the past, civilizations grew and expanded their knowledge base only to have their achievements lost to history from a lack of documentation. Even the simple act of copying important papers and books was a tedious job left to monks or scribes. Thomas Jefferson invented a writing instrument that would copy his exact pen movements in a separate piece of paper. This is so he could retain a copy of what he had sent to someone else. That was only 200 years ago. The personal computer and the Internet changed all of this. Documentation and reproduction is commonplace and written world history is being quickly digitized into readily accessible data from anywhere you happen to be. This will greatly improve our ability to understand and seek out new information, pushing civilization even further up the learning curve.

Religions will also have a great effect on how people act in a dynamically changing economy. Confucianism places a greater weight on group effort and consensus building than on individual initiative. In Japan, performance reviews and judgments are still largely time-oriented rather than task-oriented, as in the West. If you're not in the office, no one thinks you're working. There is also a distrust of information flow, as sensitive data may fall into the wrong hands—the top-down organization as opposed to the bottom-up.

The choice facing Muslims is to come up with an adequate and effective response to modern life. Islam, in its strictest sense, is incompatible with tolerance, democracy, or women's rights, all things that are modern. An act of Congress is an insult to the sovereignty of God. "Allah has sent a manual on how to treat human beings. That manual is the Koran,"[119] so there's no need for any other code. "Islam and democracy cannot coexist,"[120] says a Muslim cleric. Islamic prophets are considered to be as close to God as humanly possible. Local governments are centered on them. When the government bureaucracy exists with no democratic representation, what remains is really an autocratic combination of church and state together.

Most Arab governments maintain their power in similar ways. At the apex is a single authoritarian ruler, be it a prophet, a president, or even a royal family. Democracies in the Arab world are largely devised in order to channel and contain political movements, as we have noticed with the recent elections in Iran. Complicating things, America is also Israel's greatest defender and our policies have a sharp impact on all Arab states.

The Arab-Israeli conflict is also one of different worldviews. The physical conflict is related specifically to land, land that the Palestinians believe to be theirs but was annexed for Israel after World War II. The anti-Israel and anti-Arab emotions rank at the top of the highest and most long-standing conflicts in the entire world. Palestine traces its roots to 5,000 years before Christ and a conflict that lasted a mere hundred years is just a blip on the calendar.

America has not helped with the transition of Islamic faith into modern society. First, many Arab lands were developed by American companies for oil. The end of colonialism did not leave the Arabs freed from external meddling. America continues to have an interest in the region and remains the chief armed forces presence in the Middle East. Secondly, the 9/11 attacks made Americans group all Muslims together as terrorists. President George Bush did not portray the war against terrorism as a war against Islam, but that's what most Americans thought.

Small factions of any religion can be considered to be fanatics, even Christians. It is the challenge of Muslims, not outsiders, to recapture the spirit of Islam. "The stark choice for the Muslim world is between the revival of civilization, difficult as that is to achieve, and its secularization and the dissolution of Islam into modernity."[121] Change comes only slowly and there is understandably going to be many setbacks, but the Internet has turned the world in motion. Information will get into the hands of the people and that is the force that will bring more freedoms and democracy. Individualism and property rights are essential ingredients to innovation. Good information will lead to educated decisions.

President Barrack Obama won the Nobel Peace Prize less from his actions and more from his words of compassion and understanding of other worldviews. The exercise of exploring other religious worldviews will be transforming to the average American in that very rarely do we experience people in our melting pot who are substantially different from ourselves. Our role as a leader must become more connected with and compassionate toward others in the world, regardless of worldview. We must seek the commonality in our views rather than our differences. Mostly, we must understand that we are imperfect and that any worldview may not be entirely correct. Therefore, wisdom is the truth. The more we know, the more we will find answers to our questions about the world.

The trends of religion and demographics are powerful in predicting the world's future. As the United States is now a leader in a multi-polar world, so, too, is its primary religion. Christians will become a smaller percentage of the world population as other religions have more robust demographics. The American way of life up until now has been centered on Christianity, and the vast population of immigrants has been similar. Immigration is our key to growth as a developed economy, and as the world becomes flatter, we will have to become more religiously diverse. As American companies expand their goods and services abroad, they will hire more ethnically varied people with diverse faiths. Our economic success is dependent on how much we understand and accept these varied worldviews. After all, we are quite similar and believe in many of the same principles.

ᖋ ᖋ ᖋ

9. Innovation and S-Curves

"Imagination is more important than knowledge."

— Albert Einstein

Innovation is an important component of the world in which we live. Actually, it might be the most important! The heart of innovation is inherently human. A combination or mixture of several sometimes completely unrelated ideas come together to form a new one. Thomas Edison may have been right with his idea that genius is formed primarily from effort, but at times innovation comes entirely from chance. It is important, however, to be looking out for unexpected results or seeking new answers to common questions. Keeping an open mind is crucial.

As Robert Solow, the Nobel Prize-winning economist, has observed, ingenuity is an important component of putting labor and capital together to form output. According to his research, innovation accounted for about eighty-eight percent of the growth in output per man-hours between the years 1909 and 1949. He's labeled this all-important factor "technical change," and it may be nothing less than our country's survival strategy. Ingenuity may be the most important component but it is highly unpredictable. Early Americans had to adapt to change; if they failed, they would perish, or at least take a long boat ride back to their home country. [122]

If you believe in intelligent design or if you believe in a natural evolution of our species, you still have to agree on how human beings have adapted to their surroundings over time. "It is not the strongest of the species that survives, nor the most intelligent, but the one most responsive to change," said Charles Darwin. Our style of capitalism didn't just emerge from the Protestant work ethic, but also from the nature of animals and the theory of natural selection. Most of the world believes in some type of evolution. Scientifically, it can be proven. Evolution, adaptation, innovation, and experimentation are all human traits. Very primitive human traits. Darwin observed that change is at the heart of all human development. Innovation is the fuel of progress in human civilization. Michael Porter of the Harvard Business School says, "Innovation is the central issue in economic prosperity." America believes in this "social Darwinism" and it is the heart of our economic system.

From understanding planet movements to planting seasons, humans have sought to understand and control what they can. Early in life we are always banging things around, trying to fit square pegs in round holes, and trying to see if we can do something our big brother or sister does and do it better! There is something very human about innovation. Great is the human who has not lost his childlike heart.

If you were given the world's strongest computer today, it still wouldn't be able to innovate very well. Creative innovation consists largely of rearranging what we know in order to find out what we do not know. We must be able to look newly at things that we normally take for granted. It's easy to come up with new ideas. The hard part is abandoning something that works well today because a new process or product will work even better tomorrow. Computers aren't yet at the level of trying things with little chance of success. Someday they will be. Computers today are computational instruments that think in straight lines and not by association. Eventually computations can be made to mimic the human brain and how we discover things. That's when change really comes and takes off.

America is unique in the sense that it is so young compared to the civilizations with which it competes, such as Europe, Japan, and China. We have really done so much in such a short amount of time. The United States has been the leader in technological innovation since the late-nineteenth century...well, for most of the modern era. In 1876, Alexander Graham Bell was awarded the first U.S. patent for the telephone. Since then there have been more patents awarded to Americans than to citizens in all other countries combined. In 2008, fifty-one percent of patents were awarded outside of the United States. Of course, this is just a number, not the quality, but it does send a message that our dominance is declining. Our society has encouraged many talented individuals to leave their home countries and immigrate to the United States, producing inventions in this land. This will continue to be a source of growth for the future.

Technical Change

Technical change is a term used to describe improvements in productivity from the same amount of inputs. The United States is a leader in improving productivity. The entrepreneurial dynamic of our economy and the market-based systems upon which we rely have positioned our country perfectly for this highly turbulent, innovative era. Unfortunately, in recessions, research and development budgets are scaled back. These types of expenditure issues are thought of as temporary. Cutting-edge economies like that of the United States make progress through innovation in products, techniques, services, and communication. Emerging markets, on the other hand, grow by learning how to make things. The United States will most likely not lose its lead in innovation should the proper incentives be put in place to continue the type of business structure that has been successful in the past. Private capital and venture capital are important components of this puzzle in that bankers notoriously will not risk money on far-fetched ideas. The money for these new ideas usually comes from one of the "three Fs"—friends, family, and fools.

Innovation relies on individual insights but it is totally **dependent on communication with others**. It is usually one person alone in a lab or basement who makes a discovery that changes how things are done, but it is the communication of that idea that makes a discovery productive and successful. If a tree falls in the forest and no one hears it, it still fell, but it didn't have a human effect. A history of successful startups reads like an illustration of interpersonal partnerships. From Jobs and Wozniak, to Gates and Allen, to Brin and Page, and even Ben and Jerry, many great companies began as a brainstorming partnerships. If we could wire the brain when these occurrences happen, we would have a better picture of how the mind works in these "eureka" moments.

A recent *Harvard Business Review* article measures innovation abilities as five separate areas: associating, questioning, observing, experimenting, and networking. Of these, the first two, associating and questioning, seem to be what make successful innovators different from the average non-innovator.[123] Association is the ability to compare and contrast things. It is not a linear process as it may cross multiple disciplines and jump into varied fields of study. The broader the knowledge base, then the more ability to associate. If we lead in anything in the world, we lead in questioning authority. I should know…my wife and I have raised two teenage daughters. We know everything about questioning authority. It's how our country was born, questioning why people were given authority at birth and not by the strength of their ideas.

Computers will someday be able to think like humans, but will they be able to create like humans? Artificial intelligence will outstrip human brainpower as soon as 2020, says Ray Kurzweil, the futuristic scientist who created voice recognition software in the 1970s, the same software that I'm using to write this book. Ray Kurzweil has predicted that human brainpower and artificial intelligence will be equal sooner than you think, and that will bring in a renaissance of technological development. "Singularity" is a term to define a point in time when a mathematical equation series becomes so large it is infinite (it is also the title of his best-selling book). This point in time is when computers and humans are equal. We are getting closer. Kurzweil has created a Singularity University, an institute that helps senior executives focus on and harness disruptive technologies to prepare for such a time. It helps executives grasp the implication of fast-changing fields, assembling virtual groups with a self-sufficient goal and then disassembling them as needed.

The connection of everybody in the world is a good thing for innovation. Many times in the past, we would find two discoveries at virtually the same time in different places around the world. These inventors now have the ability to exchange notes during their trial-and-error discovery process. The ability to communicate and compute will speed up the process. When we have computers doing this, it will happen a million times faster! Yes, a million times faster— or more. Computers think at the speed of light.

Most of what happens in the world has to do with knowledge, and its creation and delivery through communication. Human beings have been central to this system as a retaining, teaching, and delivery mechanism. In fact, it is the act of getting everyone involved that strongly propels ideas forward. If you work in a marketing organization, you will know what I mean, in the form of a late-night pizza party, along with a keg of beer, throwing ideas against the wall to see what sticks. The reality sets in the next day when the ideas rarely make any sense. But it was an extremely fun project! This is evident on *Saturday Night Live* every week. Sometimes that free association is what makes a breakthrough.

Management techniques like "six sigma" get everyone involved, too. Everyone cares about brainstorming, prototyping, storytelling, and scenario-building. These are all important links in the innovation process. Human beings and communication are the important glue to connect the dots. In fact, this type of haphazard, out-of-the-box thinking has to be part of an organization's DNA. The accountants would not understand why so many people are wasting time. It looks like a beer bash to them. A case in point is Silicon Valley, where many inventive experiments look like fun.

What it Means to You

In the local hospital, you may notice a difference in how information is recorded now than it was before. We may note that the nurses working different shifts on the same patients seem to know a lot about what happened in a prior shift—that is, without actually talking about it. You might also notice that they're asking patients a little bit more information and also recording that. Imagine that? Asking a patient how he feels! This may be the result of research done by Kaiser Permanente. They set out to improve the overall quality of the healthcare experience and a consultant was hired to design work shifts. Most of the results of the project were to engineer shift changes to increase the communication among all the people who would have contact with a patient. Individuals were empowered not only by their contributions and how important they were, but also by the feedback of others, including the patients. The new procedures had a large impact on productivity and patient satisfaction, but they also had a large influence on both the workers' and patients' well-being.[124] The fact that the patient was involved also helped the healing process. The more a patient *wants* to get better, the faster they typically *do* get better. There is a lot about the power of the mind that we do not yet know.

As the core team of nurses, doctors, and support personnel went from carrying out their own individual projects to acting as connected consultants to the rest of the organization, human ingenuity was unlocked.[125] To make sense of continuing medical advances, doctors and hospitals need to form large but tightly knit groups that allow their members to get fast-breaking information and to collaborate on remedies and cures. In a sense, doctors need to link up electronically. Your local doctor may access an expert in an area, from completely different cities at possibly completely different times, extract their expert opinion, and apply it to your own situation: a virtual partnership of doctors and advisers created specifically for you. This connectivity and association is the key to our success in many industries within the information age.

The Myth of Innovation

There is a myth that innovation can't take place in large companies, that entrepreneurship is lost on the big mega-corporation. Many entrepreneurs are sworn enemies of big business. Granted, in a make-or-break business venture, the incentive is to produce something of value, push human ingenuity to its limits. However, we may be able to create that type of atmosphere within a large company. A.G. Lafley of Procter & Gamble has focused his company on innovation, and has been successful in transforming the large and stodgy consumer product business into one of the most innovative companies in the world today. A.G. Lafley doesn't care where the ideas come from, or if they have to be bought or generated internally. He designated a chief innovation officer, increased the number of design managers by more than 500 percent, created an innovation "gym," and acquired companies with bold new ideas.[126]

At Pfizer, Jeffrey Kindler has captured innovation with the "power of scale combined with the structure of small." Small, innovative think-tanks are springing up all around the company. Large companies were not always large, and the bureaucracy that was created might be stifling an ability to shift and take advantage of new markets. This is in the midst of the most disruptive change in drug research, moving from chemical-based discovery to biotechnology and genomics.

The history of innovation follows paradigm shifts along the way, changes in the prevailing worldview. Each decade seems to have a new focus of what is important, from the assembly line in 1910s, market segmentation at General Motors in the 1920s, brand management by Procter & Gamble in the 1930s, decentralized units in the 1940s, manufacturing efficiency in the 1950s, scenario planning in the 1960s, and 360-degree performance reviews in the 1970s, to six sigma in the 1980s. The 1990s was a period of outsourcing and, since the new millennium, we have entered the era of information.

Accidental Innovation

From history, we see that some of our common products were created in odd occurrences and through chance discoveries. Innovation comes in fits and starts and is not always recognized immediately.

Consider:

- Balkanized rubber was discovered in 1839, when Charles Goodyear accidentally dropped a lump of a substance he was working with on his stove.
- The inventor who discovered photography, Daguerre, made a breakthrough when he put an exposed plate into a cabinet in which a thermometer had earlier shattered. The mercury vapors in the air from the broken thermometer developed the photographic image unexpectedly.
- Frozen foods were invented when American Clarence Birdseye traveled to Labrador on a fur-trading expedition in 1916 and came away impressed with how people stored their food in ice. In 1925, he started a company that quick-froze food between metal plates and the Birdseye name lives on.

- In 1928, Scottish physician Alexander Fleming smeared a petri dish with a strain of bacteria and left it on the lab bench while he went on vacation. Mold spores found their way on the dish and multiplied. He had found penicillin.

- In 1934, four years after discovering a synthetic rubber called neoprene, the DuPont research lab created a new fiber called nylon. But the marketing department was called in to figure out what kind of uses this new product could be developed for.

- In 1945, Percy Spencer from Raytheon was standing near an operating radar transmitter when a candy bar in his pocket began to melt. Fascinated, he grabbed some popcorn and watched kernels pop next to the device. The radar range was introduced later that decade in industrial kitchens.

- The hair-growing drug called Rogaine would initially be used for blood thinning. In their exit interviews, the patients realized that their hair was also growing.

- 3M's "post-it note" was also the result of an accident in a lab when someone spilled glue on paper.

"Accidental innovation," as Sarah Jane Gilbert calls it, is an important non-measurable ingredient in the discovery process.[127] It takes considerable capability to see the value in an accident and build upon it. Louis Pasteur called it the "prepared mind." In 1960, Donald Campbell proposed that we think of creativity in two components: random variation and selective retention. One is to generate things that are not related or connected, that we can't think of an advance, i.e., the accident. The other focus is to generate ideas from the discovery; focus on what happened and its implications. The more we lead research in this regard, the more we understand how the human brain works and thus how to create computers to do this thinking for us.

Thomas Edison was the first professional inventor. He is credited with the discovery of the electric lamp, movies, batteries, and hundreds of other things. He had a huge team of people working in a big laboratory in Menlo Park, New Jersey, where he created the concept of a research laboratory. One of his coworkers asked him, "Mr. Edison, please tell me what laboratory rules you want me to observe." Edison replied, "There *ain't* no rules around here. We're trying to accomplish somep'n!"

At Xerox's famed Palo Alto Research Center, innovation was years ahead of the marketplace. Personal computers had fancy graphic displays and a mouse. That was in 1979, before Microsoft or Apple brought that technology to the masses! Researchers sometimes discover things in unorthodox ways. Scientists and designers were encouraged to take a hot shower when working on specific problems in order to unlock subconscious thoughts that may help with solutions. The research center was known for unorthodox methods in developing new ideas. Silicon Valley has never looked back!

Sometimes even experts in the field don't recognize what they've come upon:

- The telegraph's inventor, Samuel Morse, declined to buy the patent rights for the next new thing, the telephone, because it provided no permanent record of the conversation.
- When the typewriter came into widespread personal use in the 1930s, the *New York Times* editorialized against the machine

on the grounds that It destroyed the art of writing in one's own hand.

- In 1957, Ken Olsen received venture capital funding to create Digital Equipment and began to ramp up small computers for business. He later remarked, "There is no reason for anyone to have a computer in their home."
- It wasn't until 1970 that researchers at Corning designed and produced the first optical fiber for use in telecommunications. The company that was known for glass dinner plates quickly shifted to become the optical glass fiber cable leader of the world. Enough optical fiber has been installed around the world to go to the moon and back 350 times. That's a lot of china!

In 1899, the commissioner of the U.S. patent office wanted to shut it down. Charles Duell made his famous quote that "everything that can be invented, has been invented." That was probably at the cusp of the greatest innovative change of all, the Industrial Revolution. The statement was a failure of imagination. Innovation is about failure, too. Of the above examples, how many times had something revolutionary happened, but simply wasn't noticed? How many experiments were tried with no results? How many companies blew up in failure from negative cash flow from funding experiments that didn't produce immediate benefits? This is the nature of capitalism. There is a lot of failure in between the little successes.

Innovation affects you and me and the average American. The history of innovation began when man began to walk and discovered how to make fire. He developed methods of agriculture and domesticated animals. What followed was the invention of the wheel, of writing, mathematics, printing, and what we would more commonly call "civilization." The Industrial Revolution followed the harnessing of power through electricity. When we look at the timeline of these inventions, it's a pretty drawn-out affair. It would look like a flat line with a spike in the last data point.

When major events in the world are plotted together, they seem to find a logarithmic plot. In a logarithmic scale, change is calculated on the last data point, not the starting point. The difference is that the rate of change is being applied to a larger and larger base, and if the growth rate is increasing, large increases are realized. Human knowledge is calculated on its previous data point, what we knew yesterday, and change is accelerating at an accelerating rate. The rate of technological innovation is accelerating; right now it's doubling every decade. Machines will be able to process and switch signals at close to the speed of light. The speed of light is 186,000 miles per second. That's seven times around the world in a second. Compared to the human brain, that's about 3 million times faster.[128] Just think if you could complete your work at warp speed, Dr. Spock!

Knowledge is about to radically change and accelerate, disrupting many worldviews. Scientific discovery accelerates as the methods of calculation and observation are improved. Calculation is at the heart of knowledge and is essential to further push human achievement. It is evidenced in architecture, nature, and even baseball. We are quickly moving up an advancement curve that will only accelerate in time.

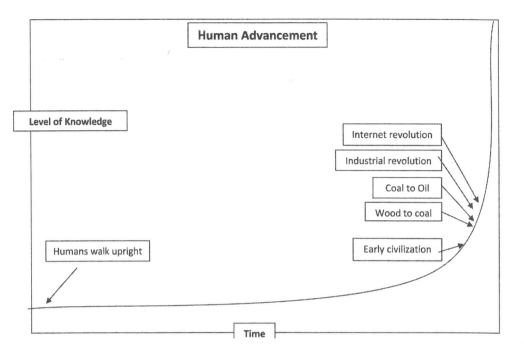

Some have observed certain cycles of innovation. A Russian mathematician observed that innovation typically comes in waves of fifty to sixty years. Named after him, the Kondratieff cycles extend back to the 1750s and document enormous leaps forward in human knowledge, followed by decades of consolidation. The first wave of the early 1800s can be associated with the textile and iron industry. The second wave of the mid-1800s was represented by advances in steam and steel, and the expansion of the railway system. For the third wave of the early 1900s, the catalysts were electricity, chemistry, and the combustion engine. A fourth wave came in the late-1950s with aviation and automobiles. The fifth wave, cresting around the year 2000, was in communication and information technology.

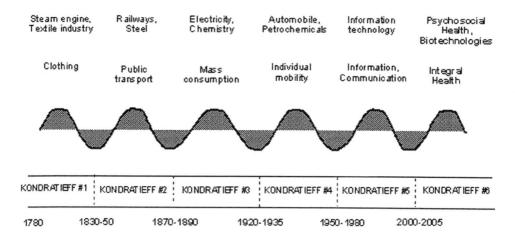

Steam engine, Textile industry	Railways, Steel	Electricity, Chemistry	Automobile, Petrochemicals	Information technology	Psychosocial Health, Biotechnologies
Clothing	Public transport	Mass consumption	Individual mobility	Information, Communication	Integral Health

KONDRATIEFF #1	KONDRATIEFF #2	KONDRATIEFF #3	KONDRATIEFF #4	KONDRATIEFF #5	KONDRATIEFF #6
1780	1830-50	1870-1890	1920-1935	1950-1980	2000-2005

Long waves, Basic Innovations and main application areas

Source: Leo A. Nefiodow: Der sechste Kondratieff. Wege zur Produktivität und Vollbeschäftigung im Zeitalter der Information. 2001

Kondratieff Cycles
(Source: *Glatt International Times*, March 2007)

〜 〜 〜

Each historical wave pushed human knowledge forward, but took years for its application to fully assimilate throughout the world economy. It takes time for people to understand how to work with innovation and new products. The theory behind this is based upon human capabilities of comprehension and adaptation.

Is it coincidence that these waves exist, or are these more a random collection of events that seem to occur repeatedly? Innovation rapidly sets the stage followed by a consolidation phase. We are just getting used to the communication and technology wave and our ability to become more productive with the use of these new tools. The next wave could easily be predicted to be about biotechnology, nanotechnology, and renewable resources. But are these waves a natural phenomenon or will the rise of rapid communication transfer **accelerate** these waves? One would expect these waves to become more compressed because of the interconnectivity of the world. Humans are learning how to use these new media. Things are simply moving much faster today and, therefore, cycles are going to be shorter.

Creative Destruction

When we think of modern-day innovation, it is all about calculation and measurement. The success of any industry is related to the freedom of information flow among suppliers, producers, designers, and customers. This information flow is, in fact, an evolving, innovative process itself. However, at the heart of innovation is disruption. It upsets the status quo. As Joseph Schumpeter, the world-renowned economist from the 1940s, pointed out, innovation is at the heart of economic progress but it is not a smooth process. It gives new businesses a chance to replace old ones and challenges those existing businesses to continue to innovate or to fail. In his most famous phrase, Schumpeter compared capitalism to "a perennial gale of creative destruction" as entrepreneurs create new enterprises through sheer force of will and determination.

The scientific community generally downplays the role of innovation in economics and society because simply it's very hard to quantify. It's not conducive to mathematical models. Even Schumpeter's theories do not instill strong well-being; they are a bit unsettling. The most important feature of technological development is not mathematical; it is social. It is not a smooth process; it comes from fits and starts, and trial and error. Unfortunately, that's the way the world works.

Scientists search for universal laws to understand everything from the heavens to the deep ocean. At the heart of science is the theory that everything can be predicted with some universal rules. Scientists are skeptical of chance discovery, at least at first. Medical science is like this. Nothing is proven until it's tested and retested. A theory is just an idea until it's put into practice and tested, and, only then, after a good bit of research. This is the brute force part of discovery.

Change is good, so get used to it. The future arrived yesterday. Entrepreneurial startups will continuously change their form and direction, even their identity, in the new world business structure. The U.S. funding for scientific innovation has usually consisted of a public-private partnership with government initiatives, including such large companies as Bell Labs, RCA, Xerox, and IBM, along with the NASA Defense Department and others. The U.S. government these days is more focused on providing services to the masses, not on strategic initiatives. Many of these large companies have been dismantled and research and development is much more decentralized. Where the government does not spend money, they can create incentives for companies. Figuring out how to create innovative think-tanks will not be the same as just duplicating what we have done in the past. A university structure, where research is networked, where experienced professionals monitor results, and experimentation is small in scale, may be the best way to innovate today. Many successful companies place an emphasis on smaller units within a larger structure that can act independently up to a time in which they need funding. As the world connects and economies become more knowledge-based, the university-type structure becomes a very critical component of innovation and entrepreneurship.

One of America's truly great assets is that we have a tremendous collaboration among our universities, companies, and research laboratories. We have already connected universities to research parks and business incubators in a kind of public-partnership, as many universities are publicly funded. Once again, innovation is a very difficult thing to pin down; it is very elusive but it can be taught and it comes from a combination of good old research and observational luck—and sometimes lucky research and trained observers.

S-Curves

S-curves are graphical representations of trends. Many natural progressions do not follow a straight-line trend. Instead, they follow a pattern where the beginning is slow, but it gains momentum and then accelerates rapidly. After reaching a point of almost unlimited growth, it then slows down, until it begins to contract. S-curves display a progression that has been used to describe anything from demand for new toys and allocation of resources in a project to Mozart's symphony production, the popularity of a movie star, and bacteria populations in petri dishes. It is a good way to think about trends in the world.

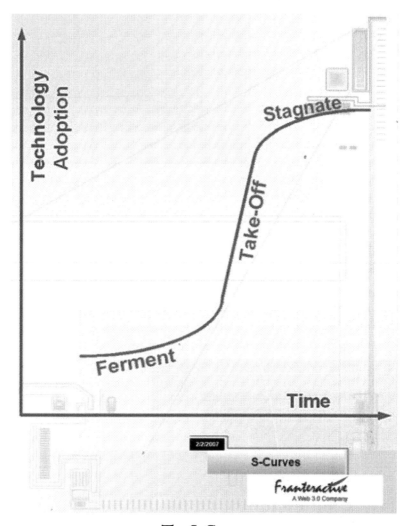

The S-Curve

S-curves can also be used in penetration rates of products, services, and society. As a product is introduced on the left side of the scale, its acceptance is slow. As the product grows market share, it does so in an increasing rate of growth from six to eight to ten to twelve percent. The delta, the rate of change of the growth rate, is increasing. At the point at which the delta is the highest, it has been accepted by the majority of the population. This is the middle point on the graph, the middle of the S, where generally fifty percent of the population has purchased the product. The delta then starts to fall, as product sales are still growing, but they're doing so at a decreasing rate, from twelve percent growth to ten to eight to six. The product's acceptance reaches 100 percent penetration when everybody owns it.

S-curves are naturally occurring trends to project human acceptance of new products and services. They can assist in analyzing the professional services being delivered by a firm. In any firm, there is generally a reasonably good understanding of whether a service is emerging, growing rapidly, maturing, or declining. A reasonable understanding of where the service falls along the curve is usually sufficient for the strategist to make an informed decision regarding the options.

A typical S-curve has four distinct phases. The chart below also shows the likely profitability of a service, according to its position on the curve. During the 'learning curve" of the emergent phase, cash flow is typically negative. Profitability peaks during the growth phase and then levels off and declines as more competitors enter the market and clients become more price-sensitive.

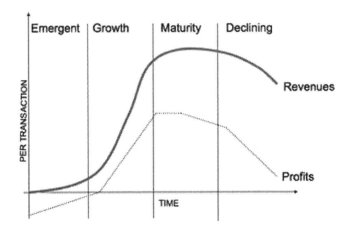

The S-Curve Illustrating Sales and Profit over Time

Innovation is being accepted into the marketplace at an accelerating rate. The time it takes from discovery to testing, product introduction, and acceptance is becoming more compressed. Disruptive technologies have the ability to unseat the more established rivals in months. In the words of Andrew Grove, the former boss of Intel, "Only the paranoid survive." As every company faces internal and external forces that are mostly unanticipated, events may combine together to make an existing business strategy unviable. Key directional decisions will need to be made or undone as decisions are correct or directions fail.

Let's look at S-curves for popular inventions, the length of time it has taken for new innovations to be accepted by the public. The horizontal axis is time in years. The vertical axis is the percentage of households with the product. Look at how each new product has come to the market and been accepted at a more rapid rate.

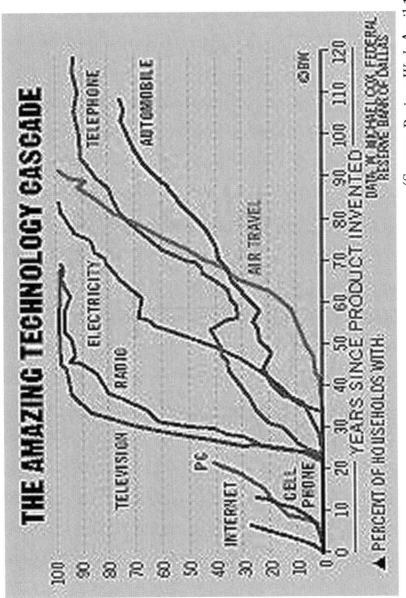

(Source: *BusinessWeek*, April 10, 2000)

This chart illustrates S-curves by product. From the invention of the product, at the lower left side of the graph, acceptance grew ever so slowly. It took over 30 years after the invention of the automobile for the line of acceptance to actually move up; meaning consumers were finally buying them. The higher the line goes, that means the more consumers that own it and the higher percentage of households with the product. It took all that time to proto-type, test, design, manufacture and bring a product to market that could be mass produced. It took eighty years for half the population of the United States to own a car. Eighty years!

After electricity was invented to power light bulbs, it took another 20 years before consumers could actually buy the system. It took an additional 30 more years for the average American to have electricity. The S-curves started to look steeper with the invention of the radio and TV. Granted, these devices are smaller than cars and electrical systems, but the same challenges of testing, marketing and manufacturing had to be solved. It took twenty-five years for the average American to own a radio or a TV.

Then the S-curves start to get steeper. It took twenty years for the average citizen to own a personal computer. This chart above was produced in a *Businessweek* article of April, 2000, so some of the S-curves are not entirely up-to-date. Look at the steepness of the acceptance of the cell phone and a connection to the Internet. The cell phone was rapidly available within five years and the internet only a few years. We are inventing new technologies and bringing them to market faster than before. The pace will only become more rapid. How many cell phones have you owned since your first one? How many iPods does your family own? Do you know anyone that still uses dial up Internet service? How has the iPhone changed the cellular marketplace?

S-curves are illustrated in many different technology markets, from VCRs to cell phones to DVD players. Small markets today could be extremely large markets tomorrow. The navigational GPS market in 2007 was under $200 million. Today it is estimated that the GPS market could top $7 billion. Video games, which amounted to all of $3 billion in 2007, could be over $10 billion in sales today. The music business has also undergone a transformation from LPs and 45s to downloads and iPods. Such transformations require paranoid executives or companies become extinct.

The chart below demonstrates S-curves through time, from the 1900s on the left, to 2005 on the right. Notice how S-curves are becoming steeper and more compressed. We started with the examples of the automobile and electricity. Those were the inventions of the early 1900s. Then we noted the acceptance of the radio and TV. Those were steep S-curves in the 1930s to 1960s. Then we noted the computer, cell phone and internet. These were all rapidly accepted in the 1990s on the far right side of the below graph.

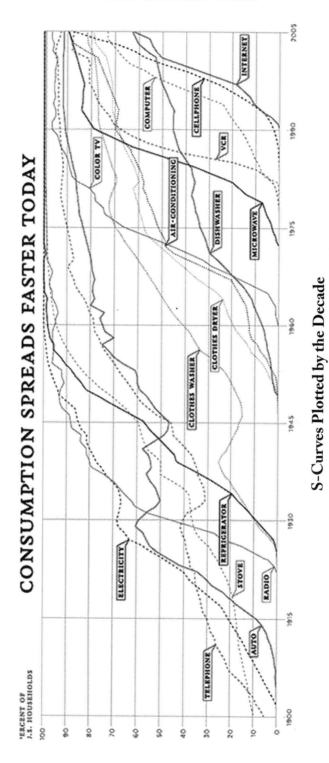

S-Curves Plotted by the Decade

(Source: visualizingeconomics.com)

S-curves are around you every day. You can see them if you look for them. Fads and customs catch on slowly and then explode. Like GPS or video games. Special items become common place after a time. Like cell phones and remote controlled car locks. Some items then become passé and stores selling these fold up and re-invent themselves. Like video stores. It is a natural way to expect a product introduction. It is also how natural forces work, not just manufactured items. The proliferation of everything from flowers to rabbits can be viewed from these power S-curves. Nature also works this way.

It's not just about **technology** either, like computers and spaceships, but technology is an "enabler" of innovation and development across all economic sectors. Nanotechnology, genomics, robotics, and broadband are all increasing rapidly from new information and ways to compute. Human knowledge is increasing in a rapidly increasing rate.

Genomics is changing the way drugs are discovered. The identification of genetic markers for disease is exploding, leading to exponential advances in prevention. Instead of creating compounds chemically, through a tedious process of trial and error, identifying which compounds have an effect on a disease, genomics is allowing biologists to understand the disease itself and then work backwards to eradicate it.

For biotechnology, the chart below shows the rapid identification of new genes connected with disease. Since the mapping out of the human genome, scientists have been trying to identify which gene combinations can cause disease. They have been successful at identifying genetic contributors to disease slowly at first. In 2007, the success rate jumped straight up! The number of markers identified went from 10 in 2006 to over 60 in 2007. (the double asterisk after 2007 indicates that it was only nine months of the year) The S-curve started slowly and after only a few years, was pointed dramatically upwards. These advances should rapidly progress.

Confirmed Genetic Contributors to Common Human Diseases

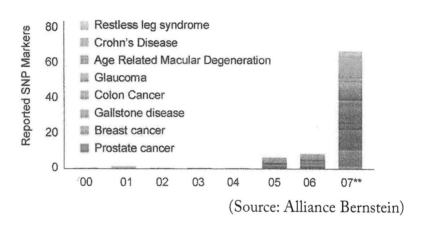

(Source: Alliance Bernstein)

What we now know about life itself is a different picture from just a decade ago. Living things are built on information. DNA is a code of life that is passed on from generation to generation. At times, the information can become changed and distorted but as we are finding out, it can also be corrected. We are what we are made of, both genetically and emotionally. The science of genomics does not pre-ordain our lives; it is what we do with those genes that counts.

Technology is also changing itself. The rapid broadband acceleration is in its early stages. The decline of the "PC" box means the rise of web-based computing, open-source software, and on-line gaming. It is amazing that 80 million people are participants in virtual games, from *Madden NFL* to *Worlds of Warcraft*, up from literally zero ten years ago. The Internet is not just used for e-mail anymore; it's used for creating virtual worlds and projecting holographic images of people from far-off places. At millions of instructions per second, computational abilities continue to increase at Moore's Law of doubling every eighteen months; the types of services that will appear in the near future are quite unpredictable. As Bill Gates has said, "Never before in history has innovation offered promise of so much to so many in so short a time."[129]

The chart below demonstrates that as we invent new applications on computers connected to the internet, they typically require more speed and capacity. A movie shown on a VHS tape has less bits of information in it than a DVD, which has less than a Blue Ray film in high definition 3-D. More calculation of information is needed for each new platform.

Expanding Broadband Applications

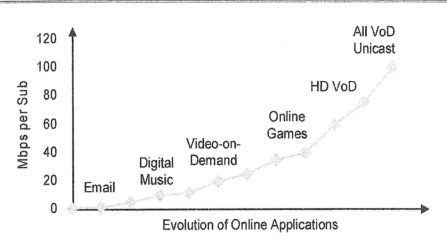

(Source: Alliance Bernstein)

∽ ∽ ∽

As more speed and capacity are made available, then programmers utilize these resources when designing new games. It is a virtuous cycle. The benefit from one isolated area of technology can make a difference to fighter pilot or a teenage video gamer. Those applying the new technology will find weakness and strength of the program that can give feedback to improve the design even further. Improvement in design depends on information flow and communication. Market systems provide that feedback loop quickly and the information age will speed up the iterations between prototype and product.

How do you make the leap from what we have now to what if? We must follow our own genetic makeup. How we are born as people gives us a framework for exploration, curiosity, and trial and error. "Kids are the most creative and innovative of creatures on the planet. Gradually it fades as people try to accommodate what teachers want and then finally what the bosses want."[130] Bringing innovation to market is a lot like surfing, since it is important to watch and catch a wave just at the right time, utilize it, and then look for its decline in energy to exit. It not so much the idea as it is getting the financial backing and then coming to market at the right time.

Necessity Is the Mother of Invention

Necessity can sometimes create solutions to problems. Cell phone usage could be thought of only as utilized by the rich. Not so! In poorer countries, cell phone operators have to find new ways to reduce the costs and the bills for customers. Given India's size, it is an extremely attractive market; however, it is filled with poverty. The country has a reputation as a center of industry, technology, and outsourcing.

Outsourcing is the key of what is now determined to be the "Indian model," an outsourced operation that is scalable and virtual. It can move up or down in size quickly and is connected to everyone in the process, even though participants may be in different companies, countries, and continents. India's biggest mobile operator is Bharti Airtel; all of its operations are outsourced to IBM, Ericsson, Nokia, or Siemens. This passes most of the risk of coping with the daily communication mechanisms to the subcontractors, whereas the company focused mostly on marketing and growth. It is not uncommon to find mobile phones in the poorest of communities in fields cultivated by peasant farmers.

Social networking can be a new source of accelerated innovation. The social aspect of sites such as Twitter, Facebook, blogs, and live communities are rapidly growing and being accepted in record time. S-curves are compressing. Intuit's QuickBooks live community is an example. Users can trade tips on how they use the software and uncover bugs from stress-testing software. Intuit's own technical support monitors the site carefully and finds that many of the users of the software know more about the product than their technical advisors. The social aspect of the program seems to have helped sales and salespeople. Plus the free tech support is saving money as well.[131]

When looking at one of the most innovative companies on the planet, Google, one can also see threats on the horizon. From Microsoft's new entrant, BING, to Twitter and other entrants like OneRiot and Aardvark, Google needs to be paranoid in order to survive and remain as dominant in search as it has been. Faster than the blink of an eye, consumers' tastes can change and the spread of that information can become universal instantaneously. It's a 24/7 public relations contest to stay in front the curve. "Even the best managed companies, in spite of their attention to customers and continual investment in new technology, are susceptible to failure no matter what the industry. Successful companies can be 'unseated' by disruptive new ideas," says Clayton Christensen of the Harvard Business School, in his book *The Innovator's Dilemma*.

In *Business Week's* 2009 ranking of the world's twenty-five most innovative companies, half of them are from the United States, led by Apple, Google, Microsoft, IBM, Hewlett-Packard, and Wal-Mart among the top ten. Look at a company like Starbucks, how they took a low-value commodity, coffee, and created a value with intangible assets, the "experience" of the daily coffee stop. It is not surprising that we are an innovative economy, but we must provide incentives for businesses to innovate. From accounting rules to tax credits, expenses for research and development should be rewarded. It is a long-term investment. Generally accepted accounting principles in the United States deduct research and development as an expense in the year in which it occurs. Conversely, plants and equipment are depreciated over many years. European rules allow R&D costs to be capitalized, spread out over many years to coincide with the revenues that have been created. There is a difference between U.S. Generally Accepted Accounting Standards (U.S. GAAP) and International Financial Reporting Standards (IFRS). The U.S. is slowly moving toward the international standards.

For more than half a century, the United States has led the world in innovation. It's been a beacon for the world, drawing upon the top experts in every field. In today's rapidly evolving, competitive, globalized world, though, the United States can no longer take this supremacy for granted. For first time in modern history, other nations are on the fast track to pass our country in this field or that. However, our economy is extremely flexible and adaptive, and can set new priorities and benchmarks to continually capture innovative change.

We are the information economy and all change begins and ends with analyzing data. The amount of data is exponentially growing and our potential as a society is only limited by how quickly we can analyze and use information. Without the benefit of federal financing, the private sector must do the majority of funding research activity. The government must get involved in direction, strategy, and incentives. The rule makers in Washington must understand our competitive advantage in innovation and information, and attempt to exploit it in years to come.

America is the information economy and the world leader in innovation. Invention is a combination of both art and science, a mixture of a broad knowledge base across many disciplines. Not only is the U.S. economy better positioned to adapt to change, we are also well suited to teach about change. Our society is dynamic, changing its focus sometimes on a headline story in today's newspaper. In a rapidly changing world, only the paranoid and adaptable survive!

10. Investing in the NOW

"The investor of today does not profit from yesterday's growth."

—Warren Buffet

Everybody today is an investment portfolio manager. Yes, that's right, because of the tremendous growth in the individual retirement account (IRA), the self-directed 401K, and self-directed profit sharing plans. Careers that used to last thirty or more years at one company are now jobs lasting five or ten years. Individuals are now more than ever in charge of their investment futures. This has accelerated with corporations dissolving their defined **benefit** plans into defined **contribution** plans. Benefit plans promised a fixed payment in the future. Companies and unions had to have a pool of funds available to pay their retirees a monthly check. These payments were going to be made far in the future and were unpredictable, depending on how long retirees lived. Conversely, today companies prefer contribution plans that only require the contributions to a pool of funds. After that point, the company's obligation is done. No more worrying about retirees living long and requiring a long stream of payments. In today's world, once a contribution is made, you are on your own.

Everyone today must be able to make the big asset allocation decisions. It is vital to get help. A financial advisor of any type is a requirement. With over thirty years of experience in all facets of investments,
even I need help. Exchanging viewpoints and floating new ideas is part
of the investment management process. I am not one of the smartest
thinkers in the world, but I read and listen to them! Sometimes two extremely astute investors will take the opposite sides of the same argument. There are seldom easy answers to the questions of the day, and
sometimes there are so many potential outcomes of current events
that it is vital to keep an open mind. So, this chapter is the most important part of the book. How does one incorporate the new worldview
and the way things change so rapidly into a solid investment strategy?

Many of the people managing your money today are portfolio
managers of mutual fund companies. Some of them may be in their
twenties and thirties. They haven't lived through multiple recessions.
I have a sport coat that is that old! Investing is the one profession
where you actually get better at it as you age. Experience counts.
Living through a crisis teaches you a lot. Agonizing over someone
else's losses because of your decisions is a learning experience. Its
wisdom and experience that helps guide you through difficult times.

Many individual investors can outperform the professionals because they do not have to answer to a committee or risk losing clients if they underperform a benchmark for a quarter or two. What
makes the client happy can be completely different than what makes
the investment manager happy. The investment manager can outperform his index by five percent but still be down by twenty percent.
What will make the client happy: the nominal return or the relative
performance? What do you think? The investment manager thinks

relative, whereas a retail client thinks **nominal**. The focus of institutional pension plans on longer-term data also helps, as most of my institutional clients would only get a quarterly report, while the retail client is on-line every night checking values and dialing up their pulse rate. This emotional detachment of the institutional pension plan may serve as a benefit for making "rational" decisions, although sometimes committees take forever to make even the slightest little decision. Analyzing money managers under a microscope is a job for an analyst. Even the best managers in the world experience poor performance. There is nothing wrong with a strategy that the market is pricing incorrectly, which it usually is.

We are human beings and we are subject to many biases, which are difficult to overcome. Each person has his or her own makeup, leading to many different possible decision-making frameworks. Each person has his or her own mood swings and life changes that can also affect how problems are solved. In general, we need to support and also refute all our ideas to weigh them properly and incorporate them in an investment strategy and portfolio. The most obvious way to achieve this is to be well-read and be able to bring new ideas to an advisor who acts as a generalist to many different specific products and services. It is also helpful to seek out someone who thinks differently than you do, to have discussions about alternative scenarios that you didn't foresee. You are what you know, and if you don't know much then leave it to the professionals. Its judgment and wisdom that make someone a great investor, not up-to-the-minute information, where every second counts.[132]

The stock market is a bit like a baseball game. There are rules. There are great teams and players. There are not so great teams and players. So, why do we play the games? Because anything can happen.

The human element enters into the game itself and can change the outcome that is predicted. On any given day, a lousy team can beat a great team. Over the course of a long season though, the great ones will come out on top. Just knowing the rules of the game don't make you a good player. It is the ability to adjust to events and adapt which makes a player.

For a baseball player, there are going to be "fat" pitches, those right over the plate, at which he will want to take a swing. Like a good batter, though, you don't have to swing at everything. There are also bad pitches, out of the strike zone. Sometimes you get hit by a pitch. Sometimes you close your eyes while swinging and hit the ball out of the park. The best batters over the course of a long season will be those who came ready to play every day, diligently prepared, and capitalize on what they do best. Baseball has a 162-game season. With four at-bats per game, a baseball player may have 650 chances over the course of a season to hit the ball for a base hit. To hit a respectable .300, a batter will hit 195 base hits in the whole season. A less respectable .250 hitter will hit only 163. This difference of 32 hits in an entire season is spread out over the 162 games and is equivalent to one extra hit every five games. If you go to the ballpark every day, you may not even notice the difference between the .300 hitter and the .250 hitter. It is all about getting on base more consistently over a long period of time.

Investors are no different. The moderate but steady returns will, most of the time, beat the volatile but high reaching portfolio. The determining factor is the end point. If you end on a high note, a bull market, most likely the portfolio with the most volatility will win. However, if you end the analysis within a bear market, most like the higher volatility portfolio will be much worse off. There is a great deal of "end point' sensitivity to any investment return. If you set a portfolio up to gain modest returns but emphasize positive outcomes, that strategy will usually beat the high risk, volatile, up-and-down "day trading" account. Compounding positive outcomes year after year is the key to tremendous growth of a portfolio. Trying to hit singles and doubles is the key, not trying for the home runs and striking out.

Stock Values

Stocks follow earnings. Over time, stock prices will reflect the earnings power of companies. As the earnings trajectory in the United States took a hit in 2008, so did all the future expectations. Some stocks are valued by looking far into the future, so even a temporary blip can have dramatic consequences to long-term valuation. We just experienced a boom and a bust back at the turn of the millennium: the buildup of Y2K. How could we have one again so soon? Much of the "medication" that was injected into the economy after 9/11, in the form of lower interest rates and easy money, created a new bubble in real estate. The lack of regulation in the financial markets also led to a bubble in securitization. These twin bubbles burst. Most economists in June 2008 thought the slowdown would be limited to housing and automobiles; it wasn't. They didn't or couldn't predict the margin call that was coming, which was primarily caused by emotion.

We can assume that the long-term growth trajectory of company earnings will be somewhat altered by our recent experiences. In the short term, it will be difficult to see the earnings power of companies, within the noise of a great recession and a muted recovery. There is a large unemployed workforce with no key industries to create jobs.

Job growth has been close to zero for a decade. Housing, automobiles, and finance had a large employee base with good job growth before the crisis. In the future, it will be slow going. We have to focus on the sectors of the economy that are growing and will be growing with the new dynamics in the world. Here in America, we need to focus on value-added, intellectual property that our market system can quickly assimilate.

The possible causes of a lower growth potential will be re-regulation, higher taxes, nationalization, zombie institutions that should have failed, decaying capital stock, and social transfers. The business cycle serves a purpose to clear out marginal competitors and capacity in the system during a recession. With government involvement, it is hard to calculate prospective returns. Government investment puts support under weak companies. There just are not many historical incidences. It will be very hard to predict how companies will grow their earnings. "Animal spirits", those emotions including greed, has to return to the markets. Investment depends a lot on the analysis of entrepreneurs, who must commit their funds to uncertain ventures for extended periods of time.

Investing is about buying cash flows. Savings is what you have left over after getting a paycheck; everyone should have some savings apart from investing. When you are buying cash flows, there is always a price that you pay, which will affect the yield. For a very stable and secure set of cash flows, you will pay a high price and get a lower yield. Treasuries are a good example. For higher yields, more risk has to be taken, with the possibility of some financial stress that may upset the cash flows in the future. Corporate bonds are a good example of these but even municipal tax-free bonds may come under stress that could affect their ability to pay interest. Evidence is California sending out IOUs as interest on their outstanding bonds, which are IOUs to begin with!

Stocks are IOUs, too, but do not carry a specified interest rate in the form of a dividend payment. This comes with ownership, but you are really just buying prospective future cash flows. When financial professionals try to value a stock, they simply try to add up all the future dividends, accounting for some growth from the earnings power of a company. The analysis is the prospect of future cash flows, either in the form of dividends or the eventual sale of the stock. If a company pays no dividends then there is no theoretical support for the stock, except for some future payout, or finding some other investor to pay you more than you bought it for. That buyer will be more enthusiastic than you about the company's prospects. Dividends should be important to long-term investors and retirees. They will exhibit less volatility and a more predictable path of growth. Stocks with no dividends are valued on future earnings and perceptions about the future can change rapidly.

Today, there is very little a "stockholder" will have a say in regarding how things are run, except for the invitation to the annual meeting and an annual report once a year. The company really doesn't care what you think, unless you are Carl Icahn and you own twenty-five percent of the outstanding shares. You are buying cash flows; it is that simple.

People will value a set a cash flows differently depending on their point of view. In fact, every day the market will value the cash flows of the securities you hold with particular regard to the most current news. At times the valuation will be optimistic and at times pessimistic depending on the news flow. It is almost as if some real estate agent comes to your house every day, knocks on your door and then tells you the value of your house. They say that depending on interest rates, mortgage lending, employment, the amount of buyers and sellers in the area and other current events, the price of your house is this particular amount. Every day the realtor will bring you a different value depending on their analysis and their mood. The stock market does this every minute.

Now, some companies' cash flows are going to be better than others. Earnings can be real or made out of accounting gimmicks. Cash flows are real. In fast-changing fields like technology, I would not want to forecast earnings out past five years; it would be too difficult to predict. As for drugs and consumer goods companies, they are a bit more forecastable. The more stable a company is, there is usually better stability in the yield or the higher price that you pay. The less stable or cyclical a company, there is usually a higher yield that you should receive for taking that risk.

The cash flows from certain asset classes used to be predictable. Not anymore. The ability of certain companies to continually generate earnings has been brought under question. If specific companies are difficult to forecast, what about industries and asset classes? How will cash flows domestically be affected by international flows and competition? With such a large amount of change in the world, what should an investor do? The age-old methods of building portfolios should be revised in the new order of the world.

Asset Allocation

"It's the end of asset allocation as we know it. In such an interconnected world, portfolios will no longer have country consideration.
Money managers will invest according to sectors and industries, irrespective of borders."[133] The world is not what it once was: predictable, stable, and full of national borders. It is a highly unpredictable,
unstable, and ill-defined place. How does one invest in an era in which
there are no likely historical precedents on which to rely? Now more
than any other time in the past, it's appropriate to have an advisor to
talk through the issues of the day. You must evaluate the economy,
but also how the market reacts to the economic news. The reaction
is more important. Equity markets are based on perception more
than reality.

The stock market is like a beauty contest. It is not always the
prettiest girl who wins! It is impossible for financial professionals to
be able to accurately forecast the next five years, let alone try to
do that if you are a part-timer. Even the full-time forecasters find it
difficult to grapple with the changing dynamics of the investing landscape. Some experienced professionals have fallen flat on their face.
It's important that you don't do the same with your own investments.
You worked hard for the money you have accumulated; grow it, but
protect it, too!

In the beginning, investing was quite simple. The right combination
of stocks and bonds over time would give investors the right amount
of risk and reward. Then the investment management business started dividing the universe of stocks into subsectors like value, growth,

or developed, international, and emerging. This process of diversification was easy in that the more slices you had, the more diversified you were, the lesser risks were, and the more you could reach for returns. Since all these markets were uncorrelated, the chance of all markets going down together was small. If one investment style failed, it was such a small part of the whole that it shouldn't have materially affected the total portfolio. This line of thinking was derived from the landmark 1952 *Journal of Finance* paper entitled "Portfolio Selection." Harry Markowitz was a young graduate student at the University of Chicago when he chose to do his dissertation on applying mathematics to the stock market.

His idea focused on linear programming, a field that employs mathematical models for manufacturing companies to maximize output for a given level of cost or to minimize costs for a given level of output. The same cost-benefit analysis could be done for investments. For a given level of risk, adjust the combination of assets that will give you the highest return. The far-reaching influence of his paper earned Markowitz a Nobel Prize in economics and the science of asset allocation began.

By combining vastly different asset classes together, the correlation effect of these asset classes—the fact that they don't move together—created a lower risk than the addition of all the sectors together. By creating a lower risk, investors could invest in more risky asset classes, like stocks, even small stocks, and emerging countries, and still enjoy some degree of stability. This is what we call MPT, or modern portfolio theory. ERISA (Employment Retirement Income Security Act) was adopted for pension plans in 1974. This regulation formally changed the thinking of portfolio construction from the prudent man rule, which said every investment had to stand on its own merits, to this new portfolio rule, that each investment will be analyzed in how it contributes to the whole. Much of this kind of work is based upon historical observations.

New developments in this field are adopted quite slowly. Investment pioneer Gary Brinson took part in a study in 1976 that demonstrated that asset allocation, rather than security selection, accounted for the variation in performance among pension plans. It took at least ten years later for institutional investors to strongly embrace the idea of a properly allocated portfolio.

But what if historical observations are not going to be accurate pictures of the future? Ever since 9/11, I personally have allocated my own portfolio differently than before with a reserve set aside for a disaster scenario. If I had lived in a foreign country with greater risks than America, I might have done this sooner. What 9/11 did was bring more of the unexpected. It was truly a "black swan," an unexpected yet material event that could not be predicted yet was highly influential in the direction of asset prices.[134] Black swan events don't have to be negative. Certain black swan events in the past could be the inventions of the Internet, cell phone, the personal calculator, the assembly line, or the conversion from coal-fired engines to oil-based energy. These are several examples of unexpected yet material events. What if 9/11 happens again? What would my portfolio do? A typical investor would place money in **traditional investments** like stocks and bonds.

With an interconnected world, though, all stocks are now moving more in unison. There is a lack of benefit from only investing in traditional assets classes. I've expanded that to include commodities and currencies, and to consider all three types of bonds: treasuries, corporate, and municipal bonds. Hedge funds and private capital are now available for the small investor through mutual funds or ETFs. (ETFs are electronic-traded funds and are just like mutual funds) Additionally, real estate, structured notes, and futures can all be utilized to enhance cash flows and reduce risk. Traditional stock diversification cannot provide the risk reduction properties like it has in the past.

I would encourage you to begin with a "one third" strategy. A third of your financial assets should be in stocks with half of that outside the U.S. A third of your financial assets should be in fixed income, including as many different ways to collect a coupon as you can feel comfortable with. Finally, a third of the financial assets should be invested in alternatives. It doesn't have to be fancy or complex like hedge funds or venture capital. Alternatives can be commodities, absolute and targeted return securities. Alternatives do not have to be risky. They can be something safe and predictable like a beach house as an inflation hedge. Alternatives could be utility stocks or those with high dividends, something that is stable.

What you are looking for are investments that do not move with stocks or bonds. For the retired person living on a fixed income, cash assets won't do at such low yields of today. Cash does not correlate with stocks and bonds but low yields will eat away at your purchasing power. There are great alternatives to money markets with liquidity and moderate risk.

You need to focus on the total portfolio. The pieces are important especially in how each contributes to the whole, but after you have chosen a new investment, give it time to work. Every month, look at the total portfolio change in value and spend little time trying to analyze all the pieces. Most investments need to be given three to five years to work. You don't see gardeners digging up their tulips in March to see how their bulbs are doing.

From this one third in each asset class, adjust according to your own risk tolerance, age, retirement goals and what you read in the news. Whenever one sector looks overvalued, you can adjust the mix. Rinse and repeat! Remember, when there is fear in the streets among asset classes, that is usually a good time to buy!

This "one third" strategy will be more conservative than a 60/40 mix, where 60% of your financial assets are in stocks and 40% are in bonds. This is the starting point for most large pension plan because it gives long term investors the right mix of growth and stability. That is the right mix for yesterday, not today or tomorrow! With such an interconnected world, correlations will tend to be higher. Stocks alone will not provide the diversification once offered by investing in different economic cycles across the globe. These cycles are now more in sync. A "one third" strategy will reduce volatility which is especially important if you are taking income from your investments, because the amount you take will be based on the principal value.

Your portfolio in a "one third" strategy will look more like a college endowment. The typical educational institution has over 45% of their long term investment assets in "other" areas like hedge funds, private equity and real assets or commodities. Their stock allocation is over 40% because most endowments focus on long term growth. Approximately half of that stock investment is in foreign securities. Their bond allocation is very low, about 12%, because most colleges do not need the income to fund expenses.[135] This large investment in "other" assets requires little or no income requirements, because these assets are less liquid. In return for the lower cash generation and illiquidity, the investor should enjoy a higher return from information that is only offered to high quality investors according to present day regulations.

For the safe investments, I've always liked gold for a disaster scenario because of its store of value. Gold is really three things; it's a substitute currency, it's a store of value, especially in a crisis, and it's a commodity used in jewelry and commercial applications. It's difficult to separate what's really moving gold from day to day, but more recently it's been a currency substitute. As the Asian economies have reached their limit of allocation to U.S. Treasury securities, gold can serve as an alternative asset class to currencies in addition to the more traditional euro and the *yen*. In times of crisis, gold is a store of value. In 2001, after 9/11, gold was the safe investment in an uncertain world. In 2008, gold did not provide the store of value because it had a price, and everything with a price was sold. With all the governments of the world in charge of the circulation of their own currencies, there is too much incentive to keep the printing presses running and create inflation. Gold is a store of value against these inflationary tendencies.

Now, should a 9/11 happen again, municipalities that are affected by the terrorist attack would go bankrupt almost immediately. That eliminates most individual municipal bonds, so national or state portfolios that invest in widely diversified bonds are the choice. Treasuries are the most liquid investment in the world and probably the safest fixed income commitment, and, regardless of interest rates, should be included in any portfolio. If you fear inflation, buy TIPS. (TIPS are treasury inflation protected securities and provide a fixed rate over the inflation rate.) Corporate bonds of various qualities, including investment-grade and high-yield, should also be considered. There are hybrid bonds that combine the qualities of stocks and bonds, like convertibles, REITs (real estate investment trusts), and MLPs (master limited partnerships). All of these income sources will seek to cushion the blow in the event of another black swan event. Only a fool (or a nineteen year old trading their grandmother's account) would put all their investment money in stocks. Risk and volatility matters. This is not your father's world where a 60/40 allocation will do the trick. Yours is a much more unpredictable, difficult world in which to invest.

The world is a different place, and 9/11 won't happen again, exactly. But the fact that it did happen, especially here in America, leads some to believe it could happen again. The possibilities are endless: Iran with a nuclear bomb, an attack on Israel, Afghanistan erupts, Pakistan does something stupid with its nukes, Russia kills off another official or another corporation, a country has a problem staying in the EU, Japan goes into another depression, Venezuela invades Columbia... you get the idea. It's during one of these moments when investors would say, "That was unpredictable. What's my stock really worth now?" It's a promise of future earnings and dividends, not a guarantee.

These events will be discounted and magnified more quickly too. It will be important to read the news and distinguish what is really "the news" and what is just noise. It's kind of like hurricane season today: You know there are going to be storms and you know they're going to be bad, you just don't know how bad and where. Ignorance is not wanting to know something. Stupidity is not admitting your ignorance. Shit happens.

With a portion of your investments, you should be prepared for a series of conflicts where the world is in a highly agitated state, from lack of jobs, lack of food, and social unrest. This is the portion of your investment portfolio in which you want to take as little risk as possible. The advice for people who wanted to invest in stocks used to be, "If you can leave the money there for three to five years, it will be okay." I think in the last two bear markets, we've learned our lesson: You need a longer time horizon and you need to be flexible.

For the equity or risky side of the portfolio, it is mostly stocks. We can slice and dice the equity universe into many different asset classes, including domestic, foreign, developed, developing, emerging, frontier, and BRIC. I don't consider the BRIC (Brazil, Russia, India, China) countries to be emerging; I consider them to be among other countries like North Korea, Taiwan, and even Indonesia that are "developing." Emerging countries would include countries establishing rules for investors. Frontier economies are those with little or no rules. Now, we can take this stock universe and also split it into small companies, medium companies, and large companies.

Correlation

Correlation is a way to measure how asset classes move together or in different directions. The subprime meltdown spread into all sorts of different securities, and investors were highly leveraged. It created a massive margin call. All stocks went down in every sector, every industry, and every country. Stocks were highly correlated. Not only that, but stocks were also highly correlated with every other asset class because things had to be sold to meet margin calls. Anything with a price was sold.

The correlations in the correction of 2008 were all high, approaching one perfect correlation, where one asset class always moves in the same direction and magnitude as another asset class. Correlations over time, though, are much lower. Correlations between the S&P 500 and emerging market stocks over the period 1970 to 2005 have ranged between .25 and .9. On average, half the time, emerging market stocks did not move in the same direction as domestic large-cap stocks. In an interconnected world this advantage is less. What this means to you as an investor is risk reduction. If you get enough asset classes moving in different directions, the volatility of the total portfolio is substantially reduced. If you can reduce the volatility, or risk, of the portfolio, then a person may be able to allocate more to assets with better return expectations. For the same amount of risk, that person may be able to attain a higher rate of return. Markowitz at his best.

Commodities, global bonds, real estate, and other alternative asset classes not only provide great return potential, but also terrific risk reduction qualities. These types of asset classes should be in everyone's portfolio. Remember, the world has changed and your portfolio has to change, too!

After the past two years, discussions of **risk** in portfolios have taken on a new meaning. Suddenly risk is not an abstraction, like standard deviation of returns, but it's the loss of real money. For some people, the loss of value in 2008 was enough to buy a car, for others, enough to buy a house, and for a few, enough to buy a Caribbean island. The way in which apparently diverse and non-correlated markets took a synchronized dive has challenged these ideas about asset allocation and diversification. The fact of the matter is that it didn't work out the way the statistical models had predicted. So maybe we should be trying more forward-thinking models and adjusting our definition of risk.

Why risk is important is that it is all about purchasing power. Do you want more or less? If you have two investments, each with a 10% return, but one is twice as volatile, which one do you want to own? They have the same 10% return. Then they are the same. Right?

Wrong! The more volatile investment will have less value over time. It's not just the annual return but also the "path" that the returns take. That path will affect the dollars that you have invested. Most returns are calculated on what we call a time weighted basis. This assumes that you start every year with the same initial investment. How many investors actually do that? Well, none! A dollar weighted return will take into consideration how much money you actually have invested and a 10% drop on $100,000 will be different than a 10% drop on $120,000. Actually, a $2000 difference. So, volatility matters. It will determine the path your money experiences in its growth. To grow your portfolio consistently with low volatility, that's the goal! We want to be more like the tortoise, than the hare!

All this talk about risk is good. By combining asset classes together that don't move together, you lower risk. By lowering risk, you have the ability to grow your dollars invested, your purchasing power. Who wants more purchasing power? How you do this today is going to be different than how it was done ten years ago. Maybe even three year ago. Correlations have now changed. So must your portfolio. In order to keep the same principles of portfolio theory working for you, a portfolio must have more non-traditional assets, like alternative investments. Without them, you will have a highly correlated, high volatility portfolio that puts your purchasing power on a roller coaster ride.

Monte Carlo

There is a way of predicting portfolio returns using the past as a guide and over-weighting certain scenarios that are more possible, using today's environment. These are called Monte Carlo techniques, and as the name suggests, they analyze many times when you can "roll the dice." These techniques incorporate historical data with the present day investing environment, adding in retirement plans and social security payments to inheritance and project how your portfolio could grow for the next ten, twenty or thirty years. It will help you understand how wealth can be transformed over time. They let an investor "pre-experience" their wealth over their lifetimes. It is a realistic snapshot of the future possibilities.

Most of what we used for risk, though, is elusive. In the investment business, we use standard deviation or volatility to define "risk" and it's based upon historical figures. There are probably some advances that will be made in this regard to help improve understanding of the path of investment returns. Even Markowitz himself said that he hoped that better methods, "which take into account more information" than just historical data, would be uncovered subsequently. Using Bayesian techniques, updating these historical numbers in light of new, more relevant data, we can overweight the present-day scenario and try to underweight occurrences that are not likely to recur. With low inflation and interest rates combined with high government stimulus, there are not many historical examples from which to choose. It's almost as if we were moving from snow-covered land along to an ice-covered lake; we recognize the difference in terrain and we need to tread very lightly before we fall into mistakes from our analysis.

Asset allocation means different things to different people. So does a "balanced diet." Asset allocation became a household word just in time for the bear market of 2008 to arrive! Well, one actually also arrived at the turn of the millennium, but diversification in 1999 was owning five different technology stocks. We've had two bear markets in the span of ten years, completely unpredictable when considering historical precedent. Today, an investor in stocks would be no better off than if he invested in 1998. Are you better off than you were in 1998? No, I'm not running for president. Did you own a cell phone in 1998? How many computers did you own in your home? Have you had any body part replaced since 1998? Don't laugh…many readers understand this. The world was materially better off in the last ten years, so I don't think equity markets reflect this. *Business Week* magazine labeled this the "great round trip," as investors have been taken on a ride that has ended right where they started. The fact is we had two strong bull markets along with these bears, with equity returns between twenty and thirty percent. As any student of the markets knows, those are abnormally high, as the bear markets are abnormally low. With history as our guide, the world is a much more volatile place.

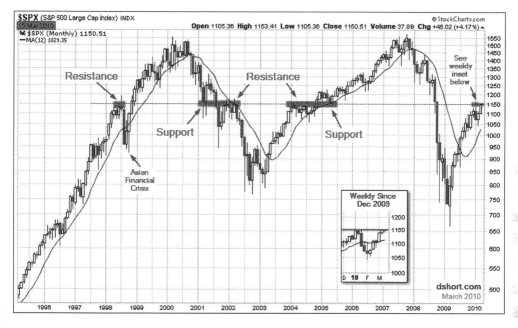

S&P 500 Price 1998-2009

(Source: Investmentpostcards.com)

Now, I cannot tell you that 2008 was the worst market historically, since there have been many others. In fact, 2008 doesn't even rank in the top ten of market corrections in modern world history. Of course, we had the 1929-1932 correction of about **-89%** in the United States. We had the NASDAQ correction of 2000 to 2002 of **-82%**. Comparable to that was Japan's lost decade, from 1990 to 2003, of **-79%**. The United States had a correction in 1973 and 1974, but London's was worse, taking **-73%** of stock values down with it. The Asian contagion market of 1997 and '98 gave us Hong Kong's returns a **-64%**. The second recession of the Great Depression was in 1937 and 1938, and produced returns of **-49%.** And then there were a couple of crashes that we don't hear about much, one in 1906 to 1907, of **-48%**. There were fears that the new automobile sector in 1919 was becoming overheated and car ownership had reached a saturation point, forcing the market down **-46%**. Finally, rounding out the top ten of stock market crashes, was 1901, when the market was spooked by the assassination of President McKinley, coupled with a severe drought, forcing stock market returns **down -46%**. So, historically, stocks have done something like this before. It's rare, but it has happened before, and it is the nature of capitalist economies to have failures. In this brave new world, anything is possible.

Panics and downturns are part of the free-market system. Looking at the last 200 years of the S&P 500, or its equivalent, returns ranging from zero to ten percent in stocks were registered about two-thirds of the time. The rest of the time, investors experienced a negative or in excess of ten percent return.[136] Although the stock market's long-term return is ten percent, you rarely get it exactly. What you will get as an owner (stock buyer) rather than a lender (bond buyer) is better returns over time. Over longer periods, like ten years, you have about a ninety-five percent chance of being positive, eighty-six percent chance of earning better than five percent, and a fifty-six percent chance of earning over ten percent. Over twenty years, the numbers get even better. I'm going to go with a ninety-nine percent probability that stocks will do better than bonds over just about any twenty-year timeframe. Say you don't have twenty years. Well, unless you are eighty, you do! You should be investing, not just clipping coupons, because there is a likelihood that you will live longer than you expect and the Social Security checks will not be coming. This horrible period through which we have just come is the exception, not the rule. People have lost half their money in the stock market, twice—once in the tech bubble and once in the financial collapse. Dust off your history books and you will see what we're witnessing currently is an atypical point in time. Confidence in stocks is low. The time to buy stocks is when confidence is low.

As investors have returned to the markets, it hasn't necessarily been reflected in economic growth. That might be a disconnect for you, but financial markets don't always follow the underlying economics. Over time they will, but in the short term there will be massive counter-movements. Hence, many investors spend an inordinate amount of time wading into forecasts of an economic recovery that, even if correct, will not reward an investor. It's possible in the next five to ten years that GDP will expand strongly, but the stock market could do nothing. From 1964 to 1981, GDP grew 370% in the United States. Sales of the Fortune 500 companies more than sextupled. Yet the Dow Jones Industrial Average went from 874 on December 31, 1964, to 875 on December 31, 1981. It's these points of time that are difficult to figure out. Warren Buffett once described his investment decision-making process as if he were not going to get a newspaper for ten years or might be stuck on a deserted island. He invests for the long term. It's these low points that will drive an investor crazy.

Rebalance

Is breaking up the hardest thing to do? No. Probably the hardest thing to do, at least in investing, is to rebalance. It requires buying things when they're out of favor and selling things when they're in favor. It will not win any friends on the golf course. An astute contrarian investor is always out of step, talking up the wrong stocks at the wrong time and seeming completely misguided. If you took all the major asset classes of stocks in which to invest, you would find similar twenty-year returns. They're all about the same! Equity styles really converge to a mean return. So that means to you, as an investor, when things are below mean, they're attractive, and things above mean are not. This principle can be utilized within a narrow asset class; for example, large-cap growth has a strong five-year run versus small-cap value or emerging markets. Over time, most of the investment returns in stocks will be quite similar and will regress to some number, let's say between ten and twelve percent. Some of these times seem to go on forever, like the tech boom. The time that asset classes sometimes take to regress back to the mean can take a lot longer than you think, and you can run out of money waiting for an asset class to "catch up" to the mean.

Imagine you're driving a car down the road on a six-lane highway, and your lane slows down. You naturally want to get in the faster-moving lane, but as soon as you get in that lane, what happens? Yes, you guessed it, the lane you're now in slows, and the one that you were in starts moving faster again. The same can be said for checkout lines at your local supermarket. There is a human element in making these decisions. Now, if you traveled from New York to Philadelphia and traversed in and out of lanes to always get in the fast-moving lane, how much faster would you really get there than someone who stays in the same lane for the whole trip? Yes, you might get there faster, but you also run the risk of an accident. Diversification or asset allocation is the equivalent of having a car in every lane, and the time that you take to get to your destination is less than the average of all lines together, with a lot less risk of getting into an accident.

Human beings are social animals. Alan Greenspan himself noted that there was a tremendous urge by Americans to "keep up with the Joneses,"[137] Whether this can be defined as greed depends on your point of view. There is a competitive nature of most Americans that is embedded in our culture. When all the cars in the highway are moving very fast, there's an inclination to keep up. Many times a car traveling at the speed limit appears to be moving much more slowly than all the other cars. When everybody's speeding, taking on more risk and leverage, nobody notices, but over the hill an accident may be waiting. The cost of driving too fast is received in the pain of declining values in your 401(k). The financial industry has to understand that its typical client has very little investment expertise, so the use of target date funds that target a person's retirement date and changes the asset allocations appropriately are probably the best **vehicle** for the retail investor.

The trick of investing is to get someone else to do the driving for you, to resist the temptation of the human behavior of switching in and out of lanes. The vehicle that you choose for investing has a lot to do with how much influence you have over the driver's wheel. If you're in a trading account, you're driving while listening to the radio, getting stock market reports, and figuring out travel delays, all at the same time. If you're in a mutual fund, you're letting someone else do the driving and you're focused on the bigger picture, expected time of arrival, and the risks that you're taking along the way. If you're in an annuity, someone else is both doing the driving and checking on the traffic; you're focused on what you might have for dinner tonight. An investor has to judge how good a driver she is, and the investment business is not some mythical town in Minnesota where everyone is above average. If you're not in the business, chances are you're going to be a horrible investor and you need advice. If you are in the business, you better get back to school because things have changed a lot, and if you're going to be helpful to your fellow man or client, you need to know how the world has changed.

If you follow fund flows, in and out of mutual funds, you will find that the average retail investor does just the opposite of what they should be doing. The average stock return of the retail investor is about the same return one would obtain by investing in treasury bills over time. According to the Dalbar studies, stock returns for the period of 1986 to 2006, of about 12% were mostly enjoyed by the large institutions, whereas the retail investor's return was less than five percent over the same period.[138] Since inflation averaged three, the retail investor did have a positive real return, but it was substantially below the potential. The bond index return over that period of ten years was about 9%. The average retail bond investor attained about a 2% return, making that a negative real return after inflation. Why did investors do so poorly? They are driven by biases that influence their behavior, such as the timing of purchases and sales in "hot or cold" investment styles. Investment performance looks great just when you should be selling, not buying.

Most people have what I call "Home Depot portfolios." Have you ever gone into a home improvement store to pick up one thing and left with ten items or more that you "need"? Most investors collect stocks like stamps: "I have this one and that one." There is no balance and no overall strategy. People begin to invest in $5,000- or $10,000-increments. They grow their net worth substantially over time, but still invest in these small amounts in proportion to the total. If you are worth $1 million, a $10,000-investment is one percent. Even if that investment doubles, it won't do much for your total net worth. You must change your investment amounts in proportion to make you decisions meaningful. Otherwise, you may be spending a lot of time thinking about things that are almost inconsequential to the total picture.

Institutional investment committees tend to focus on the bigger picture. They are less emotional, long-term oriented, and more structured. Some have guidelines for equity ownership and when they fall below a certain percentage in stocks, they have to purchase equities, or they would be in violation of the investment policy. They can realize most of the returns that are available in the market. You should build your investment account on the principles of an institutional style by formulating an investment policy statement and sticking to it, making gradual adjustments over time. Always focus on the **total portfolio**, paying attention to the components and the role that each investment plays in the total construction, but measure your progress by the path of your total financial assets.

To make investing even more difficult, five-star mutual funds are not as consistent as we're led to believe. Typically, the performance of what propelled a fund to a five-star ranking is made before such accolades. The chance that a fund remains top-performing is actually less than a flip of a coin. Of top quartile managers in the ten years ending June 2008, 90% of them under-performed by at least 5% in any one year of the ten. Over 63% under-performed in any one year by 10% or more. You would have assumed that your investment manager was either sailing on his boat, in the midst of a messy divorce, retired already with the portfolio now being managed by a nineteen-year-old, or being completely unmanaged. Appearances aside, the manager may have done nothing wrong but simply stuck to the thing that made him successful in the other nine years.[129] There was a study that I read that said that using the worst-performing relative performance would have been more beneficial than using the best relative performance. The under-performers tend to bounce back. I'm not ready to call that a strategy.

When markets do correct, it's hard to do nothing, but that may be the best thing to do. As Nick Murray once said, "The more times you change an investment strategy, the worse your returns will be." The ride will be volatile, but you will be better off in the long run being an equity holder rather than a bond holder. When corrections come, that's when your advisor really makes his commission. Calm down, take a walk in the park, and don't let the inevitable recessions and corrections upset you. Better yet, when markets do correct, rebalance. Buy when others are selling. See…the top line rises! This is the price value of the S&P 500.

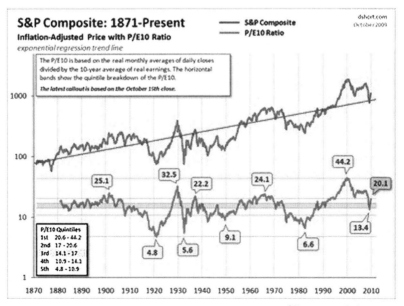

(Source: dshort.com)

The Eighth Wonder of the World

Compounding of interest is the eighth wonder of the world. If you took $100,000 and were able to compound it at 25% per year for ten years, what would you have? Before you read ahead, think of this: $100,000 with a 25% growth, in the first year, you'd have $125,000. Second year, you would not have $150,000 because it is 25% compounded on the **new** balance. You'd have $156,000. That's a small additional increase in principle, but it can have an enormous effect over time. In the ninth year, with the returns and annual compounding on a higher portfolio value, the total would be $745,000 and with another 25% return, in year ten it would total $931,000. The original $100,000 after ten years would be close to $1 million! Now if we could only find something that's guaranteed to be up 25% per year! It is a lofty goal. Let's break this down into bite-size pieces.

The long-term total return on stocks is about 10% per year, but if we find industrial sectors of the economy that are outperforming the overall market, we might be able to get another 3 or 5% above market returns. There are certain regions of the world that are growing much faster than the developed markets. These stock markets do offer the potential for above market returns as well, another 3 or 5% above global market returns. Now we come to the more complicated concept of currency. As we've discussed in a previous chapter, the long-term depreciation of the dollar is almost a given, not every year, not by the same amount, but a given over the long term. How much can we attribute to foreign investment appreciation just from the U.S. dollar depreciation? For the ease of mathematics, we will call it 3 to 5% per year. So, first we get 10% from stocks, then 3 to 5% more from being in the right sectors, 3 to 5% more from being in the

right countries and regions, and about 3 to 5% from being outside the
United States. There you've got a 25% potential. It is a pretty lofty
goal, but it is the return **potential** from a concentrated, long-term-
oriented strategy.

In the real world though, a 10%-15% return is more likely the
overall result from an all stock strategy but the two main points
are, first that compounding works wonders and secondly, that concentration is more important than diversification in growing assets.
Compounding works to your advantage in positive years, because the
return is calculated on a higher base value. From our $100,000 begin-
ning portfolio value, a 10% compounded return over ten years would
provide a $259,000 ending value. A 159% cumulative return. This is
a doubling and a half more on the initial value. Not too shabby! It is
those negative returns that could hurt. A *negative* 10% or 25% return
on a $100,000 portfolio results in a much smaller capital loss when
compared to a $1 million portfolio. As your portfolio grows, keeping
to a more consistent and positive strategy will usually is the best approach. Singles and doubles.

Instead of diversifying all over the world in many different mutual funds and receiving market-like returns, investors should pick
and choose the best opportunities. By owning ten different mutual funds, with 100 stocks each, an investor actually will own 1000
stocks. The S&P 500 index only has 500 stocks in it. How can you
beat the market? You are the market! Each individual stock holding
will be so small in proportion to the total, it will be almost meaning-
less. Look for the best pitches. That doesn't require any day trading or market timing. You can do this yourself, not by buying hedge
funds and giving away two percent of your principal every year and

twenty percent of your profits. You can do this by simply using mutual funds or ETFs.

ETFs are mutual funds that are traded like stocks. Mutual funds typically value all their securities after the close every night and publish a net asset value. ETFs also publish a net asset value but, during the day, investors can trade these securities, anticipating an increase or decrease in the underlying value of the securities. ETFs now total almost $1 trillion in a short period of time, leading them to be one of the fastest-growing areas of investment management. The mutual fund industry, $7 trillion at the end of 2008, is still quite a bit larger, but ETFs are growing extremely fast. With daily announcements that have an effect on the value of your securities, it's nice to have the flexibility to be able adjust portfolios. An investor in ETFs today could deposit $25,000 or $25 billion and build the same portfolio. Many formerly illiquid asset classes are available in this form. The beauty of ETFs may be in that an investor will focus more on the **macro overall asset allocation** rather than the individual components. When you assemble a portfolio one stock at a time, you can wind up with something quite lopsided. One or two positions usually dominate a retail investor's portfolio and far too much time is spent on picking individual stocks. Greater opportunities for risk management are available to those who view their investment portfolio from the macro level, or from the top-down.

There are many misconceptions about the risks associated with foreign stocks and the seeming lack of information about foreign markets. When I was young, I lived in Holland. Do you think Dutch people invest 90% of their investment portfolio in Dutch companies? Of course not! The Dutch first think of their own country in combination with Europe and then as a contributor to global trade. Because of their great country's size and scope, how large our equity market is, and its large barriers of oceans, Americans have become overweighted domestically. The United States market capitalization today is under 50% of the world's total. It is 42% of the MSCA All-Country World Index.[140] In order to make a simple allocation decision, based simply on opportunities, domestic investment should be about 50% of your stock portfolio. I know this might be a leap of faith for most of you, but you can move toward this goal over a long period of time. And if you've reached an age when income and security are more important than capital appreciation, or foreign stocks are "foreign" to you, by all means stay right here in the good old U.S.A.

Any investor has to evaluate not just the "return on the investment but the return of his investment," as Will Rogers said. Very few of the original Dow Jones industrial average members are still standing today. From the year I was born in 1957, only seventy-nine of the original 500 remain as independent companies.[141] In the next fifty years, how many of today's 500 will still be available investments? When we look at companies' earnings in the ten years between 1990 and 2000, we found many companies that were able to sustain a ten percent earnings growth over one year. One hundred and forty-five of the S&P 500 companies were able to achieve it. For three consecutive years of 10% earnings growth, we see only 52 companies, and when we measure for five years, we only find 22 companies of 500 that were able to sustain it. When we move on to six, seven, and eight consecutive years of 10% growth, we find only a handful of corporations. Companies that are able to sustain 25% growth, as you can imagine, are very few. Again the law of averages would say if you find a company that's able to sustain earnings growth consecutively over five or six years, chances are it's got to stumble. One should always be on the lookout for signs that it's losing leadership. Anyone can fail and all companies eventually fall short of expectations.

Market Forecasting

Market forecasting has become even more popular with the advent of new shows on CNBC, as even the most juvenile analysts can be asked their opinion on the markets. The extent to which this has been taken is demonstrated on Jim Cramer's show; part circus act, part Maury Povich, and part hedge fund manager, Kramer has a following of stock traders. As people call in to the show and mention a stock of interest, Kramer will shout out almost immediately, "buy," "sell," or "hold." I don't think Kramer did the same kind of research when he bought his last refrigerator as he does when he gives his rapid-fire opinions. Hopefully, people don't believe he's a palm reader and can actually define the future. Market forecasting is relatively easy if you follow the market. The best forecaster is usually the market itself.

The only sound basis for forecasting is historical fact. That makes it difficult when, as we have demonstrated before, much of what's going to transpire in the immediate future hasn't ever happened in the past! Classroom economic theory doesn't cut it. Most people come with a bias; they've developed a theory and then they will select the facts to support it. It's important to let the data lead you to a conclusion and not try to enter the market with any "gut feeling." Financial markets are leading indicators, one of the government's ten indicators for anticipating economic activity three to six months in the future. Granted, sometimes they do not correctly forecast, but they probably will do so with a higher probability than even the most astute market expert. Financial markets move earlier and respond faster than economic activity. Economic activity will move earlier and respond faster than the statistics that are reported in the news. Market forecasters need time to evaluate the statistics, establish trends, and make some sense of a collection of data points.

Markets reflect changing expectations of not only current buyers and sellers, but of future expectations of buyers and sellers. The information embedded in prices is almost like a survey or census of participants. It is the weighted average opinion of the people trading at that particular time, not everybody, and only those who feel the need to buy or sell. The majority of investors have no say in this. It is only the people who are trading, maybe one percent of the holders, that will determine prices. It's almost as if it's the tip of the iceberg, not what lies beneath the water.[142] In some days, it is the tail wagging the dog!

Global Macro

According to Henry McVeigh, managing director of Morgan Stanley's global macro and asset allocation, we are entering a period of the "renaissance" of global macro investing. This term defines an all-inclusive investment strategy of any market in any region at any time. It may sound extremely risky to you, but in fact may produce less risk than what you're doing currently. The S&P 500 is your father's investment index. The world is now global! Use the MSCI All-Country World index. Most importantly, a global macro strategy will give an investor some strategic and tactical abilities during these volatile markets. Strategic could be considered a more long-term asset allocation, for example, to overweight the emerging markets. Tactical would be much more short-term, for example, to overweight technology in a short upgrade cycle.

The unprecedented amount of government stimulus globally offers opportunities to, as Bill Gross at PIMCO says, "shake the hands of the government," or partner with them to make money. Many of the government programs to buttress the financial system can be beneficial to an investor. Many banking institutions have access to government funds with essentially no interest rate. This has to help their financial strength. Since interest rates fell to zero, governments also took it upon themselves to purchase securities in the open market, the so-called "quantitative easing." It is easier to make money when there is a big elephant investor helping you in supporting prices.

As the market moves away from the crisis in 2008, correlations will decrease again, offering other ways to diversify portfolios. The world is extremely interconnected and it's important for someone to understand that. Correlations in stocks will remain high. There are also many opportunities that are regional or localized and are somewhat uncorrelated from the overall global economy. There are many investment vehicles that are not traditional but can provide potentially strong returns in an uncorrelated manner.

It used to be when the United States sneezes, the world caught a cold. Not anymore! The United States has a sizable say in the world economy but it is not the tremendous influence that it has been in the past. In some regions, the spectacular growth that has been experienced in the last decade has resulted in a boom in net worth and disposable spending that paused briefly in 2008, but has continued upward. This is the case not only in the BRIC countries but in other areas as well. Since the Berlin Wall fell in 1989, there have been billions of people brought into the market economy. Not only with the collapse of communism, but with the freedom of information available to the average citizen, free markets and democratic elections have been introduced to every country in the world, except for just a handful. Obviously, when the Berlin Wall came down, most people did not understand its significance or immediately adjust to the new world. It has been only twenty years since that event and it looks like they finally caught on. This explosion of capitalistic consumers is the equivalent of creating a new American middle-class every few years.

Demographics is something to which an investor should pay attention. If you follow the baby boomer generation of 1946 to 1964, you will see that some amazing distortions to our economy have occurred. How the S&P 500 is composed can give us an insight as to where the investor dollars are flowing. Let's look at how the S&P 500 stock index has been overwhelmed by what baby boomers do. When baby boomers were growing up, they needed shoes and clothes to go to school every year because, as you know, they grew a few inches every year. Their parents needed to go to department stores to shop for them. That industry is in the consumer cyclical sector, which became the largest sector of the S&P 500 in 1986 at 14%. Later, during and immediately after college, they consumed mass quantities of foods and beverages. That industry is in the consumer staple area and it became the largest sector of the S&P 500 in 1990, comprising 17% of the index. After leaving college, the baby boomer bought his first house and went to a bank or a finance company, propelling that sector to the forefront. Finance as a sector became the largest component of the S&P 500 in 1997 at 17% of the index. Then the PC revolution came upon us and, you guessed it, technology became the largest sector of the S&P 500 in 1999 at a whopping 30% of the index. All the while, as the baby boomer was getting older, a new sector was rising. At only 6% of the index in 1980, 10% in 1990 and then 12% in the year 2000, healthcare for a brief second of time became the largest sector of the S&P 500 in 2008, as finance collapsed and technology was yet to rise again.

Sector Shifts

Sector Weights in the S&P 500

	1980	1986	1990	1997	1999	2006	2009
Consumer Staples	8%	12%	17%	16%	12%	9	12%
Consumer Cyclical	10	14	11	9	9	11	9%
Health Care	6	7	10	11	11	12	13%
Finance	5	10	8	17	15	22	15%
Energy	27	12	13	8	6	10	12%
Technology	10	9	7	13	30	15	19%
Utilities	6	8	7	3	3	4	4%

Source: Standard and Poors

(Source: Standard & Poors)

If we follow the demographic trend, we probably could have figured this one out. Healthcare will be a viable investment sector for years to come. A lot of investing is just common sense. Themes do matter and will work over time. There are predictable, long-term, and investable themes.

- The Internet has opened the information era. Broadband is enabling people to source and sell at any time and any place. Information flows from anything to everywhere and is delivered with more segmented and regionalized coverage. Personalized media will market to your tastes and past behavior.

- Emerging consumers in developing and emerging markets are growing by 25 to 50 million people per year and will be moving up the consumption chain from essential goods to demanding urban consumer products and services. The billions of people who have entered the globalized economy in the past twenty years are just getting started.

- Agricultural land is in short supply and techniques are desperately needed to expand output. The world's demographics are forecasting a continued migration to the cities and an explosion of poorer people in need of food and water.

- Genomics/biotechnology is changing how drugs are being discovered and will prove to be more accurate and effective. Genomic drugs, specific to your genetic makeup, now account for 20% of all U.S. drug sales; this is up from about 7% in the year 2000. That's a trend that's going to grow from mass markets into personalized medicine.

- Nanotechnology, the science of small, is the ability to alter things at the molecular level. It is just beginning to affect the food you eat, the clothes you wear, and the car you drive.

Nano-engineers will be able to modify and build molecules that will alter everything, maybe even you!

- There is a lack of fossil fuels in the world to power the world's future growth. China's thirst for energy will only further tap limited resources and force prices up. The trend is unsustainable. Better oil usage must result, combined with the advance of solar, wind, battery technology, and nuclear power, with needed discoveries of other energy sources.

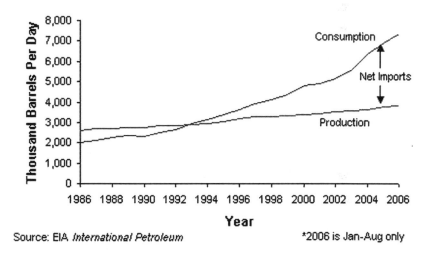

Source: EIA *International Petroleum*   *2006 is Jan-Aug only

China's Oil Production and Consumption, 1986 - 2006

(Source: eoearth.org)

ⱱ ⱱ ⱱ

How investors interpret these trends can get cloudy and tough economic times create uncertainty, but these trends will continue. It is pointless to try to anticipate short-term movements in the market since there is always someone who knows just a little bit more than you. But it's relatively easy to spot these big trends; do your homework so that you have the emotional stability to stick with them.

More recently, government stimulus programs everywhere have caused central banks to print money at a historical rate. In the movie *All the President's Men*, the *Washington Post* reporters used a confidential source named "Deep Throat" when the Watergate break-in was first investigated. Deep Throat said to "follow the money" to determine who was behind the activity. The money led all the way to the White House and resulted in the resignation of Richard Nixon. In investing today, follow the money! There are large money flows from sovereign investors, governments, and hedge funds. Large investment pools around the world are searching for good investments. These savings flows can distort market movements and reinforce trends. Liquidity-driven investing is going to be a theme for the next three to five years. Where that money flows will move asset classes and could conceivably create another bubble. The trick is to try to wring out the human emotion and the irrational pricing of these themes in the marketplace.

If you were going to invest in themes that would be prevalent in the world and 10 or 20 years from today, how would you go about doing this? Many companies that will be dominating the economic landscape in 10 or 20 years may not even exist today! The dominant companies may go through transitions or spinoffs to focus on particular markets. It is impossible to forecast which companies will be the winners. It is important to hold a basket of potential winners, knowing that some will fade. However, this basket of winners may all belong to a very narrow sector of the market. For example, in healthcare, there are many ways to invest in the graying of America, from nursing homes and nursing itself, to providers of health services and drug companies. With the government focusing on universal insurance, it's very difficult to figure out the winners and losers, especially since, at the time of this writing, nothing's really been figured out yet. Some trends that look like they have staying power are the rise in bio-genomics and DNA identification, increased use of artificial body parts, smaller things getting even smaller through nanotechnology, and the use of technology for patient records both by the doctor and for the patients themselves. These are the trends that you can invest in today and feel confident that they will exist 10 or 20 years from now, although in a completely different form than today.

Which new cell phone, computer, replacement body part, or so-cial networking site will be popular in 10 or 20 years? It's anyone's guess, but it's worth thinking about because, by directing your portfo-lio to these trends, you could not only avoid disasters and bankrupt-cies, but you could also realize stronger earnings growth than in the overall market.

Trends

In 10 or 20 years, there can be enormous risks to the global mac-ro environment. Global growth today depends a lot on the U.S. consumer, although less than in prior periods. U.S. consumers still make up over a quarter of global consumption. Real estate could have difficulty recovering with the enormous amount of supply from foreclosures for many years. The unemployment rate in the United States could remain extremely high without industries like finance and home-building putting people to work. The last decade did not create the jobs like in previous times. How Europe and the United States continue their mutual relationship is also a question, as well as the U.S. and Japan, let alone China. China may overstretch its imperial reach. Russia may become resurgent within Eastern Europe. Rogue regimes like North Korea and Venezuela could erupt. The Middle East will go through transitions, but how they play out is yet to be known. These are all risks to the future economic environment.

Demographic trends in the world will mean large population growth in poor countries. Climate change may have adverse repercussions for feeding the world. The U.S. will be reinvesting in roads, bridges, and public transport, as the emerging economies will be building out their own infrastructure. Large population growth in the poorest countries with less modern religions means a smaller working population in the developed countries. And in combination with these trends, the world is in the most innovative period in its history, with change accelerating. Countries and companies that are able to change will prosper. These are just some of the trends that we can predict today, but there are many more that will be unforeseen for some time to come. For these, we must keep an open mind and stay current with news, research, and technical events.

So at the end of this chapter on investing, I think it would be appropriate to comment on where we are in the overall stock market trend. We can separate the possibilities into really three basic trends: number one, we are in a new bull market that just began in March of 2009, as the market will move to new highs within a few years and continue upward. The second option is we are in a bear market where the market will test the lows of March 2009 and possibly move lower, in combination with a global recession and eventual lack of government stimulus propping up weak economic activity. Or our third possibility is, after a strong surge upward, rebounding from the 2009 lows, the market meanders in a narrow trading range for many years, essentially moving sideways. The odds favor the third scenario since many historical markets appeared to follow the same pattern of bust, rebound, and sideways movement for long periods of time. It is also quite likely in the context of the government stimulus around the world that is hitting its peak in the fourth quarter of 2009 through the second half of 2010. With many of the developed countries already taxed to their limits with excessive amounts of debt, it's going to be difficult to continue the stimulus programs. At the same time, if things deteriorate, the governments may step in.

There are no historical precedents to guide us through this period and the market will be expecting the worst at times and anticipating the best at others. It is going to be a trial-and-error world. There are going to be successes and failures, and some experiments will work and others will not. The market does not like uncertainty, and will be bouncing between the thrill of victory and the agony of defeat.

A strategy team of Morgan Stanley Europe provides the chart below and shows what a typical secular bear market looks like based on the average of the past nineteen major bear markets around the globe. (This chart was from the late summer of 2009 and points to an "X" that we have already passed.)

The Four Stages of the Typical Secular Bear Market and Its Aftermath

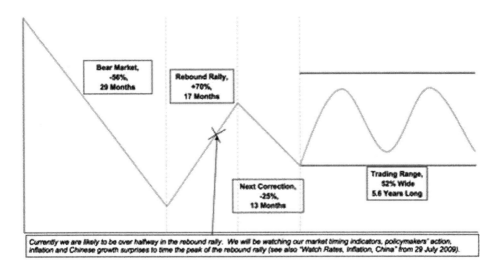

Bear Market,
-56%,
29 Months

Rebound Rally,
+70%,
17 Months

Next Correction,
-25%,
13 Months

Trading Range,
52% Wide
5.6 Years Long

Currently we are likely to be over halfway in the rebound rally. We will be watching our market timing indicators, policymakers' action, inflation and Chinese growth surprises to time the peak of the rebound rally (see also "Watch Rates, Inflation, China" from 29 July 2009).

Note: Chart represents the typical secular bear market based on our sample of 19 such bear markets as shown on slide 5.
Source: Morgan Stanley Research

(Source: Morgan Stanley)

❧ ❧ ❧

The emerging markets, with current account surpluses, large foreign reserves, and growing consumer consumption, may be able to continue to grow more quickly. They very well could be in a new bull market that takes them to new highs. Commodities also have good supply and demand trends, especially in the energy complex, which could take them to new highs as well. Oil over $150 a barrel? Yes, now more likely because it has been there already. The United States is in a very precarious position with regard to its demographics, the amount of debt that has been incurred not only by the government, but by the consumer, and by the level of entitlements that has been promised to many citizens. A few years of new simulative policies to avoid another Great Depression have been appropriate. However, the time to let private enterprise take the handoff is now! The Federal Reserve must walk a tightrope between deflation and inflation, since both price movements are difficult to stop once they've begun.

The Federal Reserve must remain extremely diligent and run the risk of making too many changes in reaction to market indicators instead of the status quo. There is no history book that can really teach us about the new order of the world or the situation through which we just lived. History repeats itself but never exactly, and this time, combined with the **speed** and the **size** at which the world moves today, it makes it difficult to learn the past's lessons and apply them. Boom and busts are part of the capitalist system and should be expected. Look out for the real trends rather than the wiggles. Seek to find what is really happening in the real economy, not just what is reflected in stock prices. There are opportunities in any kind of market. There's a kernel of truth to every bull market as well as every bear market.[143]

Be prepared for both good and bad scenarios. Accept concentration and volatility on the risk side. They are the pathways to performance. "Shun the shuns" of the world: diversification, correlation, and standard deviation.[144] These are technical terms that get you away from thinking about what you are investing in. An overly diversified stock portfolio will do nothing more than the market averages. Correlations work sometimes, but then, in market panics, they won't. Try to find investments that are truly non-correlated. Standard deviation should be left to the statisticians. Risk is about loss of money! Calculate the potential loss of capital. You should try to identify the value that your portfolio has "at risk."

Try to unpack your assumptions before tackling a problem. The "rules of thumb" of historical rates of return, mean reversion, and asset allocation should all be questioned. Within reason, think of themes in the world that are long-term, predictable, and investable. Be an investor, not a mathematician!

So, what is America's strength? What do we do well?

11. America—What Are We Good At?

"The winner is the chef who takes the same ingredients as everyone else and produces the best results."

—Edward de Bono

We, as a nation, have accomplished a lot. Americans have created many things that were deemed impossible. We have pushed human civilization further than even dreamers would have imagined. Our market-based economy is where it all starts and ends. The information era will enable the people of the world to be connected and vote with their money and voices. Socialist systems will be slower to react. However, where there are ideas of combining socialist structures with market mechanisms, we must keep an open mind.

The future of the world depends on us. This is an opportunity to focus on what makes us great, where we can exploit our model of economic capitalism and utilize it to our best advantage. Where diverse opinions arise from varied backgrounds and viewpoints, we must listen attentively. Where there is conflict, we must see opportunity. How should we plot our course in this new order of the world? By emphasizing our strengths! Let's review what we do well.

Agriculture

The United States is agriculturally diverse, almost to the point of being entirely self-sufficient. Taking the benefit of our extensive land mass in applying technology and logistics makes us a leader in food. We are talking about food that can be traded with the world: wheat, rice, corn, vegetables, cotton, pork, poultry, dairy products, fish, nuts, and grains. Although the United States produces only ten percent of the world's wheat, it is consistently the world's biggest wheat exporter.[145] With the United States' large size and geographic variety, we span most of the world's climate types in a mega-diverse ecology. The agriculture industry is the world's largest and generates international trade reaching upward of $100 billion, but it only represents about one percent of the country's GDP.

The farm in America was the family, and the family was the farm. In the year 1790, of the 4 million people that had settled in the United States, ninety percent were farmers. Much of America's history in the early years was a function of the boom and bust cycle of agriculture. Many leaps forward in human civilization initially came from improving the practice of farming. As inventions improved efficiency, it also reduced the amount of people involved in this industry. Consolidation and industrialization have forced most single-person farms into cooperatives or networks of large farming organizations. Two hundred years ago, it would have taken 200 to 300 man-hours to produce 100 bushels of wheat. Today, it would take three man-hours of labor. In the 1930s, about twenty-five percent of the country's population resided on the nation's 6,000,000 small farms. By 1997, only 157,000 large farms accounted for seventy-two percent of sales, with only two percent of the U.S. population residing on farms.[146]

Where America excels in agriculture is where technology meets the field. In 1970, the Nobel Peace Prize was awarded to a plant ecologist, Dr. Norman Borlaug. "He saved more lives than any man in human history," said Josette Sheeran, executive director of the United Nations World Food Program.[147] Dr. Borlaug transformed agriculture through high-yield crop varieties and other innovations, helping to more than double world food production between 1960 and 1990. He is known as the father of the "Green Revolution." The disease-resistant varieties of wheat seeds produced much more grain than in previous yields. It improved life for people in the regions of Asia, the Middle East, South America, and Africa. In Pakistan and India, grain yields more than quadrupled.[148] From this start, a huge worldwide industry developed with Monsanto, Archer Daniels Midland, Cargill, and even DuPont involved in the business.

Altering crops through breeding practices changes the genetic makeup of a plant to develop crops with more beneficial characteristics. Crop alteration has been practiced by humankind for thousands of years, but lately society is cautiously watching this. Genetically altering crops has become controversial. Genetically modified organisms (GMO) are organisms that, through injection of genetic materials, have been altered. "Franken-food" is the result, but again it creates the desired qualities for crops. These qualities can be seeds that are drought-resistant or need lower water requirements. Whether eating a genetically modified food also genetically modifies the consumer is in question. Companies in this area have pulled back from directly altering foods on the vine to their work on seeds. Currently, American seed companies dominate the global seed market.

Genetic engineers someday may be able to solve problems of irrigation, drainage, or increased yields with lower fossil fuel inputs. Herbicide chemicals also allow plants to tolerate exposure to seasonal weather patterns. Improvements are going to be especially important as the world moves from 6 billion people upward.

With the advent of climate change and global warming, weather forecasts will also play into when and where to best plant fields. Technology will be introduced into primitive areas for irrigation control, plant foods, and herbicides. There are massive challenges ahead if the planet is altering its climate cycles. There is an urgent need for world coordination in technology, crop variants, disease reports, and distribution. The United States has been a leader in agricultural and development. It is an important part of our history and an industry in which technological innovation is greatly and vastly improving methods and techniques. The time is now for us to continue in this leadership role.

Brands

The most recognizable brand names in the world are American. The most important aspects of any business are intangible: its people, symbols and slogans, quality, name awareness, and company name. Assets like proprietary resources, patents, trademarks, and channel relationships don't show up in a financial statement except sometimes entered as book value, or the price you paid for them. These assets are the primary source of competitive advantage in future earnings of the company and they're difficult to measure. Brand names bring emotional attachments that make a connection between a brand name, its symbol and slogan, to a buying impulse on the part of the consumer. Moreover, many companies have been hurt financially by the change of a brand, a price promotion, or brand extension that affects the overall image of the company. To protect this value, many companies have created a management position to be guardian of the brand.

What is the value of the brand name? The standard practice of adding on a "brand-name premium" can lead to higher estimates for value. One of the benefits of having a well-known brand name is that firms can usually charge a higher price for the same product, leading to higher profit margins and thus higher value for the firm. Interbrand, a division of Omnicom, is a branding consultancy created in 1974 with a keen interest in the valuation of international brands. Every year they release an analysis on the "World's Best Global Brands" and the 2009 ranking lists half of the world's most viable brands to be American, with eight in the top ten.[149] Interbrand ranks only the strength of individual product brand names and not a portfolio or a company-wide image, like a Procter & Gamble or a Pfizer.

In first place is Coca-Cola, which retained its ranking from the prior year with a brand name that's worth $68 billion, or about 55% of the total market value of the company. That means the market is valuing Coca-Cola at $123 billion, of which half is solely the "brand." In second place is IBM with a brand name of $60 billion and a market cap of $158 billion. Third is Microsoft, with a brand name of $57 billion and a market cap of $249 billion. General Electric, McDonald's, Google, Intel, and Disney round out the top ten. During times of lower market valuations, these brand names can be acquired cheaply.

There is a bit of creativity when it comes to evaluating these brands, something with which an accountant is sure to find fault, but there is a value here and we have to attach one. First, it calculates how much of a company's total sales fall under a particular brand. Secondly, it calculates how much of those earnings are derived from the power of the brand, and, finally, it attempts to look at future earnings and arrive at a present value. The final result values the brand as a financial asset, but not one that you would find on the balance sheet in the financial statements of each company. The interesting thing to note is that many of these brand names are equal to more than half the total value of the company when analyzing the current market valuation as of the end of 2009.

These brand values can change over time, for example, how finance companies are on their way down in the rankings and technology companies are on their way up. Citigroup has recently ranked eleventh in 2005; this year it was ranked thirty-sixth. American Express, J.P. Morgan, Goldman Sachs, and Morgan Stanley all have had the value of their brand names challenged. New to the list were Ralph Lauren Polo, Campbell Soup, Adobe, and Burger King.

The United States takes its branding seriously, and companies can be acquired solely for the cachet and consumer allegiance to its brand. An analysis of the top ten brand names from a decade ago indicates little change, except for the rise of Google. Brand names don't change in value much from year to year. There is no doubt that upstart consumers in the emerging markets will desire the cachet of brand names; they already do. However, as these economies mature, they will create their own value brands; the annual ranking will most likely change as the world does.

Capital Markets

The United States has been the dominant country in financial markets for decades in stocks, bonds, commodities, money markets, derivatives, and insurance. The history of stock exchanges began in Holland in 1602, when the Dutch East India Company issued the first shares on the Amsterdam Stock exchange; it was the first company to issue stocks. Around the time of the Industrial Revolution, the center of the world became America. And the markets are many.

The stock market is a public market for trading and issuance of share ownership in companies. At the end of 2009, the size of the world stock market was estimated at about $45 trillion, with the U.S. accounting for about 35% of that number. The New York Stock Exchange is the largest physical exchange of its kind in the world, but as trading becomes more electronic, this leadership may become cloudy. There is no central location for an electronic exchange. The NASDAQ is a virtual exchange, or all trading is done over a computer network and the rise of computers has created huge trading "black pools" to match orders instantaneously. The balance of power in equity markets is shifting.

The U.S. bond market is the largest market for domestic bonds, accounting for over forty percent of amounts outstanding, followed by Japan, with only sixteen percent.[150] A quarter of the amount outstanding in bonds were mortgage-backed securities, approximately another quarter was in corporate debt, with the remainder in treasury, federal agencies securities, and municipal government bonds. In different markets, we can trade spot prices, forward prices, and future prices, or purchase currency swaps or options on certain interest rate scenarios.

In money markets, which involve very short-term securities, the United States is again the leader. Within certificates of deposit, commercial paper, Fed funds, treasury bills, or repurchase agreements, the United States has the most depth and breadth of any short-term market in the world. In the United States, federal, state, and local governments all issue paper to meet funding needs, and corporations issue commercial paper on their own credit, bypassing middlemen.

In commodities, the largest world exchange is the New York Mercantile Exchange, with competition from Japan, China, India, and the Euronext Exchange in multiple locations. In the five years up to 2008, the value of global exports of commodities increased by 17% per year, with commodity OTC derivatives increasing more than 500 percent.[151]

Derivatives are a market unto themselves. They are securities that are based upon other security or asset values, where their prices are "derived" from their source. Many of these simply cancel each other out and serve to distribute risk around the world. If anything has exploded in the world, it is derivatives. Notational value stood at about $200 trillion in 2004, but the recent value outstanding of all derivative positions was an estimated $800 trillion, or ten times the size of the entire world economy.[152] Where the United Kingdom remains the leading derivatives center, the United States is the only other major location, with twenty-four percent of global trading. Most derivatives contracts are related to interest rates, where an issuer can hedge the prospect of a wide difference in interest rates incurred throughout the life of a bond. The derivatives market has been accused lately for its alleged role in the recent financial crisis in that most of these securities are traded over-the-counter. This means that agreements are made between two parties, without middlemen to enforce rules, regulations, and standardization, as well as provide some assurances that buyers and sellers will make good on their contracts.

The dollar is the most traded currency in the world, accounting for over half of the daily share of transactions, as reported in the foreign exchange market.[153] The next most important currency is the euro, followed by the *yen* and the pound sterling. The Chinese *yuan* is not freely traded and therefore does not account for even a fraction of foreign exchange transactions. Should the Chinese want to become a world leader, this will have to change. The foreign exchange market is the largest and most liquid financial market in the world. The daily turnover was reported to be over $4 trillion by the Bank of International Settlements.[154] Once again, London accounts for about 34% of the total, making it by far the global leader for foreign exchange, with New York second, accounting for about 17% of all transactions. Tokyo followed up in third with only 6%. Of the top currency traders in the world, three of the top ten are based in the United States in the form of Citibank, J.P. Morgan, and Goldman Sachs.

Although the United States has taken a great deal of blame for its deregulatory free-market philosophy of the recent decades, we also have to take credit for the benefit of financial innovation to the world economy.

Chemicals

Chemistry fuels America. Every physical industry and sector of the economy directly depends on chemistry. If you "drive it, build it, wear it, or bottle it, chances are you're working with the products of chemistry."[155] The chemical industry is one of America's largest, with about $1 trillion in sales every year. The U.S. produces about 25% of the world's chemicals, more than any other country. More than ten cents of every dollar exported outside the United States is from the chemical industry, accounting for almost $200 billion in annual exports.[156] Over a million people are employed in the business of chemistry nationwide. These value-added intellectual products are the key to America. Chemical and pharmaceutical companies were awarded about 200,000 patents, or ten percent of the total, with pharmaceutical companies being the top patent-awarded industry.[157]

The chemical industry is a keystone of the U.S. economy, converting raw materials into more than 70,000 different products. Dow Chemical, DuPont, and Lyondell are three of the largest chemical companies in the world. DuPont has been the leading chemical company, successful in innovation and in branding its material products into household names like Teflon, Corian, Kevlar, and, of course, nylon. DuPont has not only invented a great deal of things, but has been awarded numerous prizes for advancement of technological knowledge.

The United States, with its innovative culture in research and development and explicit property laws and regulations, is best suited to lead the world in chemical-based applications. Chemicals can have adverse side effects, and a rigorous testing and experimentation structure must be followed in order to protect humans. This is an area in which we can encourage both established companies and entrepreneurial startups, in addition to providing a much more rigorous educational array of alternative studies for young chemists.

Consumer Products

Consumer products are primarily foods and beverages. The world's largest restaurant provider in the world is based in Lexington, Kentucky. It has 36,000 restaurants in 110 different countries and over one million employees. Half of those restaurants are outside the United States. One of largest in China, it has 3,500 restaurants in that country alone. It is not McDonald's! It is the combination of KFC, Taco Bell, and Pizza Hut that is the company known as Yum Brands. With $11 billion in sales last year, it is second to McDonald's $22 billion in global sales, but has roughly the same number of restaurants in the same number of countries.

The United States is the world leader in consumer products because we have the world's largest consumer base. Two-thirds of the total production of the country is driven by personal consumption. Because the U.S. is 40% of world GDP, the American consumer is about 25% of the world's consumption. We matter, not only in our own country, but throughout the world. We know a lot about bringing consumer goods to mass market and we are positioned to sell our products to the new emerging consumer in developing economies.

One of the first things an immigrant will learn about our great country is the abundance of food and product choices in the average supermarket. There is at times a dizzying array of choices to make on a typical shopping trip that only Americans take for granted. We in America enjoy an extremely competitive, widespread, and robust consumer product choice. Since the U.S. is the largest market in the world, consumer products companies have to make it here to be globally successful. In some more developed countries around the world, a limited supply of narrow-based choices is the norm, and the developing areas lack access to basic food and water. It is important for the American consumer to travel outside the country to experience this firsthand. When my family travels outside the United States, one of our first excursions is a trip to the local supermarket to evaluate the level of products and the uniqueness of each province and county.

Total sales for the top 250 consumer products in 2009 exceeded a half trillion dollars.[158] Over a quarter of those total sales were concentrated in the top ten largest companies, of which four were American, with Philip Morris and Hewlett-Packard taking the first and second positions. Procter & Gamble and Dell Computer were in sixth and ninth position, respectively. Nine of the top 25 companies in the world are also American, including Motorola, Pepsi, Tyson Foods, Coca-Cola, and Mars.

By far the largest category of consumer products is foods, beverages, and tobacco, accounting for almost half of the sales in the consumer sector. The United States has six of the top ten ranked companies. Electronic products come second in consumption percentage, and, as you can imagine, the United States positions well with three in the top ten, but manufacturing electronic equipment is not our specialty. Where we do excel is in personal and household products, with Procter & Gamble leading the way, followed by

Kimberly-Clark, Colgate-Palmolive, and Avon.   Moving to fashion goods companies, the United States places seven in the top ten, including Nike, Ralph Lauren Polo, and Levi Strauss. Since Americans have a very high percentage of homeownership and some of the largest homes in the world, you would think we'd also be strong in home improvement products. Correct! Eight of the top ten companies in the home improvement field are American, with the top six positions filled with companies like Black & Decker, Masco, Sherwin-Williams, and Stanley.

U.S. companies operate in a mature market with barriers to entry and a sophisticated consumer. Those in emerging countries are growing rapidly with a smaller base. The challenge for U.S. companies will be to identify markets that generate new growth and then position strategies to successfully sell in these new markets. We will excel by partnering with existing networks, creating educational marketing programs, utilizing the existing organizational structure, and collaborating with local companies. U.S companies have to learn cultures, etiquette, customs, and language in order to be successful.

In India, there is an automobile for under $2,000, the "Nano". Computer manufacturers worldwide seek to offer personal computers for under $200. Manufacturers need to find ways to lower costs and sell products with minimal packaging. The rise of a handful of powerful low-price retailers like Wal-Mart has wreaked havoc for consumer product companies as margins have been negotiated down to bare, break-even levels. Wal-Mart itself, the world's largest retailer with $400 billion in sales, operates in fourteen countries, with over 4,000 stores in the U.S. and almost 3,200 stores outside the United

States.[159] According to Forbes, Wal-Mart's sales in 2006 were greater than the economies of 144 countries.[160]

Defense

The U.S. military is considered to be by far the world's leading military force, hands down. It's the most sophisticated, well-trained, technically superior fighting force in the world. The U.S. defense industry is big business, accounting for twenty percent of the U.S. federal budget and about ten percent of GDP.[161] In 2009, the U.S. Department of Defense expenditures are expected to be $650 billion. This does not take into account military spending outside of the Defense Department, which is estimated to be $200 to $400 billion more. The U.S. counts for about forty percent of the world share in defense spending, more than the next ten countries combined. It is not only important for defense, but is an example of the technological, innovative know-how of valued-added goods. Not only government-owned enterprises are involved, but the defense industry private sector establishes the United States as the leading force in military products and services.

After World War II, our nation suffered from a "winner's complex," when it seemed to us internally that we could do no wrong and whatever we attempted to do, we achieved. Then came the conflicts in Korea, Vietnam, and, more recently, Iraq and Afghanistan. With over half a century of world military dominance, the United States is always looking over its shoulder at number two. For years, during the Cold War, that was Russia. Since the fall of the Berlin Wall, there was supposedly a "peace dividend" that reflected a reduced expenditure needed in defense systems. Although a reduction in expenditures was realized in the 1990s, the year 2000 represented a starting point for a doubling of the U.S. defense budget. This was in response to a much more complicated and terrorist-oriented war in far-off places, with enemies that are difficult to pin down.

The U.S. is the police of the world, with 761 military bases in 151 countries.[162] Since it is an all-volunteer force, combined with the fact that most jobs require a high degree of educational background, the U.S. armed forces have higher personnel costs compared to the militaries of other countries. Only China has more standing troops than the United States, with a population that is over four times our size. Top defense contractors are a who's who of American ingenuity, including Boeing, Lockheed Martin, Northrop Grumman, General Dynamics, and Raytheon, with government revenues representing over half of these businesses. Private military companies also combine to form provide specialized expertise to make these public numbers much larger than estimated.

By land, the United States has 1.4 million active military personnel, and another 1.5 million in reserve, in addition to half a million people in paramilitary units. It has over 30,000 land-based weapons and 5,000 more pieces of towed artillery.[163]

By sea, it is by far the dominant presence on the oceans, with more aircraft carriers than the rest of the world combined. China is expected to launch its first one in 2010. The United States has twelve, along with fifty Navy destroyers, seventy-five submarines, and over 1,500 naval vessels, making it by far the largest in the world.

By air, it is even more dominant, with over 18,000 aircraft and almost 5,000 helicopters. With almost 14,000 major serviceable airports, the United States has the largest air network and infrastructure in the world. With space, the next frontier, our leadership will strengthen.

We have the most advanced air logistics structure combined with the largest system of roadways and railways that make our country a fortress of self-defense. Trends within the industry emphasize technology with information systems, lasers and optics being the most important areas of foreign interests. Many of the technological fields such as chemicals, nanotechnology, computers, and electronics are where America exhibits its leadership. In addition to this, we have space and marine systems that are far and away the world's most advanced and sophisticated. In information systems technology, communications, simulation, and sensing, our areas of high intellectual input are protected with many patents, as well as classified processes and materials, for national security interests. With stealth aircraft, drones, and advanced optics and lasers, the United States is continuing to push forward in its leadership role. With this interconnected world, there are obviously challenges with regard to information flow getting into the wrong hands. There has been an increase in suspicious reports from foreign contacts and there have been many recent reports of computer hacking intruding into networks. This is a national threat.

From the beginning of time, there have always been advances through the years in how battles were fought. These times are no different. The rise of the drone aircraft more recently is a great example of how technology can change conflicts. Lieutenant Colonel Chris Gough was interviewed recently on *60 Minutes*. He flew F-16 combat missions over Kosovo, but now the unit he commands has no jets—just pilot-less planes. "Physiologically, the stimulus and response are exactly the same. I'm not going 400 miles an hour, which means when I pull the stick, I don't get 5 Gs on my body. I have much more ability to process and to comprehend what's going on in the battlefield and the information just conveyed to me, and am better able to relay that information to who needs it."[164] The Air Force has 116 Predators that can stay up in the air for twenty-four hours at a time. One can be miles away from its target, flying undetected through the clouds, while zooming in on an unsuspecting enemy. Ten thousand feet above, the Predator is able to zoom in and send back a very precise image of a person standing on the ground. This is an example of the type of technological innovation that it's important for the United States to continue.

With the rise of China, there has also been a rise in stress about the aim of that country's military. As China rises to a military power, possible conflicts with Taiwan, Tibet, and even India, in addition to the new resource-dependent connections that it has around the world, make China a possible threat to United States' dominance. However, China is far from an advanced military power. It is trying to find the right mix of military might, cultural influence, and economic clout to make it as a world power and secure in the world.[165] In fact, the United States spends approximately ten times the amount that China spends on its military today, has unquestionable superiority in the land, sea, and air, and has advanced logistical systems to support it. China has acted as a soft power in the world, with more intimidation than actual conflict, and tends to be much more self-oriented in its policies and actions than even America. We can rest assured, at least for our lifetimes, that America's position as the world's police force is secure. However, we must also allocate resources appropriate to our own internal needs, and it is time that we analyze many post-World

War II arrangements and focus on more timely and strategic areas. It is certain that the American military is too far-flung and overreaching, and it is time to take a hard look at what we're doing and the reality of what it's costing.

Drug Discovery

America gets a bad rap on healthcare, especially the delivery of healthcare services and its cost. In the United States, life expectancy at birth today is about eighty years, which is a few years shorter than the overall figure in Western Europe. In the past two decades, our country's rank in this area has dropped from the top ten to around 40th in the world. Cancer survival rates in the United States are the highest in the world; however, the one problematic factor is the population percentages for overweight and obese individuals. Studies tell us that a third of our population is tremendously overweight. What does miss the headlines is that the United States is a leader in medical innovation.

The U.S. drug industry is the largest in the world. Innovation happens here more often than overseas. And there's tremendous innovation coming. The drug industry is in the midst of its own revolution. From the invention of penicillin, most drug discovery takes place in a trial-and-error process, with large libraries of chemicals tested for their ability to modify a target disease. Viagra had its beginnings as an experimental drug for relieving chest pain. When the researchers scrapped the trial due to poor results, they found the patients did not want to return the trial pills. Researchers gave this objection little note until they heard rumors about the medicine's sexual side effects.

Up until this point, the world of drug discovery was controlled by chemists whereby a target was identified, such as a disease, and a large library of chemicals were tested for their ability to change the target. Many petri dishes and drops of chemical compounds resulted in days upon days of tedious results-based analysis. However, the world is rapidly changing this model in the way of bio-genomics. This type of research is the opposite of trial and error, as the genetic makeup of the target is identified and scientists work backwards to see how to change the target and what interferes with it. From here, molecules are formed that contain the key ingredients that will eventually be put into human beings. The bio-genomic process eliminates many of the iterative testing phases and in trials goes right to the patients with the particular disease. Only a small part of the earth's biodiversity has ever been tested for pharmaceutical activity and there are many organisms living today in the world that evolved defensive and competitive mechanisms to survive. We haven't even begun to scratch the surface here.

Drug companies recognize this revolutionary change, as their pipelines of chemical compounds are slowly giving way to biotechnology. The drug companies have the money and the biotechs have the ideas! It's been only ten years since Dolly, the first mammal to be cloned from an adult cell, was introduced to the world sheepishly. It was at that time the greatest achievement of a science that was only a few decades old. Ten years ago, only seven percent of total U.S. drug sales were for biotechnology innovations; today, that number is over twenty percent and the momentum is growing.[166] Matching genes with disease is rapidly accelerating as there has been an explosion of identifying which genes cause disease. A lot of this is directly related to the increased computer processing speeds and capacity.

The next few years will bring a convergence of two other revolutions with genomics: nanotechnology, the science of very small things, and robotics, creation of instruction-oriented mechanical devices.

A few decades from now, if you have a cancerous tumor, a glass of water may contain a nanotechnology robot, a "nano-bot," that has a genetic code for which it is searching and will seek and destroy. "There are very few diseases or conditions, including infectious diseases, aside from physical brain damage, that cannot be carried out using nano medicine," says pioneer Robert Freitas, Jr. This will come from the ability to build complex medical nano-robots to molecular precision. Just as sensors are used to determine if stress is being increased on certain joints of buildings, sensors can also be inserted into human beings to determine if chemical imbalances are appearing and diseases are forming.

The old system of creating blockbuster drugs for mass distribution is falling to the advantages of personalized medicine to one's own individual DNA. It took fifteen years to sequence the HIV virus. In 2003, science tests took less than a month to sequence the newly emerged SARS virus. With the most recent "swine flu," drug companies were scrambling for new virus protection vaccines within a matter of weeks.

Physicians are beginning to look at people's DNA as a way to track potential diseases or illnesses in a preventative way. Today physicians have tight control over all medical information but the Internet and DNA genome sequencing cost is allowing individuals to carry their own individual characteristics on a flash drive. Affordable gene sequencing will enable individuals to do their own research and, as we know, they'll generally do it well because their life depends upon it.

The cost of sequencing DNA has fallen from about $1 million per person to about $10,000 today. This decline is because of Moore's Law, which, when announced in 1965, predicted the exponential rise of computing power with the costs also exponentially falling. Technology is a friend of gene sequencing. The microprocessor was the technological enabler of disruptive innovation in the computer field, but it also makes products cheaper and more convenient for biotechnology research. Predictive human genomics is here!

Today, almost all U.S. healthcare is delivered by small practices, most of them composed of solo physicians of groups of five or fewer. These practices rarely work closely with the hospitals where their patients are admitted and almost never interact with research scientists except through medical journals and conferences. If we replace today's thousands of small, isolated outposts with interactive technology that allows them to collaborate, participate, and investigate alternative methods for solving clients' problems, human ingenuity may create even more favorable results. Your "team of doctors" will see you now! The United States is a leader in technology and in data storage, so it's a natural evolution that we are a leader in medical innovation and service as well.

Education

The United States has one of the strongest education networks in the world, and it may surprise you, but some experts say that higher education is America's best industry.[167] According to The Times' higher education survey, the United States has 13 of the top 20 universities in the world, with Harvard retaining its number one ranking for the past six years.[168] In the top ten are Yale, Chicago, Princeton, MIT, and the California Institute of Technology. Another survey by Shanghai Jaiao Tong University, in their annual survey of academic rankings of world universities, finds that the United States takes 11 of the top 15 places and 31 in the top hundred. Though these surveys are subjective and in some cases weighed by peer review, these findings nonetheless place America in a leadership role in higher education.

The basic literacy rate of our country is approximately ninety-nine percent. Whereas most public education is operated by state and local governments, higher education takes the form of a competitive environment of public and private institutions. Local community college open-admission policies attract more economic-oriented students, where the majority, some eighty percent, attends public universities.

Though many countries emphasize tests and memorization, America's schools teach people to think. In America, people are allowed to be bold and challenge what is taught, even though it may lead to failure. Here in America, failure is almost a badge of honor. Many tests in America are as much about memorization as they are about the application of those things that are important. It's almost as if the American style of higher education trains the brain to help itself find answers. A balance of right-brain and left-brain activities may be the best educational curriculum. Technical knowledge complemented by liberal arts educations can unlock the true innovative human being.

Globalization of the world is going to demand intelligent students. The United Nations says that the number of students worldwide pursuing post-secondary education has quintupled from 1970 until 2007, moving from 29 million to 153 million students, while the world population less than doubled.[169] Educating students is big business; it is a $1 trillion-business worldwide. We have created an educational system that works, is practical, and is profitable. With innovation being America's calling card, think-tanks and entrepreneurial startups surrounding these universities are the key to keeping our leadership strong.

A decade ago, there were 3.5 million Chinese attending universities. In 2008, that number was over 21 million. Much has been said about Chinese universities graduating more engineers than America, but I remember the Soviet Union also had more scientists and engineers than anyone. It's all about what they're trained to do. The Chinese university system may not be the structure for the working world today. In China, there is a "misalignment between the university system and the needs of the economy," says Robert Ubell, who heads a New York University program in China. "Chinese graduates often have few practical skills." Since most of the elite universities are funded by the Chinese central government, they have been largely exempt from financial problems, but also subject to bureaucracy and status quo. Ironically, the government has enforced curricula of math and science on these schools, which has resulted in great manufacturing advances, but few sophisticated marketing and management minds. Can you name just one Chinese brand name? It can't be just about copying great ideas.

In Europe, many universities are practically free. But the overused and under-funded network of universities is going through a capitalistic process of rewarding research professors over teaching professors. "In Germany, professors juggle scores of students, whereas the top American universities nurture a handful."[170] Slowly, the German education model is weaning itself from the public payroll as private endowments are now rising to fund universities. But along with other countries, Germany has to brace for an extra amount of students caused by migration and a minor baby boom.

In the Arab world, most of what students typically learn is religious or traditional. A listing of the world's top 500 universities includes not one single Arab institution. In trends of international mathematics and science study, out of 48 countries tested, all 12 ranked Arab countries fell below the average.[171] The strength of religious beliefs can be overwhelming in a curriculum, where state primary schools in Saudi Arabia devoted over 30% of their time to religion. A quarter of the kingdom's university students devote the main part to Islamic studies, more than engineering, medicine, and science put together. A third of Egyptian adults have never heard of Charles Darwin and a large minority thinks there's no evidence to back his famous theory. In Pakistan, only around half of adults can read, schools lack basic necessities like water, and the bureaucracy is cumbersome. Again, the public school is religious-oriented, which offers little education beyond memorizing the Koran. That's why private schools have been blossoming up around the country to now almost 60,000 and around one-third of Pakistan's 33 million students attend a private school. This is far more than the less than 2 million in the state-run religious schools.[172]

What we have here is valuable: a higher education facility that breeds thinkers and innovators. But, of course, we are American; we need to do better. Education is an investment into our future. In a knowledge-based world, it is our currency. We need to reward and award the great thinkers of the land as much as we do investment traders and football players. As Americans, we must be more open-minded than ever before, grasping different ideas from many parts of the world to amalgamate them together in forming new and better ideas.

Entertainment

Americans love to be entertained and with more leisure time than in most societies, we've made it big business. The world's first commercial motion picture was exhibited in New York City in 1894 using Thomas Edison's invention. The industry quickly moved to Hollywood to escape many of Edison's patents, and the rest is history. Americans are the heaviest television viewers in the world, with the average viewing time reaching five hours a day in 2006.[173] Americans listen to radio programming on average just over 2.5 hours a day. The music and video industries are morphing into on-line businesses with the Internet's open access structure. It is changing the businesses as we speak. The entertainment industry is one of our country's strongest competitive advantages; it utilizes our creative and innovative skills and creates lasting profitability.

Hollywood has produced the most commercially successful movies in history and American films dominate the global film industry. The big five companies, 20th Century Fox, RKO, Paramount Pictures, Warner Bros., and Loews-MGM, dominated the industry for decades.

Today, these movie studios have merged or been acquired by conglomerates like CBS, Walt Disney, Time Warner, or Liberty Media, but the United States is still the largest film market in the world. Technological innovation has propelled 3-D in movies like "*Avatar*" to sports events on the small screen.

Television has also been dominated by news conglomerates, and cable has helped make it a more decentralized business. No longer do the big three networks monopolize a select group of channels like they used to. The switch from analog to digital TV has eliminated the ease and convenience of rabbit ears to catch radio waves from wherever you happen to be. This has almost required the use of a cable or phone line to transmit digital images, changing this industry forever. Again the major players are Comcast and Time Warner, or phone companies like Verizon and specialized services like Dish TV and Direct TV.

Almost nonexistent in the year 2000, digital music downloads reached 11 million in 2007, whereas CD sales peaked in 2002 at $15 billion and have declined slowly since, reaching $10 billion in 2008. Because of the reduced revenue in downloads, the "music" business has changed to a "live performance" industry, with recording artists now relying more on live performances and merchandise for their income. The sale of vinyl LPs is limited to antique stores and county fairs. Inexpensive recording hardware and software make it possible to create high-quality music in a bedroom and distribute it over the Internet to a worldwide audience instantaneously.

There are over 1 million worldwide Internet gaming participants in the videogame industry. The release of *Madden EA Football* every year is a much-awaited event. The upgrade cycle of Playstations, X-boxes and Wii all require additional purchases to "keep up with the Joneses," or at least with your on-line playing partners. Gosh, even Warren Buffet plays bridge on-line. There is no telling where these trends will take us. We are creating virtual universes where people can act out their fantasies, own an island, and shop for mega-yachts. All this is pushing the video gaming industry to create more revenue and, in so doing, is creating more technological know-how and innovation that will spread across multiple industries like medicine, sports and defense.

Finance

Finance is one of the largest sectors of the United States, representing between 15 and 20% of the S&P 500's market value in the past ten years. It has accounted for an enormous amount of new employment and profitability throughout the country. Domestic financial services accounted for 13% of the country's pre-tax profits in 1980, but that rose to 27% in 2007.[174] Of the 145 million people working in the United States in the year 2000, 7 million of them worked in the finance, insurance, and real estate businesses.[175]

Assets of U.S. financial corporations reached over $30 trillion before the crisis in 2008, with about half owned by capital market companies like broker-dealers and security issuers, and the other half owned by banks, credit unions, and savings institutions. These two sides of finance were created by the Glass-Stealgall Act of 1933, which separated banking from investment institutions in order to provide some wall between the volatile industry of investment banking and finance from the banking system that pays checks, extends credit, and takes deposits, the lifeblood of the economy. The act was repealed in 1997 to allow more flexibility to banking institutions in a deregulated environment and to compete worldwide. It obviously needs to be rethought whether some type of structure walling off the banking system is needed going forward.

Markets are just a form of human exchange and should be encouraged. Amartya Sen, a Nobel Prize-winning economist, says, "To be generally against markets would be almost like being against conversations between people."[176] A healthy economy requires a financial system that provides liquidity and promotes efficient allocation of resources and dispersion of risk. As Niall Ferguson pointed out in his book *The Ascent of Money*, finance builds the foundation of human progress; it is an essential part of improving human history. And history is filled with step backs after huge leaps forward. Finance is what America does best; it is a service that is intellectual and innovative, and provides value for participants most of the time.

Retail banking is a highly fragmented industry in the United States with the largest company, Bank of America, only having about a three percent market share. Business banking and commercial finance is much more consolidated with the large "too big to fail" institutions dominating in size and scope. As we have recently learned from finance, a high concentration of risk in one small area of a large company can be detrimental to not only the total company but also the companies with which it does business. There's an inner relationship, interlocking many of the large financial companies in the world that needs to be understood.

Does financial innovation help individuals? Absolutely, we have witnessed high homeownership rates from securitization. Financial innovation has produced some noteworthy victories in electronic clearing, the development of futures, forwards, and mutual funds has all had a tremendous positive impact. Does financial innovation help the management of risk? Absolutely, as banks are able to offload concentrated exposures to other parties. Surely, these two points were pushed to extremes. The point in time in which risk is misrepresented or either just simply misunderstood is hard to pinpoint.

Finance does not only have implications for America but for the world as a whole. Many countries have a much more direct relationship between bankers and borrowers. In Japan, companies will traditionally turn to the same one or two banks for financing. In Germany, banks have cross shareholdings with borrowers and representatives on their boards. These are in direct contrast to the American style of securitization and subordination. Both styles have their own advantages and disadvantages, but when it comes to complex decisions of whether to fund a new entrepreneurial idea, it's often better to leave the job to the wisdom of the crowds rather than the groupthink of the committee.

Freedom

The United States' ideal is based on freedom. We created this nation on the proclamation that "all men are created equal," and that they were given certain "unalienable rights." Most of the people who came to America were leaving Europe because of religious persecution. When the United States defeated Great Britain in the American Revolutionary War, it was the first successful colonial war of independence. The Bill of Rights guaranteed many fundamental civil rights and freedoms. Included are the rights to free speech, the right to bear arms, the right to religious freedom, and the right to assembly. It also covers the freedom against search and seizure, cruel and unusual punishment, and even the right against self-incrimination. That's when a hardened criminal says, "I'll take the fifth." He is invoking his Fifth Amendment right in that his testimony may actually harm himself. That's a freedom that few nations observe.

What is freedom? Is it the idea of being free? Is it the idea that you won't be interfered with in your rights as an individual? It is not only the right to speak and believe what you want, but, as FDR pointed out, it's also the freedom from fear and from want. Liberty is a condition in which an individual has the ability to act according to his or her own will. Adam Smith, in his *Wealth of Nations*, said, "Basic institutions that protect the liberty of individuals to pursue their own economic interests, result in the greater prosperity for the larger society." Freedom also created an "invisible hand." There is a link between freedom and prosperity. In fact, studies show that higher economic freedoms correlate strongly with higher per capita income and with higher self-reported happiness.[177] People do care about how society provides them opportunities to undertake new projects and allows them to make choices based upon their own personal preferences. According to the Cato Institute, higher economic freedom promotes participation and collaboration. Higher economic freedom may also be significant in preventing wars.

When you ask immigrants why they came to America, the freedom to pursue their own path, use their own labor, and protect their own property is the most common answer. Economic freedom provides the right of property ownership and the freedom of movement for labor, capital, and goods in the absence of coercion or constraint beyond that necessary to protect other citizens. The Index of Economic Freedom is a series of ten economic measurements created by the Heritage Foundation and the *Wall Street Journal*. It measures the degree of economic freedom in the world's nations. The United States always shows up strongly in these measures.

America scores above the world average in business freedom, investment freedom, financial freedom, property rights, freedom from corruption, and labor freedom. Laws and legal frameworks support entrepreneurial activity. Foreign investments in domestic capital are subject to the same rules. Financial markets are open and are among the world's most dynamic and modern. The judiciary system is independent and of a very high quality. In business freedom, the overall ability to conduct business is strongly protected under regulations. Starting a business typically takes six days! This is compared to the world average of thirty-eight days and, in some cases, years. Trade tariffs are also among the world's lowest. Monetary freedom, or the ability for a citizen to retain value in the country's monetary unit, remains high as well because the government attempts to keep inflation rates at manageable levels. Investment freedom is widespread as even the smallest investor can take their piggyback to a bank and invest in some far-off foreign enterprise, completely legal and legit. As one of the world's most dynamic and developed financial markets, the U.S. has regulations that are generally straightforward and consistent with international standards.

Where freedom in the United States is probably most important is in property rights. Property rights are guaranteed. Contracts are very secure in that the judiciary system is well developed and protects intellectual property as well as physical land and buildings. If your own labor is considered property, the U.S. has the most highly flexible labor regulations, which enhance overall employment and productivity growth. We are one of the largest workforces in the world and also one of the most flexible. Although it is difficult to see the benefit with high initial unemployment claims every week, this highly flexible, dynamic workforce can focus on a new industry like bees to honey.

Freedom House has also published "Freedom in the World," an annual assessment of the state of political rights and civil liberties. According to their most recent survey, 90 countries are considered "free," with their 3 billion inhabitants comprising 47% of the world's population. These people enjoy a broad range of rights. 58 countries, representing just over a billion people, are considered partly free. Rights are more limited in these countries in which dominating ruling parties make policies that could be prejudicial or corrupt. The survey found that 45 countries are not free, with 2.5 billion inhabitants or 23% of the world's population. One half of these people live in China who are denied the most basic political rights and civil liberties. Also amongst the "not free" are Cuba, Iran and North Korea but surprisingly also Saudi Arabia, Vietnam, Thailand, Egypt and Russia.[178]

Freedom of the press is also measured by Freedom House. The degree to which each country permits the free flow of news and information classifies it as "free," "partly free," or "not free." The United States remains one of the most open, with some of the strongest ratings in the world. Also among the top are Germany, Canada, the United Kingdom, Japan, France, and many other European countries. The bottom of the list is rounded out by North Korea, Libya, Cuba,

Venezuela, Zimbabwe, Iran, and China. Media freedom has been under threat during the global recession, with many of the Eastern European countries prosecuting media sources. "The Iron Curtain is still there," says a media watcher at the Organization for Security and Cooperation in Europe.[179] Political meddling in elections is widespread but so is government force in exerting control over public broadcasters and newspapers. Russia, famous for the one-candidate ballot and the 98% voter turnout, is rigging its elections like in no time before. In a recent election, a Moscow independent candidate was simply not registered and the corruption in the election received almost no public attention. Even in Italy, Silvio Berlusconi, the prime minister, is forcing pressure against two left-leaning newspapers and demanding damages for disparaging him in public. He controls three of Italy's seven main television channels, with another three operated by the state-owned corporation. His family owns a leading daily newspaper plus a weekly newsmagazine and the country's biggest publishing house.[180]

Some of the most basic freedoms that we enjoy in America are not available in other countries. Freedom of information is also freedom from misinformation! Some Russian textbooks rewrite history to include more benevolent memories of Lenin and Stalin. In China, textbooks have the habit of bending the truth to suit the Communist Party or to reinforce moral messages. In some countries, freedom's progress actually may have come to a halt or even gone into reverse. That is the most recent conclusion of Freedom House. Over the past half-century, it seems that the advance of democracy and basic freedoms was on the rise. First, the Europeans let their colonies go, and then the Soviet empire fell and, with it, the communist monopoly of power. Apartheid ended in South Africa. Recently, however, through political elections and censorship of news sources, It seems that freedoms have been violated.

With the Internet transferring news around the globe instantaneously without interference, we have to believe that this is simply a step back due to the more recent economic challenges. The United States is the leader in freedom. It may not have the highest "ranking," nor are we the most advantageous economically speaking, but as the largest economy in the world, it is amazingly free. The fact that I can write exactly what I think and have it published easily is a testament to letting ideas bubble up into bigger ideas. Innovation begins here with an idea and a discussion of that thought. Without the freedom to assemble and discuss, innovation is lost.

Government

The United States is the world's oldest surviving federation. It is a constitutional republic as defined by the regulated systems of checks and balances offered in 1789, when the structure of government was changed from a confederation to a federation. The government reflected a new style of structure at the time, favoring elective government officials with a less powerful chief executive, as opposed to the existing monarchs, priests, dictators, and emperors of the past. This system was based upon more diffuse power and individual liberty dating back to the Greek philosophers.

The U.S. is a federal union of fifty states and possessions. The most recent state was Hawaii, which achieved statehood in August of 1959. In creating it, the framers of the Constitution sought a more balanced representative government, which would last through highs and lows of the society and not be dependent upon a "leader." The legislative branch makes federal laws, has the power of money flow, and can remove sitting members of government. The judicial branch approves, interprets, and overturns laws. The executive branch is the commander-in-chief of the military and appoints cabinet officers. The power of veto is only granted today on an entire bill. The president cannot take out his pen and mark out specific lines. State governments mostly have this right of "line-item" veto. This is something to consider in this day of large earmarks and out-of-sight budgets.

State governments have the greatest influence over most Americans' daily lives. Each state has its own written constitution, government, and code of laws. They handle the majority of issues most relevant for citizens within their jurisdiction. Most states operate within a balanced budget environment, where severe budget cuts are made in times of recession to equate revenues with expenses. Conversely, in times of expansion, budgets usually expand as well. This type of government spending is very pro-cyclical or can magnify the volatility of the business cycle.

The founding fathers imagined a world of limited government interference from daily activities. It is interesting that the founding fathers did not think of themselves as statesmen first but rather as farmers, lawyers, or bankers. It is almost as if they believed that government should be so small as to not be a full-time job, except for that of the president. If they were alive today to witness the type of system that they created, they may not be able to recognize it. Although individual rights are still the cornerstone of the society, the full-time statesmen with monetary incentives to stay in office and after office may not be what they had in mind. Nonetheless, they would be astounded that the structure has had no major changes throughout almost 250 years of feasts, famines, wars, and civil conflict. The fact that human economy has progressed so rapidly and has been managed within the same government structure is miraculous.

Although often criticized, the form of government that we have is very stable and representative of the people. Although one could debate how little power each citizen really does have in the scheme of power brokers and special interests, it still remains the best social system of which to be a part and to get your voice heard. Many times, an issue with strong following can cause change rapidly in our political system. In the information age, this type of government will be able to change and respond to issues rapidly.

Green

The United States has come late to the green movement compared to Europe, but is rapidly becoming a leader and the environmental mindset is becoming more common among our citizens. Environmentalism is central to United States' history and the National Park System, which began in 1916 and is the world's largest. Public support for our environmental concerns is widespread, as became clear during Earth Day demonstrations. The U.S. Environmental Protection Agency was established in 1970 and, following that, there was an enactment of a whole series of laws and regulations pertaining to waste, pesticides, polluted site cleanup, and protection of endangered species. In the 1980s, business interests and political contributions turned our government away from an environmental agenda, which continued for several decades. More recently, regulations having to do with capping carbon emissions, environmentally friendly rules, and recycling have been on the forefront. Big business is starting to notice.

The United States has the world's largest organic foods and beverage market, which has reached sales of billions of dollars and is continuing to grow rapidly. The United States has become a leader in green buildings, where lighting, building materials, and even sewer systems are designed with a low environmental impact. Unfortunately, most of our houses and buildings were all designed with the assumption of an endless supply of cheap fossil fuels, but that central tenet is changing. We are a leader in environmental impact analysis, with conservation biology an important and rapidly developing field.

We are part of nature, not separate from it, and that principle is guiding a grassroots democracy toward key green values. The so-called "green-collar worker" is one area of increased employment opportunities in the environmental services sector. From organic farmers to environmental lawyers, or even local unions installing solar panels for homeowners, the green movement is here to stay and is growing. Ecological sustainability is in the interest of our country and the world.

We are also a leader in the consumption of energy, but slowly there is a groundswell demanding change. Our energy use in transportation is the world's largest and is predominantly powered by gasoline from crude oil. With the rise of the price of gasoline, the number of miles driven has dropped considerably and conservation measures have risen, but our country has a long way to go in oil conservation. There is some substance to the theory that we have reached a "peak oil" scenario at which the world's consumption is increasing, with new oil discoveries decreasing. It is certain that we have reached a point of exhausting the easy-to-recover oil and are now working on technological innovations to extract oil from tar sands, deep water, and new methods of horizontal drilling, which allow better extraction percentages. With higher prices for oil, profitability will be present to develop new technologies to harness new sources of energy and wean ourselves off of oil dependency.

Most likely we will be moving toward fewer gas engines and more hybrids that only fire up if the electrical power is insufficient. Natural gas is readily abundant in our country and moving heavy trucks to that alternative would make a large bounce in our oil deficit. The cost of an electric plug-in for your car is substantially less than filling up at the gas tank, although maybe not as environmentally healthy. Most of our electricity is produced from burning coal, which is also polluting. Smaller homes, smaller cars, more locally grown foods that don't need to be transported, and more public transportation are directions that we must take and will. It's not a question of being environmental; it's a question of economic survival. If our country was more self sufficient with our energy sources half of our trade deficit and many of our foreign policy actions would be greatly reduced. We need strong energy policies at all levels of government to shift decisively away from polluting energy sources toward clean and green.

Currently our energy needs for electricity are supplied by a mix that is about half coal, about twenty percent nuclear and natural gas, and about six percent hydro. Other renewables such as generation from solar, wind, geothermal, biomass, landfill gas recovery, and even ocean waves constitute about three percent of our national fuel mix for electricity. Other renewables are expected to rise considerably, but even with enlarged expectations, these cannot be thought of to power more than ten or twenty percent of this country's power. Currently, there are many nuclear power plants on the drawing board as the industry was effectually shut down since the incident at Three Mile Island in the 1970s. Solar is becoming more popular with technological advances and a large capacity glut forcing prices to decline. Wind power is also popular, becoming a topic at municipality meetings that want to attract the income and self-sufficiency. Technological advances in ethanol creation have moved from corn to switch grass and offer increasing sources of energy for the future.

The carbon issue is more complex than meets the eye. Whether you believe in global warming or not, carbon dioxide emissions are pollution. We have passed emission regulations with the reduction of acid rain before. Carbon emissions have been regulated in Europe with a cap and trade process. It is likely that the United States will pass such a regulation that caps most polluters at current rates and will allocate permits for their emissions. As these permits are reduced and encourage lower emissions in the future, the cost for reduction will be thrust upon the polluters as they will have to buy emission credits on an open market. Those companies that can reduce their pollutants below the expected level can sell these credits and reap the benefits from modernization. Europe has been operating under this kind of system for almost a decade and although it has mixed results, at least it's a step in the right direction. It will be important to have international agreement to these standards because if one side of the planet is concerned and the other is not, the regulations are costly and not effective.

Information

The sector of the economy called "information technology" is really two different industries; **technology** is that sector of computing, whereas **information** is about knowledge. Since America is in the knowledge business, with value-added techniques and services being our strength, we need to understand the workings of both information and technology. The market-based system is an information-based system as each buyer and seller has access to multiple sources of information when making a decision. Never before in human history has so much information been available to such a large percentage of the world. America's strength is in translating that informational knowledge into things, products, and services for the world.

The Library of Congress is listed as the world's largest library, with more than 32 million catalogued books and more than 61 million manuscripts.[181] It is home to over a million issues of world newspapers spanning three centuries, the world's largest collection of legal materials, 5 million maps, 3 million sound recordings, and more than 14 million photographic images. The library also serves as a legal repository for copyright protection and registration and as the base for the U.S. copyright office. It adds an average of 10,000 items per day to its inventory.

The digital age is just beginning as the Library of Congress has just begun a multilingual digital library. On October 28, 2008, Google stated they had 7 million books searchable, including those scanned by their 20,000 publisher partners. Google has been scanning books using a high-speed camera that photographs at a rate of a thousand pages per hour. Rapidly, the information of all humanity will be available via a handheld device.

In 1962, the Department of Defense formed an information-processing group to further computer knowledge. There were three basic locations in Santa Monica, California, the University of California at Berkeley, and the Massachusetts Institute of Technology. The first computer linkage via telephone was made between the University of California at Los Angeles and Stanford Research Institute at 11:30 p.m. on October 29, 1969. It was the beginning of the Internet. The Internet has sent the world into a hyperbolic knowledge shift. We are truly in the information age.

Nowhere in the world do you have access to such information as here in the United States. From Dun & Bradstreet to Hoover's, from government publications to industry councils, the ability of a person to obtain information on just about anything is unparalleled. English is still the most prevalent language used on the Internet, but will eventually be surpassed by Chinese simply due to population.[182] America is the largest user of the Internet, with 250 of the 340 million citizens having access to the Internet with a penetration rate of over seventy-four percent. Someday soon, it will be fashionable to be at a library but maybe just for the coffee!

Many companies are swamped with information, from feedback from their clients to data on deliveries to the 360 reviews. The real challenge is making good use of what the information is telling you. The survey by Fortune and IDG research found that just a third of companies surveyed thought they were highly successful at integrating customer data into business decisions. With the information age comes specialization and personalization. Generic "one size fits all" marketing is no longer in sync with today's segmented population.

The information age allows buyers and sellers to provide feedback on their transactions instantaneously, like the A+++ on eBay. Entire industries can be changed with access to information. When you made a reservation for an airplane flight a decade ago, did you have a Travelocity.com to get you the best price, at the best hour, on the best day? Back in the 1990s, if you called on Sunday afternoon or Tuesday night, prices would be different. Then along came the Internet and now everyone knows the prices all the time. The industry's pricing power has collapsed. The days are also over for the real estate broker that has access to listings exclusive to a community. Realtor. com has changed the ability for anyone to look into that exclusivity. Any industry in which profitability is derived from being a closed system, keeping their information a proprietary secret, will eventually be overcome by the information industry.[183]

America is in the best position of any country in the world to take advantage of information-based market systems. "Imagine a world in which every single person on the planet has free access to the sum of all human knowledge," posits Jimmy Wales, founder of Wikipedia.

Ingenuity

American ingenuity refers to the ability to apply ideas to solve problems and challenges. There is no example better than what happened here in America in the seventeenth and eighteenth centuries. The self-reliance of the early colonial settlers in New England describes a "make do" attitude with the materials on hand. The difficulty of crossing an ocean was met with a dire challenge of creating food in a territory that was hostile and less fertile than the European home. Harsh winters, Indian conflicts, and lack of basic material needs and governmental assistance were all elements to bring out the best in these new Americans. Innovation is our lifeblood; without it we would have died long ago.

Human ingenuity has led economic developments, but it can also be seen in the development of social organizations, institutions, and communication. In solving a problem, one must evaluate alternative solutions based upon resources available, and then choose the method that best solves the problem with the right tools. Much of this is not taught in school. It is an application of prior knowledge, trial and error, and collaboration that is able to discern patterns and paths of possible alternatives. It can be said that our culture is built on failures because every successful businessperson has a few failures in their past to describe.

As the complexity and the speed of the world increase, it is going to be so much more important to have creative ideas to solve problems that have never been solved before. There are no history books to refer to, only projections about what may happen. The challenges that we face today are historic. Using old solutions to these problems will not be as effective. It is the American innovative ingenuity that will throw many new solutions on the table as the people of the world choose new paths in the new order of the world.

Knowledge is good. However, if it is not used, it is worthless! It is the application of what we know that will help us solve the problems

of the world and advance toward our goals. The ability to tap that knowledge from anywhere is a relatively new thing; only in the last ten years has the mobile telephone turned into mobile broadband. This universal knowledge will serve as a catalyst to ingenuity.

Insurance

As one of the safest places on earth, we are also the most insured. The United States is the largest insurance market in the world, with over $1.2 billion in premium income in 2009 in almost a thirty percent share of worldwide insurance.[184] Seven of the top ten insurance brokers in the world are based right here in the United States. Topping them all is Marsh & McLennan, with $11 billion in brokerage revenue. Aon is second, with over $7 billion in revenues. Prudential and Met Life are two of the top ten insurance companies in the world. Warren Buffet's Berkshire Hathaway is for a large part an insurance company. The other top property and casualty insurers are State Farm, Allstate and St. Paul Travelers.

The bailout of AIG, once the world's largest insurance company, in September of 2008 did disrupt the market, but regulations ensured that many of AIG's insurance products were walled off from the speculative mortgage-backed excesses. Unlike with many other investment firms, insurers are typically not faced with a flood of withdrawals and usually have investors' funds for the long-term. They also usually employ less leverage than banks and have longer-term liabilities, like paying out life insurance. The vast majority of insurance companies have enough capital to absorb the losses of 2008 and 2009, with the exception of a small number of firms.

The insurance industry is exposed to the economic cycle but surprisingly, global insurance premiums grew in 2009 reaching over $4 trillion worldwide. Advanced economies account for the majority of insurance written but emerging economies are both growing fast and desiring more sophisticated financial services. Insurance is all about dispersing risk. By buying a home and insurance, you are supported in the event of losing your home to flood, fire, or other damage. Insurance companies will take in the premium earned and invest it should a claim arise. Financial innovation in insurance products will also benefit the average American to plan for retirement and protect their families.

Law

The United States did not invent law. Adam Smith is not only known for *The Wealth of Nations*, but also for his first book, *Theory of Moral Sentiments*. He traced the evolution of mankind's ethics to our nature as social beings who feel bad if we do something that harms another. Through this sympathy and empathy, we created a civilized society. We formed courts of law to help us govern our economy as it became more complex and over time we rely on these institutions to reinforce values that we deem important.

The United States has over a million lawyers, approximately one out of every 265 citizens.[185] India also has over a million lawyers but with its population so large, its ratio is much higher per citizen. Brazil, with a half a million lawyers, one in every 326, comes in second.[186] Italy, Spain, France, and Germany each have only about 100,000 lawyers, averaging about one lawyer in every 500 citizens.

The system of law does a fairly good job of protecting innovation through patents, copyrights, property rights, intellectual property, and proprietary knowledge. Many civilizations had laws of conduct and property, but not so formally written down. The type of law that we practice here in the United States is called common law; developed in England and influenced by the Norman Conquest, it was inherited by almost every former colony of the British Empire. This type of law relies more upon the precedent that courts make in interpreting and judging laws. This can be illustrated by anyone who has been in a court case, or read about it, where lawyers would cite a particular case for similar attributes to the present one. From criminal law to civil law and enforcing contracts, the system of laws and support for them in the United States is most likely the widest in the world.

U.S. courts pioneered the concept of the **class action**, by which the burden falls on class members to notify the court if they wish to be bound by a collective judgment, as opposed to the results of your own trial. Another unique feature is the so-called American Rule, under which parties generally bear their own attorneys' fees (as opposed to the English Rule of "loser pays"), though American legislators and courts have carved out numerous exceptions.

Around the world, cultures are not as forgiving in some cases; not paying your debts is the ultimate disgrace. In England, which has about a tenth of the number of bankruptcies per thousand people as the United States, it is considered a scarlet letter; executives from bankrupt companies have difficulty finding new jobs and generally are socially shunned. In Italy and Greece, bankruptcy is not even an option unless it is connected with a business. The law of Europe is as changing as each country's unique legal system operates alongside the laws of member states of the European Union (EU). The EU is not a federal government, as established by the European Court of Justice, but the community constitutes "a new legal order" in international law.

In Asia, Japan has attempted to borrow a lot of the structure of U.S. bankruptcy law, but its cultural values still discourage it. Within Asia, traditional Japanese culture emphasizes the group over the individual, similarity over difference. Thus, the Japanese feel that it is embarrassing and shameful to need to resort to the law. The objective of Japanese courts is less about declaring a winner and loser, and more of establishing a compromise between both parties.[187]

China has no personal bankruptcy system, but is developing a rescue system for ailing businesses. Socialism and communism also have a great effect on attitudes and culture in China and the resulting bankruptcy laws. A Ministry of Justice was dismantled in 1959 but was reestablished in 1979. Law schools were reopened and there are now over 200,000 Chinese lawyers from only 5,000 in 1981. The most developed and most significant Chinese bankruptcy laws focus on state-owned enterprises. These are companies that are property of the state, and bankruptcy is viewed as a leadership failure, a loss of face for the government. Yet, scores of them operate at a loss. Market share and sales are important, whereas profitability is sometimes not even measured and in some cases irrelevant. It is very difficult to place an SOE into bankruptcy and government permission is needed.

America's business environment is much more dynamic than those of Europe or Asia, for many reasons—and our generosity to capitalism's losers is one of them. America leads the developed world in bankruptcies. "We've worked hard to build the best—and, not coincidentally, the most generous—bankruptcy code in existence."[188] America has constructed bankruptcy law through financial and legal innovations that have helped debtors get a fresh beginning. Nonetheless, "our system works so well that other nations are trying to move away from their harshly punitive treatment of insolvent debtors, and closer to our free-and-easy, all-is-forgiven model." In 2008, there were over a million bankruptcies in the United States' courts. Of those, two-thirds were chapter 7, liquidation bankruptcies, while about a third were reorganizations. Personal bankruptcies may be caused by a number of factors. In 2008, over 96% of all bankruptcy filings were not business-related; they were personal, in the midst of a recession, with the majority involving medical bills. The *American Journal of Medicine* says over three out of five personal bankruptcies are due to medical debt.

Within property rights, the U.S. grants more patents than any other country in the world. The total value of intellectual property is estimated at more than $5 trillion, according to the U.S. Patent and Trademark Office.[189] An estimated 75% of the value of publicly traded U.S. companies is now in intangible assets, according to *The Economist*. Intellectual property-based businesses and entrepreneurs drive more economic growth in America than any other source, including government. In pharmaceutical research and development, it can take years if not decades to move a drug from the chemical composition to animal and human testing and on to a marketable, generally prescribed drug. That needs protection from generic copying to reward the long-term investment that has been made. The life of a product patent is twenty years in United States. In artistic, creative industries, intellectual property must also be protected for seventy years after an author's death or, in corporate ownership, for longer. In technologies it is important to not only patent total works, but also each component. The camcorder idea was submitted to the patent office in 1977. It was rejected as absurd! A modern camcorder is a combination of many different patented technologies. Although the initial patent application for the camcorder was rejected, Jerome Lemelson remained persistent as an inventor and eventually amassed a fortune from his ideas and created a foundation to help entrepreneurs (the Lemelson Foundation).

We Americans must recognize that there's no single path of legal development and that it is unreasonable to accept a one-size-fits-all solution to many different societies in their approach to the rule of law. We will most definitely have differences in the rights and values that we cherish, even amongst ourselves. Since the majority of Americans are Christian, the act of forgiveness is embedded within our bankruptcy law. We have the most robust legal system in the world to support the complex market mechanisms of an innovative society. There are obviously areas for improvement, especially in regard to large awards for people who have fell victim to some product or service, so-called tort reform. There are some effective legal procedures in other countries of the world that we should incorporate with our own. The fact is that once you're here legally, you have rights, basic rights that are like those in no other place in the world!

Language

English is the de facto national language, but it's not official. There are U.S. naturalization requirements to standardize English, but this is

largely up to state jurisdictions. Spanish was spoken by twelve percent of the population at home and is the most common second language. New Mexico has laws providing for the use of both English and
Spanish, and Louisiana has laws for both English and French. California
has mandated the publication of Spanish versions of government
documents. Chinese is the third most widely spoken language, with
2.3 million people speaking it, and French the fourth largest, including
Creole from Louisiana, with 1.9 million speakers.[190]

Americans speak the language of the world. The English language
was obviously developed in England during the Anglo-Saxon era
but actually traces its roots back to Germany, the Netherlands and
Denmark in the fifth century (400AD). One of the German tribes
was the "Angles". [191] Americans may not know this if they have never
traveled outside the country, but English is the "international language". It is the official language in over 50 countries including Britain,
Australia, Canada and many countries in the Caribbean and Africa.
Due to the extent of the vast British Empire, this language circled
the globe and is the common first or second language among many
countries. It is probably the most dominant of the United Nations
six official languages, (the others are Arabic, Chinese, French, Russian
and Spanish) A basic knowledge of English is required for advanced
studies in science, engineering, technology and medicine. It is also the
language of the seas and of the internet.

Americans enjoy a language that most people of the world recognize as universal. This may have tremendous implications for our
country as the innovation wave accelerates and many new discoveries are made public. The common language explaining these advances will be English and many discoveries will be disclosed first to

the world in our language. "The importance of the Internet grows rapidly in all fields of human life, including not only research and education but also marketing and trade as well as entertainment and hobbies. This implies that it becomes more and more important to know how to use Internet services and, as a part of this, to read and write English." [192]

Logistics

The United States is the world leader in getting something from one place to another. From Federal Express to UPS or the Department of Defense, from roads to airlines to mass transit, the United States dominates this physical but also informational business. Wal-Mart has built an empire as the largest retailer in the world based on a worldwide information network and logistical system. Of the world's thirty busiest airports, sixteen are in the United States. [193]

"The concept is interesting and well formed, but in order to earn better than a C, the idea must be feasible"; so said a Yale professor in response to Fred Smith's paper proposing reliable overnight delivery service. He went on to start Federal Express in Memphis, Tennessee, in 1971. In its annual report, it boasts that it connects more than ninety percent of the world's economic activity door to door within two to three days. [194] Fred Smith not only created a company, he created an industry with global competitors like UPS and DHL. These companies don't just deliver; they help plan, implement, and control the movement and storage of materials and products. At times they assist their partner companies in finishing goods, repairing devices, and serving as an outsource for specific needed services along the transportation link. The worldwide logistics business in revenue is in the hundreds of billions of dollars.

Logistics began as part of the military, as officers managed resources to the places where they were needed. Maintaining one's supply lines was crucial to winning a war. With Henry Ford's invention of the assembly line for automobiles, businesses came to need to coordinate resources in a sequence to carry out production. Just-in-time production techniques were developed to exactly coordinate when components were needed. Today, logistics management is crucial to succeeding in a globalized world. It is an informational business. More and more technology is being applied in the form of bar codes and radio coded boxes to determine exact whereabouts along the line of delivery. Many companies have built up their own logistical networks to support their own business, such as Amazon. com. America should continue to lead the globalized world in logistical management.

Melting Pot

America is known as a "melting pot," a term that has its roots in the 1700s. America is a salad bowl of different cultures, nationalities, ideas, and religions. We are a multicultural nation. In much of the rest of the world, different languages and customs keep people apart. Not here! Current trends in America have seen increasing intermarriage among all the various groups. But the United States' culture is Western, largely derived from the traditions of European immigrants with influences from many other areas, such as the traditions brought by slaves from Africa. More recently, immigration from Asia and Latin America has been added to the mix. It is a heterogeneous "melding pot" in which immigrants and their descendents retained distinctive cultural characteristics.

Although the acceptance of certain races and religions has not always been smooth, generally, over time, the cultures have mostly become assimilated. Americans don't view their nationality as separate from their ancestral identity. America means a combination of many different races and cultures. Immigrants need not completely abandon their culture and traditions in order to meet the goal of the melting pot; in fact, the varied influences around our country are many. Go to any major city and you will witness sections of concentration of certain races or countries. They are culturally unique in their own small area, but connected to the whol.

Economics also has a lot to do with immigration into the United States. There are many reasons immigrants come to the United States, but mostly it is due to the condition of their homeland. At $7.50 an hour, the U.S. minimum wage is approximately six times the prevailing one in Mexico, which is in turn higher than most in Central America. People who emigrate here basically want to live a better life and provide for their children, so that they can do the same. For others, it is a simple choice of basic survival.

The illegal immigrant population is estimated to be about 10 to 20 million people, representing about two to four percent of the country's population. Most of the illegals are from Mexico, and twenty-four percent are from other Latin American countries. The problem with illegal aliens is that it stresses the existing social systems. Families are emphasized in the policies toward immigrants, since those with families in the U.S. are given preferred treatment. We should recognize that immigration is one of the keys to our growth in the future and create policies and incentives to encourage the educated and talented people of the world to come here and live. America's melting pot is the world's largest today.

Nano-Technology

Nano-tech is the study of manipulating atoms at the molecular level. There is an enormous revolution happening in this industry that will probably affect every product in the world. The United States stands as the leader in nano-tech research and applications, and because of its strong technological base, will probably remain the leader for decades to come. It is certainly one of those industries of the future that can employ a lot of people. If you've not heard of nano-tech before, you will, because it is probably going to be just as influential and life-changing as electricity, automobiles, or computer chips.[195] These inventions created waves of innovation and development not only particular to their specific industry, but across the economy as a whole. Nanotechnology is a promising candidate for initiating a new decade-long wave of advance.

Nanotechnology can be everywhere, in car tires, toothpaste, tennis rackets, clothing, and sunscreen. The word "nano" comes from the scientific notation of ten to the minus-ninth power, or one-billionth. To put the scale in context, it is the difference in size between a marble within your hand and the earth. Nanotechnology is not easily defined or listed as a product ingredient; instead, it provides the toolset, a way of engineering the world, much like an architect does in building a house. As computers allow us to compute faster and faster, nano-tech will allow us to make things smaller and smaller. There are challenges with any new technology and the potential has yet to be fully realized by the general public. It would be prudent to say that we are at the leaping off point between lab room experimentation and product development. Processes, materials, and applications are being scaled down into the micro-atomic realm to fully exploit properties of materials. It has the potential to create many new materials and devices, and wide-ranging applications in medicine, electronics, energy production, health, consumer products, and foods. Have we left anything out?

The great physicist Richard Feynman described a process to manipulate individual atoms and molecules. In his talk entitled "There Is Plenty of Room at the Bottom," which he gave to the American Physical Society meeting at Caltech in 1959, he described a process that wouldn't be physically possible until the early 1980s. In 2000, the United States National Nanotechnology Initiative was founded to coordinate federal research and development dollars with private enterprise. The United States dominates the field, with more dedicated nanotechnology centers than the next three nations combined (Germany, UK, and China).[196] Government nano-tech funding in the United States is almost double that of its closest competitor, Japan. United States has issued more patents than the rest of the world combined, "highlighting America's unusual strength of turning abstract theory into practical products." Many countries spend a lot on research but can't turn that science into a profitable business. These "ivory tower" nations have impressive research facilities but can't translate this into commercial ideas. This is exactly what America is good at doing.

To get a little bit more detailed than what nano means and how it can influence materials, look no farther than DNA. This type of nanotechnology uses molecular biology to automatically arrange particles into some useful combination that can change the existing structure of something. The process is in mechanically manipulating individual molecules into well-defined structures out of DNA and other basic building blocks. Nano- can also be used as a self-assembly mechanism, as materials can be automatically arranged into some useful construction.

The United States is far and away the leading country of nanotechnology companies throughout the world and is quite balanced among its nano-tech initiatives. Half of all funding for nano-tech research and development comes from private sources, venture capital, and private capital. A third comes from the federal government, and the remainder comes from state government initiatives, sometimes through university settings. This is quite unique when compared to Europe, with a much smaller percentage coming from private sources and most funds originating from government initiatives. When it comes to the creation of new jobs, the NSF estimates that about 2 million workers worldwide will be needed by the year 2015, with half of them needed right here in the U.S.

Yes, there may be some unintended consequences for nanotechnology creations. There are serious concerns about the effects of these innovations and what action is appropriate to mitigate these risks. There needs to be a forum of open public debate about these implications and the possible health consequences of exposure to manipulated materials. But the issue is clear; the United States must maintain its lead in nanotechnology development, especially in the commercial application of scientific innovation. It is prudent to be precautionary, but such a course could cost us the opportunity to define an industry. As a nation, we should "continue to develop commercial applications for nanotechnology while simultaneously pursuing efforts to standardize risk assessment protocols."[197]

Optimism

We are members of a society that could very well be called the "United States of Optimism," so says Richard Reeves in *Business Week*.[198] We have been through periods of time even more tragic than today and it was "optimism and hope—often irrational, always American—it got us going again." There is something to be said for a people that rarely look backwards and see change as the norm. That sounds like an economy that will adjust and continue to adapt and excel in the future. It was Winston Churchill who said, "A pessimist sees difficulty in every opportunity; and an optimist sees the opportunity in every difficulty." Optimism is the inclination to anticipate good outcomes. It can be seen as constructing beneficial scenarios upon actions and events instead of anticipating adverse events. It is also part of America. "American optimism" is found in the dictionary. And it is derived from our nation's beginnings. It is also integral to the psychological well-being of its people. Combined with optimism in America is an open-mindedness to be ready and willing to receive new ideas favorably, an ingredient that is essential to our success as a leader of the world. Especially a world that is changing so fast!

As most of our citizens have immigrated to this country mainly from Europe, this country has offered a clean slate. The forefathers of America seemed to grow during tests and challenges. It is the true mettle of a man that is tested in periods of stress and strain. Positive thinking may be the only hope of salvation from an impossible situation. In the midst of hard times, we are able to sustain the belief that things will be better again one day. This "positivity of life" is an example to the rest of the world.[199]

America may be onto something here that has yet to be extensively verified by the medical community. Personal optimism correlates strongly with self-esteem, with psychological well-being, and with physical and mental health.[200] Optimism has been shown to be correlated with better immune systems in healthy people who have been subjected to stress. There is a lot about the human brain that we don't know, but a positive attitude can have a huge and material difference on someone's life and health.

At the beginning of his presidency, Barack Obama was urged to take a more upbeat tone by many political advisers. Although he had to set expectations low, there was much talk of "green shoots" that were developing in the economy that could result in more predictable growth. These obviously have a domino effect on confidence. Expectations have a lot to do with how people act and optimism is an important component of confidence in the future. Of course, consumer sentiment surveys aren't an exact science, and often what people say they feel and actually what they feel in reality do not match. But there is something to be said about self-fulfilling prophecies. If one projects a scenario of events taking place and is optimistic, that person has visualized and pre-experienced a scenario that is now more likely because of the emphasis on it. Olympic athletes do this repeatedly before an event. Imagine the most positive outcome. This is similar to preparing for a presentation, when professionals visualize the action beforehand and, in so doing, make the subconscious more able to transact and transform this thought into action. It is important to be optimistic because you could be creating your own destiny.

Americans are also considerably more optimistic than people in other countries. In the December 2008 Harris Interactive Financial Times survey, majorities in France, Italy, Spain, Great Britain, and Germany were more **pessimistic** about their economic situations, with percentages ranging from 52% to 63%. By contrast, a majority of Americans, 54% were **optimistic** about their future. In a separate question of the poll, 83% of French said they were pessimistic about their country's economic status. In America, the proportion was 52%. This is at a time that most experts would proclaim to be the largest economic challenge since the Great Depression. The Harris polls regularly ask Americans about their overall life satisfaction. A few years ago, a Harris poll said 58 % of Americans reported being very satisfied with the life they led, compared with an average of 31% in 15 different European countries.[201] American optimism is also a detriment, however, as sustainable positive beliefs can ignore the suffering of people and the negative implications of our actions. For our country, irrepressible optimism won't be enough for the long term; performance will matter.

Imagine a society that would take no risks, fund no startups, create no new products, or update no regulations. An optimistic society is better able to allocate capital into an idea that might be innovative and technologically superior to established products. "A society in which no one is overly optimistic and no one takes too much risk wouldn't advance much."[202]

Philanthropy

It may not surprise you that the United States is the world leader in philanthropy. What might surprise you is the degree of that leadership that comes from private and individual sources. Donations by American individuals touched $300 billion in 2007, 2008 and 2009 according to *Giving USA 2009*, and were extremely diverse and widespread. Total aid, transfers and investment in developing nations was over $200 billion by the most recent estimates. That totals a half a trillion dollars in transfers. Not only is that the largest in the world, it is larger than the GDP in all but twenty of the countries in the world.

The United States' official assistance with developing countries in 2009 was $29 billion which is an increase over the prior years despite the world financial crisis.[203] That is not the whole story; in fact it is just a fraction of what we give to the world. "To judge the United States by its official development assistance would vastly misstate generosity of the American people," says the Report on Global Philanthropy and Remittances from the Hudson Institute.[204] Total U.S. engagement with developing countries was over $200 billion in 2007 and despite the financial crisis, probably remained at high levels in the past two years. (There is a lag in reporting these figures as so many different sources of information must be counted.) Private capital flows totaled half of the amount, the largest among donor countries and accounting for thirty percent of all international private capital flows to developing countries.

Work in the United States also provides an economic base for millions of separated families across the globe, as workers send portions of their paychecks back to their home country. From America, these are monies that have been earned in the United States from our open economy. According to the World Bank, total worldwide remittances in 2009 were over $300 billion with about a quarter of these originating from the U.S. The financial crisis has disrupted currency exchange rates and employment trends having a large effect on these payments. When measuring the total assistance to developing countries, combining the official aid, private philanthropy, and remittances, the United States provided almost half of total world assistance by donors. The amount of our country's leadership in giving and providing is unprecedented in the world.

Although Bill Gates and Warren Buffett get a lot of press for their combined philanthropic pledge of billions and billions of dollars, there are many other Americans who need to be noted. Gordon Moore, the Intel cofounder who predicted two decades ago that computers would double in speed every 18 months, has donated half of his Intel stock to environmental and scientific causes. George Soros has pledged billions to the building of open and democratic societies. Eli Broad, the KB home founder, has given billions to public education, arts, and science. James Stowers, the founder of American Sentry, has given a billion dollars toward biomedical research. Sam Walton and his heirs have given $1 billion to educational causes. And it doesn't stop there; from Michael Dell, Paul Allen, and Larry Ellison to Oprah

Winfrey, Kirk Kerkorian, and, yes, Michael Bloomberg, these most generous philanthropists recognize that the gift that they've been given
needs to be given back. Although Ted Turner is more known for his
$1 billion gift to the United Nations, he is the largest landowner in
America, owning approximately 2 million acres, the size of the states
of Delaware and Rhode Island combined.[205]

The Internet is transforming the way we think about charity. Since
the popularization of the Internet and the ease with which to transfer
money, the total official flows of philanthropy, remittances, and investment have exploded. Social networking sites such as Facebook and
Twitter are changing the face of philanthropy, as people get connected and hands-on with their interests. Small-scale social networking
philanthropy is connecting with the younger donors and encourages
many first-time donors. Social investing is also popular and a beginning for future philanthropists.

Giving is just the beginning; being able to make a difference in
how the money is spent is much more time consuming. At the
most recent World Economic Forum in Davos, Switzerland, Bill
Gates said we must not lose sight of our long-term commitment
to expand opportunity for the world's poor and we must address
the current disparities in health and education around the world.[206]
As commodity price escalation and currency exchange rate volatility in 2008 cause shortages of basic food, modern structures cause
great pain to the poorest in the world. Despite the volatility in the
economy, philanthropy represents an amazingly stable portion of
America's wealth with the aging and passing of the baby boomer
generation.

A billion people on our planet don't have access to a clean drink of water or go hungry. Now is the time to change the world.

Research and Development

Research and development is the creative work undertaken on a systematic basis in order to increase the body of knowledge of a product or service. From that knowledge base, new applications and new products can be created. The United States is by far the leader in research and development and has been for many decades, accounting for 35% of total world expenditures in the past three years. In 2009, we spent upwards of $398 billion in research and development with over $400 billion expected in 2010.[207] The next largest country was Japan, with $148 billion, and after that China, with $102 billion.

With R&D making up approximately 2.5 percent of our GDP, we are second to Japan as a percent of our economy, who spends close to 3.5 percent. However, the R&D expenditures of our country have been strong for many years, creating an innovative culture that thrives in creating and adapting to change. Where China has recently greatly increased research and development expenditures, the total spending still remains under 1.5 percent of their GDP and had been under one percent until as recently as 2002. Europe as a total spent $278 billion in 2008, but that is spread among Germany, France, and the United Kingdom almost equally. India and Brazil, part of the BRIC emerging market nations, have substantially smaller R&D budgets. Russia is difficult to measure but ranks along with its smaller BRIC counterparts.

Generally, research and development investment reflects that organization's willingness to forgo profit because, in the United States, these are taxed as expenses in the year in which they are incurred. However, the benefits and research development will extend for many years. Expenses for research and development should be rewarded. It is a long-term investment. The U.S. is slowly moving toward the international standards which capitalize these expenses over many years; however, some additional incentives may be needed. Every aspect of our economy is involved.

What is different about the United States is that most of the increase in spending since 1985 has been from the private sector, as federal support has been relatively constant for the last twenty years.[208] Total research and development spending remains strong. There are only a few areas in which the United States may lose its leadership position, but there are many other advanced technologies where ongoing U.S. leadership is almost assured, especially in areas related to medical advances and defense applications. However, in key areas such as renewable energy and advanced electronics, the competition has become strong.

Despite the advantages of a market-based system, research and development expenditures affect the short-term profitability of enterprises, which could lead to short-term decision-making for the benefit of quarterly profits. Conversely, more socialist systems can direct funds over many years without the need to disclose results to the general public. There are advantages and disadvantages to both economic systems, but to date, the profitability-and-incentives-based market systems have proven to be superior. State-run and -funded enterprises can help focus the country into narrow areas of expertise. Collectively, the world's faster-growing economies are on track to catch up to U.S. investment, so in years to come, the playing field may be more level. R&D spending by companies in 2009 was led by Microsoft, with IBM, Johnson & Johnson, Pfizer, Merck, Intel and Cisco rounding out the top U.S. companies.[209] The recession will show little effect on R&D spending in 2010 as it is expected to increase in the United States, with about $100 billion funded by the federal government. Initiatives with the most interest are in the energy field with renewables, such as solar and wind, taking top interest. Oil exploration technologies and nuclear generation are also high-focus areas.

Our research and development focus seems to be part of our economy's fabric. A market-based system requires an obsession with what is sold. Profitability drives what is made. In a socialistic-based system, it's all about market share, and profitability as a goal usually comes second, or not at all. Therefore, it is not a system that has a pricing mechanism to allocate capital to the best allocation of resources. "Not only do our economy and quality of life depend critically on a vibrant R&D enterprise, but so does our national and homeland security." [210]

Small Business

Did you ever have a lemonade stand? We live in a suburb of Philadelphia in a housing development of about 100 homes, and it was good fortune that we bought the model house, which is strategically located at the front of the subdivision. Maybe a hundred cards will pass by our house in the span of a weekend afternoon: a perfect place to make some money on a hot summer day by selling lemonade, cookies, or anything else that's in the pantry. It's part of our American culture of entrepreneurship. But that's where the casual analogies end.

Small business, those firms with less than a hundred employees, represents upward of ninety-nine percent of all employers in this country; they also employ half of all private-sector workers and provide 60 to 80% of the net new jobs annually (64% of net new jobs over the past fifteen years).[211] Small businesses pay 44% of total U.S. private payroll, and produce more than 50% of non-farm GDP, roughly $6 trillion in 2008. Small business accounts for over 90% of the U.S. exporters of goods, and produced about 30% of our export value. It's interesting also that small business produces over ten times more patents per employee than large firms.[212] Small businesses are the strength of America.

Conventional wisdom would suggest that many people who can't find a job in large companies become entrepreneurs. However, self-employment does not seem to be swayed much by the economic cycle. The largest industries of the self-employed involve housing, especially construction. Studies have observed that self-employment grew steadily in the two decades after 1979, remaining relatively constant over the twenty years. More than 86% of firms in the construction sector are considered small. For their part, though, small business owners have struggled during this recession, especially with regard to credit and access to capital. Some surveys have shown that owners are less willing to expand their small businesses due to the economic shocks that we've taken in the past decade. From the tech boom, to 9/11, to the housing bubble and commodity prices increases, they have all contributed to a more volatile business environment, which makes it difficult to plan confidently for the future. A top concern has been the high cost of health care insurance in conjunction with lower levels of final sales.

America must recognize that small business is critical and vital to our economic recovery and our ability to compete in today's global marketplace. The Small Business Administration was created in 1953 as an independent agency to assist the interests of small business concerns. It does have an extensive network of offices and partnerships, both public and private, to help small businesses flourish. The website at www.sba.gov has many electronic links to sources of information and can be an example of a government agency connected to robust and diverse information sources. Federal agencies today target almost 25% of the purchases of goods and services to small businesses.

Small business will be a large part of moving the economy ahead as entrepreneurs continue to spur new innovation and create employment. "Innovation is an essential ingredient for creating jobs, controlling inflation, and for economic and social growth. Small businesses make a disproportionately large contribution to innovation. There is something fundamental about this unusual ability of small firms to innovate that must be preserved."[213] The Kauffman Foundation, a nonprofit research group that promotes entrepreneurship, said more Americans started businesses in 2008 than in 2007. Small companies have historically begun hiring first in a recovery, but this time analysts expect the pickup to be weaker. For such a vital part of our economy, we must direct stimulus and incentives toward small business.

Space and Aerospace

If there's one industry where our leadership is dominant, it is in space, aerospace, and communication satellites. From the building of passenger jets, stealth bombers, and the space station, to the Mars mission, satellites, and NASA research and development, the United States is the leader of things in the air. We spend more on space than all the other nations in the world combined. A $17-billion budget for governmental initiatives alone dwarfs Europe's $4.5 billion, China's $2 billion, Russia's $1 billion, and India's $.5 billion.[214] It is not just about money and how it's spent; it's about results and practical innovations. In the book *Inventions from Outer Space*, author David Baker has documented the many new products to bubble out of space research and become exercise machines, infrared satellite imagery, tap water purifiers, exercise sneakers, robot hands, and, of course, clothes that offer protection from temperatures reaching nearly 3,000 degrees Fahrenheit.[215]

As of September 2009, over 500 humans from thirty-eight countries have reached an altitude of 100 kilometers or more, an altitude of about sixty miles from the surface of the earth. Of these people, over 330 were Americans.[216] Only twenty-four people have traveled beyond earth's orbit, and three of them have gone up twice.[217] Twelve people have walked on the moon. They are all from the U.S.

NASA was established in 1958 and has led U.S. efforts in missions to the moon, the Skylab space station, the space shuttle, and exploring the solar system with robotic missions. It was John F. Kennedy, in his inauguration speech in 1960, launched the goal to set a man on the moon by the end of the decade. We made it by a few months; on

July 20, 1969, Apollo 11 landed the first man on the moon. From that point on, NASA has been the dominant space program in the world. More recently, the direction of NASA is to land on Mars, creating a moon base and continuing robotic missions, as well as maintaining the International Space Station. The highly successful but expensive space shuttle missions have contributed to the general body of knowledge that an aircraft can land from outer space on a runway, opening the opportunities for commercial aircraft to do the same for outer space adventurers.

In the annual Space Competitiveness Index, it is not surprising that the United States has maintained its leadership in all categories of competitiveness, although other countries have risen.[218] European space progress continues as countries of Europe deepen and broaden their institutions. As a space pioneer, Russia needs to move quickly to develop commercial applications for its space program, but is also a leading partner in the International Space Station. Japan and China both have strong programs, with the Japanese more market-based, and the Chinese more governmental. Canada and India are the only other countries noteworthy for space programs.

The aerospace industry, which produces aircraft, employs over half a million people, mostly in highly technical engineering jobs. The United States is a large exporter of aerospace goods throughout the world, as the technology and quality of our products are unsurpassed. It is a high value-added industry that includes airplanes, as well as guided missiles, space vehicles, aircraft engines, and related parts. Most of the government funds are geared toward defense work. The development of new metals and special alloys caused some fighter jets to take unusual shapes to elude radar and penetrate heavily defended

air space. There are many more innovations in defense aerospace that
I could discuss, but they're classified, and if I told you, I'd have to kill
you.

The world's largest and most innovative private airplane maker is
Boeing. Its 787 "Dreamliner" will be the first plane made primarily
of composites, engineered materials, making it lighter yet stronger
and more fuel-efficient. It is truly the world's first "global" airplane
since most of the parts and components are made outside of the
United States. Over forty of the world's most capable top-tier sup-
plier partners at 135 sites around the world have served to bring
this airplane to market.[219] It is an engineering feat in itself to imagine
the complexity of coordinating suppliers and products in order to be
successfully fitted together and launched. The jet may incorporate
health-monitoring systems for the pilots to ground-based computer
systems. Maybe they can also nudge the pilot if he falls asleep.

The satellite industry is big business for communications, weather,
navigation, and military uses. More than forty countries own satellites and nearly 3,000 of them are operating today in orbit. The
United States is the leader in GPS, which provides the military with
significant control advantages in a conflict. Not only having the most
sophisticated systems available militarily, the United States also leads
in the ability of the average consumer to purchase systems with accurate and customizable service. Virtual reference stations (VRS)
networks, mostly at the initiative of local governments, universities,
and the private sector, provide positioning available at the centime-
ter level. The GPS industry is estimated to have reached $10 billion
in global annual revenue and market values of companies surpassing
$30 billion.

Sports and Fitness

America is a leader in the study, practice, and appreciation of the science of human movement. It sounds ironic when so many studies have stated the high number of Americans that are overweight, but it's true. America is the leader in physical fitness outlets, sports teams, Olympic training, and sports businesses. Although many major U.S. sports have evolved out of European practices, there are many that we call our own. Some of these are big businesses onto themselves, such as American football, baseball, basketball, tennis, and golf. American sport inventions include snowboarding, cheerleading, skateboarding, volleyball, and lacrosse (from the Native Americans). The two most popular sports in the world, soccer and cricket, do have a following, but they are second-tier in this country.

As far as professional sports go, it may surprise you that golf, although not invented here, is big business in the U.S. A comprehensive study, commissioned by the World Golf Foundation's GOLF 20/20 initiative, has determined that golf in the United States generated $76 billion in direct economic impact in 2005, up significantly from $62 billion five years prior. That would make the golf business larger than the motion picture and video industries.[220] In addition to golf's direct revenues, the direct, indirect, induced, and total economic impact of golf on the U.S. economy was $195 billion in 2005, creating approximately 2 million jobs with a wage income of $61 billion. That is larger than the economy of some developing nations!

NFL football revenues were over $7 billion in 2007, not including the estimate of many of the offshoot industries that it supports in measuring its total impact. That doesn't include the billions of dollars in college football, which if you have ever been to one, is big business! Major League Baseball sales were $6 billion in 2007. Not including all the college, high school and little league revenues from "America's game". Sports are big business!

The American fitness center industry is generally regarded as being a decade or more ahead of its international counterparts. Health clubs are popular in the United States—Bally's being number one, with $1 billion in annual revenues. There are over 30 million members of health clubs, representing ten percent of the U.S. population. During the 1950s and 1960s, physical education experienced tremendous growth. By the 1980s, almost half of Americans said that they did something regularly to promote their physical well-being. Today, many programs emphasize overall total fitness and wellness. Baby boomers are enjoying renewed interest in old techniques, such as yoga and cardiovascular, as well as Pilates, massage therapy, and spinning classes. In addition to the health benefits, cognitive performance can also be enhanced by physical education. There's a growing body of research that supports a relationship between physical activity and brain development, and also cognitive performance.

If sports and fitness were solely about the Olympic Games, we've dominated! Since the beginning of the summer games in 1896 (which doesn't include the ancient games), the United States has won almost 2,300 Olympic medals, over 900 of which were gold. The next country is the combination of the USSR and Russia, with just over 1,300 total medals (504 gold). As for the winter games, the reunified Germany is tops with 358 total medals. Second is Norway, with 303 total medals and the United States is third with 253 medals, 87 of them gold.[221] The Olympic development team in any sport in the United States is highly regarded as a representation of the best athletes in the land.

States

We are the United *States* of America, and there are a lot of advantages to being a collection of smaller units within this day and age of empowering people. Citizens here feel connected to their neighborhood, town, and county before their state, but states can have a tremendous influence over their livelihood and economic well-being. States are competitive with one another, attempting to attract new businesses, immigrants, and other citizens to their tax base. In industry, states must seek to find those things they could and can do well and then excel at doing them.

States compete to be the most free and desirable places to live. A good environment would attract more people to come and live there, which would create more money for the state, and would also attract more business. It is really pretty easy in America to pick up from one state, buy a house, and transplant your family to another within the span of thirty days, maybe less. The attractiveness of taxes, schools, infrastructure, and proximity to occupations are usually top on the list. States or towns can and should compete to have the highest quality of life and lowest cost of living, which would benefit everybody. States do compete against one another for certain prized economic projects, providing incentives like tax rebate, prized location news or enterprise zones within a city, accessibility to labor force, and expense subsidies.

Today, almost all of the fifty states have balanced budget requirements, most of which are written into their constitutions. While
legislators can find "creative" ways around such limits, they are
standard operating procedures for state governments. That being
said, state governments are very pro-cyclical; as revenues from taxes increase, so do expenditures in boom times, and, in recessions,
both contract. There is not an automatic stabilizer to counter the
economic cycle in state budgets. All fifty states use taxes to fund
their budgets. These are primarily taxes on income, but each state
does so with its own formula. On average, state and local governments combine to tax nearly ten percent of your income. The differences can be extreme.

In New Jersey, the top-rated state, the tax rate is twelve percent,
whereas, in Wyoming, it's only seven percent. Taxes differ substantially
for corporations among the states, with Iowa having the top corporate tax rate at twelve percent, all the way down to zero in states like
South Dakota, Wyoming, and Nevada. California's GDP is larger than
all but eight countries in the world. The current tax system is indeed
taxing, with the top one percent of California taxpayers depended
upon for fifty percent of the state's income tax money. The highest
personal income tax rate is 10.5 percent, a high price for small business, which pays the personal income tax rate.

States also compete against one another for business. Most states
would do better in assessing their own internal competitive strengths
and trying to attract industries that are similar. Some states with
high unemployment rates, like Michigan, would do well to encourage
research and development in similar industries to automobiles, such
as the manufacturing of solar and wind energy units, assembly of large

electronic goods, or other machinery applications. States would do well to encourage immigrants to locate there as small communities can offer comfort to those entering a new world.

In a sense, the United States is a microcosm of how the rest of the world works: many countries competing against each other for business. Most countries do not have the benefit of fifty competing states or counties within it, each with the ability to create laws and regulations particular to its own competitive advantages. Within each state is the ability to create and innovate. It's almost as if we have fifty different research units, all collaborating and moving toward the same goal. The competition among them creates innovative solutions to problems instead of maintaining the status quo.

Technology

In the 1960s, if you wanted to deliver some information to a partner across town, you had to hire a physical courier to hand-deliver a package. In the 1970s, overnight delivery was established that could get your message there by the next business day. In the 1980s, the fax machine was the modem of choice for delivering messages not physically but over a telephone wire. In the 1990s, telephone rates dropped so considerably and plain paper faxes made for cheap, almost instantaneous communication. Today, a financial analyst compiles information on complex spreadsheets and word processing documents, clicks a button, and a thousand people get the information around the world instantaneously over the Internet. From a $2,000-courier to $200 for priority next day, to twenty dollars for FedEx, to a two-dollar phone call, to twenty cents in the Internet era, and dropping eventually to two cents, the costs of communication are nearing zero.

Technology is the enabler of the communication revolution. At a zero cost, communication volume will explode!

In August of 2000, the market value of technology companies represented 33% of the S&P 500's total market capitalization. That represented a fivefold increase from a 5% weight in 1992. At the end of 2009, the weight was around 18% and was the second largest component in the index behind finance. Information and technology is our country's strength. From Google to Apple, Microsoft, IBM, Oracle, Dell, Hewlett-Packard, and others, the United States is the leader in innovation within technology.

How long will it be before everyone in the world owns a phone? Some areas of the world are surpassing 100 percent density. Granted, 100 percent does not mean all people own phones since some own multiple phones, but some areas of the world are approaching this magic number. From that point we ask: How many will be connected to the Internet? As most phones today are smart phones with the capability of connecting to networks with broadband speeds, most of the 6 billion people in the world will soon all be connected. Mobile broadband subscribers will soon pass those that sit in front of a computer screen.[222] Already net books can cost as little as $200, giving the user access to mobile broadband just about anywhere.

Your TV today is smart. It knows the programs you want to watch and records them. The information that's available on the screen during an average sporting event is more than a baseball team manager had a decade ago sitting in the dugout of the World Series. The ability to sift through information on Yahoo finance today is more than a CFO had a decade ago about his own company.

Tomorrow, what will be next? Which television-viewing angle would you like to see? Will you be able to visualize what Derek Jeter sees when he stands up to the plate in game five of the World Series and looks at the pitch coming at him at 100 miles an hour? What about the blood pressure of the batter? What is the percentage chance of him hitting the ball to left field in a 3-2 pitch count during a night game? What is the most likely pitch that he will get in these circumstances? These are all informational pieces that can easily be obtained and displayed at your wish. Televisions will become personalized and three-dimensional.

Another extension will be holographic videoconferencing. For example, in the future, I may want to attend a conference in New York City but can't make it there physically. I call up a computer company that rents robots and from a few keystrokes on my PDA, I've input a holographic image of myself so when people see this clone at the conference, they see me, and I see them through my visual 3-D glasses. As someone stops the clone for conversation, I know who it is, slap him on the back, and say, "Great to see you." In fact, technology could get so good that you will not know if you're talking to a person or clone. That's a few more decades out. And if you want to know which country is poised to develop and utilize this fantasy, look no further than the United States.

There are several technological revolutions that are happening concurrently; examples are in cloud-computing and virtualization. Virtualization allows computers to multitask. Cloud computing brings access to unlimited amounts of storage and capacity. No longer is your computer's hard drive where all your information is stored. It's on a shared drive where you can view the inputs of others.

Documents, e mails, and other data will be stored "in the cloud," making them accessible to anyone you allow and anywhere you happen to be. The network effect will geometrically expand communication. Not all of the information will be factual or true and sources will be important to reference. Technology has lowered the cost of information, but it has multiplied the value of wisdom.[223]

Eventually computers will complement human brains and it wouldn't surprise me to find computer-like implants in humans to greatly expand our computational and memory abilities when needed. You won't need to be born a genius! One of the enablers of the information revolution is Jeff Hawkins, best known as the creator of the Palm Pilot. In 2002, he founded the Redwood Neuroscience Institute, where he leads a small group of researchers working at the intersection of neuroscience and computers. The brain is a computer, but right now it is difficult to actually know how it processes information. He recognizes the importance of learning through trial and error, which is slow and tedious but has repeatedly pioneered new ideas and products, opening up new markets. With a market to sell into, other contributors have brought their ideas to modify or change the product for more sustainable commercial success.[224] It will be difficult to program a computer to do these things but not impossible.

As the headlines pass that Acer may overtake Hewlett-Packard as the world's largest seller of personal computers, most observers would say that America is losing its technology leadership. Granted, the United States used to account for 31% of high-tech industry exports worldwide in 1980. Today, that number is below 20%.[225] At the same time, the applied technology industry has grown bigger. The United States is spending more as a percent of U.S. GDP toward technology than ever before, more than any other country. While we are being challenged from the rest of the world, specifically China, in technological innovation, there are also ingredients for success here that don't exist there. Our immigration policies, ease of business creation, access to funding at multiple stages of company creation, labor availability, exposure to entrepreneurial experience, fully transparent financial markets, and good old Yankee ingenuity will continue to provide a strong structure for technology companies.

Trade

The United States leads the world in trade and has led in the creation of the world's trading systems. Market systems rely on information to determine prices, regardless of the distance between buyers and sellers, borders or nationality. World trade is world growth! From many separate countries, we have become an interlocking, interdependent, and interracial global economy. The Internet has further connected the globe with the ability to sell or source, regardless of time and place. In this interconnected world, there are unprecedented opportunities for companies, but they come with new challenges. Most of the problems in world trade have informational solutions. From instantaneously informing supply chains to shifting work loads across different work forces in separate time zones and responding to currency fluctuations, the more information the company has, the more flexibility it will have. To IBM, who helps build information into 17 of the world's top 25 supply chains, a smarter business needs smarter thinking.[226]

The United States is the largest importer of goods and third-largest exporter in the world. A quarter of U.S. GDP is tied to international trade, up from only 10% in 1970. Our largest trading partners are Canada, China, Mexico, Japan, and Germany. Our largest export commodity is electrical machinery, while vehicles constitute the leading import. Our nation's GDP is composed primarily of services, which are rapidly growing as countries around the world develop. Never before has world trade been so important to our country.

The U.S., as the leader in free trade, has also become more reliant on the rules of the system, primarily from the World Trade Organization. The WTO is an international body that establishes standards and rules and where complaints can be heard and ruled upon. The WTO now has 146 members; this is up from just twenty-three in 1947, and could easily rise to 170 or more within a decade.[227] The creation of the multinational trading system after 1945, with America's leadership, was the result of avoiding the trading blocs that had been closed and hostile to other parts of the world. America's vision was that the welfare of nations was connected with the "friendliness, fairness and freedom of world trade."[228] The network of multinational initiatives like the Marshall Plan, the International Monetary Fund, and the World Bank, with the general acceptance of tariffs and treaties, has provided the framework for international rules. Free trade and free democracies encourage the exchange of ideas, which is essential to peace and prosperity. Trade has expanded twenty-fold, with billions of people being lifted out of poverty from the ability to connect, supply, and take from the world economy.

There's a struggle in world trade against the forces of openness and interconnectedness, which has been brought on by the financial crisis of 2008. More than ever, America's interests lie in opening the world economy more to a strong, rules-based multinational trading system. America's leadership is more important today because of the large role of information flow in the increasingly interconnected planet. Information is our business. The retrieval, analysis, and evaluation of information are how market systems work in America and beyond. Even though some may think the U.S. can achieve prosperity on its own, it is increasingly dependent on international trade and the ability to tap lower costs and better efficiencies throughout the world to allocate resources of labor and capital toward higher value and more profitable lines of industry.

The United States has led the way for decades, promoting free trade and globalization. It is important that we don't take a step back and create barriers to entry and heightened tariffs. There could very well be some political movement to protect an economy within the midst of an ongoing recession, but that needs to be resisted. Not only will the world economy perform better and grow more quickly through globalization, but "relations between countries tend to go a lot better when there is a liberal, open, international economy."[229]

Venture Capital

Our nation can be called the "United States of Entrepreneurs," as we lead the world in venture capital-funded companies. Venture capital is that investment in a company that is extremely risky. These are companies that generally would not obtain bank financing or governmental subsidies. Venture capital-backed companies are those for which traditional sources of funding are just not available. As a result of investing in these companies, investors can profit ten times their investment or more when these companies are eventually brought public, acquired, or receive another level of financing. But there is a high failure rate, with 18% of venture capital-backed companies in the ten years between 1991 and 2000 failing. Another 35% are still private or may have quietly failed also.[230] Venture capital investors are usually pension funds (42%), finance and insurance companies (25%), endowments and foundations (21%), and individuals representing families. But, indeed, some of these people are just like you and me, funding a cousin or daughter or their friends to develop an idea and bring it to market.

To illustrate America's dominance in this area, we can look at a survey of venture capital in the second quarter of 2009 from Dow Jones Venture Source. The $5 billion allocated to United States companies was almost four times that allocated to the rest of the world combined.[231] Some of America's greatest companies have been venture-backed, and these aren't just any companies; these are global leaders. Technology dominates venture capital-funded companies like Intel, Microsoft, eBay, Apple, and Google. However, there are also companies that were backed by venture capitalists early in their development, like Home Depot, Starbucks, Staples, Whole Foods Market, and Pet Smart. These companies together employed almost a million people in 2006.[232] A survey of venture capital-backed companies in 2008 identified more than 12 million people working there, generating nearly $3 trillion in revenue.[233] Looking at the Inc. 500 list of the fastest-growing private companies in the U.S. from 1997 to 2007, the study found that approximately 16% of companies had venture-capital backing.[234] The venture capital industry is dominant in American due to our vast financial structure, but also because of the number of skilled workers, the amount of knowledge and expertise of the business environment, the stable political and economic environment, and the amount of regulatory protection for intellectual capital.

America is a highly adaptable society and small business owners find the transition from corporate worker to entrepreneur
easy. American schoolchildren are raised on stories about Benjamin
Franklin and Thomas Edison. When I was in college, the best thing to
tell your friends was that you were in a band. Today, college kids brag
that they're in a startup.[235] There are three main reasons for America's
dominance in this area, with the first being our mature finance, private capital, and venture-based industry. We simply have been doing
this longer than anybody else. Secondly, we enjoy a close link between universities and entrepreneurial startups, which are sometimes
located on the same campus, allowing the exchange of ideas between
theory and practice to flow back and forth. This may be the key
to keeping this leadership alive. But thirdly, immigration is also an
important ingredient to the venture-capital community. A quarter
of America's science and technology startup, accounting for almost
half a million people employed, have had somebody born abroad as
either their CEO or the chief technology officer. In 2006, foreign
nationals were named as inventors or co-inventors in a quarter of
America's patent applications.[236] In all, between the years of 1970 and
2008, total venture investment totaled $456 billion in 27,000 or more
companies, representing 21% of U.S. GDP as measured by revenue
generated. This is big business!

Venture capital committed in the United States averaged about
$50 million annually from 1990 until 1997. At that point, the innova-
tion of the Internet leapt forward and, in 1998 alone, committed capital almost doubled; then it doubled again in 1999 and *again* in 2000.
Since 2002, an average of $250 million per year in committed capital
has been the norm. As you can imagine, technology has been the largest source by sector of venture investing, taking up over 80% of the

total in 2000. New ideas for investment now involve more energy and environmental technologies, bio-pharmaceuticals, and nanotechnology. Healthcare accounted for almost 30% of venture funding in 2008, and energy startups are now gobbling up increasing amounts of new fund flows, reaching 15% of all deals.[237] New capital funding is providing Coulomb Technologies a way for electric car drivers in San Francisco to plug into their parking meter stations. Venture capital is funding FitBit, who tracks your movements, exercise, and sleeping patterns to organize them on a website where you can track your wellness progress. It is also funding Genocea BioSciences, which uses technology developed at the Harvard Medical School that can rapidly test experimental vaccines in a simulated version of the human immune system. These are just some of the ideas that are on the forefront of discovery.

The United States has a cultural advantage in startups from its ease in taking business risks, to low tax rates, and easier bankruptcy procedures. European entrepreneurs have to grapple with a patchwork of legal codes and an expensive regulation system. In Japan, it is the fear of failure and that society's punishment for bankruptcy. Over the past twenty-five years, the rate at which Japan creates new businesses has been about a third to half of that experienced in the United States. In China, with the lack of reliable regulations and accounting rules, combined with the requirement of partnership with a Chinese company, venture investments are growing rapidly of late, but it still remains quite small in proportion to the developed markets.

Entrepreneurism, private capital, and venture capitalism are all generators of not only new ideas and markets, but employment as well. America is the world's venture capitalist.

Voting

Americans take voting rights for granted, but recent events around the world show how important the freedom to vote is to people. We not only vote in elections, but we vote every day with our dollars. Since the U.S. is a market economy, your dollar votes count! We're an extremely vocal country with multiple outlets to voice your opinion in this information age. Not only is our voting machine efficient and fair, it is also issue-driven, with a robust collection of candidates competing at even the local level. We are a country of free speech, where you can voice what it is on your mind. Many times voters decide elections with one or two issues that separate candidates who eventually win. The average voter has the ability to tip the balance of power. Unlike many European countries, with coalitions and socialistic corporations, the United States is more apt to change and be changed by voter outcry.

One hundred and thirty-three million Americans voted in the 2008 presidential election. That represents over half the voting-age population, which most presidential elections attract. Many other developed countries do have higher turnouts of 70 and 80% percent, but there are great disparities between areas and income levels in the United States. We have a very strong two-party system, which is too well-established to be seriously challenged in federal and state elections. However, the balance of power has been oddly "balanced" since the Civil War. This tug-of-war provides a competitive situation, in which the party in power must please voters or be thrown out. It is also a system that gets things done since, once the party is in power, it is usually absolute!

There are always improvements to make, like term limits, campaign reform, and empowering our populace to make their votes heard. Term limits would eliminate the present seniority system and force Americans to look for able leaders with new ideas, just like what happens in the private sector. Campaign reform would better align interests of politicians with their many constituents, not just a few. We have a great system; now, let's make it better.

Women's Rights

It would be an oversight to ignore the large movement in our country toward the equality of all people. We are not there yet, not by a long shot, but we are moving in the right direction. Far from being "the" leader, we are "a" leader in equal rights. Today, women make up half of the workforce.[238] We have made great strides closing the gap in pay that they experience versus men. According to the Center for American Progress, women still only make about 77 cents to every dollar made by a man. That is just a moderate move from the data thirty years ago for college educated workers but more impressive for those with just a high school education.

In the early 1900s, less than 20% of all college degrees were earned by women, and about 5% of the doctors in the United States were women. By 2006, the figure had risen to about 50% of college graduates and over 38% of all doctors. Women make up almost 50% of the medical student population today. The United States in general offers more opportunities to any person, irrespective of race or sex.

It wasn't until 1920 that the United States formally allowed women to vote with the addition of the Nineteenth Amendment. Voting rights for women were introduced into international law in 1948, when the U.N. adopted the Universal Declaration of Human Rights. In 1966, the National Organization for Women (NOW) was created with the purpose of bringing about equality.

In most countries around the world, women have the right to vote. In some Arab countries like Saudi Arabia, they do not have that right (or even the right to drive a car, for that matter), whereas in Kuwait, Oman, and the UAE, the right to vote has just recently been achieved. The Vatican still does not allow women to vote.

Women's rights can be seen as a parallel to human rights. In that area, the U.S. is an example to the world and is moving in the right direction. The way we try to treat people equally and understand other cultures, races, and ideologies is part of our melting pot. It may be our very best asset in the new order of the world.

So I hope this has surprised you. America does a lot of things well and is the leader in many key industries. We can't be the leader in everything and no longer is our dominance in the world guaranteed. We are the sole superpower but other powers are rising up to challenge us in areas and industries. Americans must realize this and understand how the dynamics have changed. We are entering a world that is led by many nations from Europe to Brazil, China, India, Russia, and Japan. All nations contributing their views together will now chart a path for the world.

∾ ∾ ∾

12. America—What We Don't Do Well

"We can evade reality. But we cannot evade the consequences of evading reality."

—Ayn Rand

Okay, you have gotten this far in the book and you feel inspired that the world isn't falling apart, but also feel we have been too one-sided in our appraisal of America's position in the world. Yes, we do a lot of things well—maybe a lot more than you thought—but we have some work ahead of us to make us better in the things that we don't do well.

We have developed a beautiful country and dynamic system to further human civilization. We have tremendous responsibility to push forward because no one else can really lead by example like the country with largest and most developed economy in the world. We must set the direction and seek to be better at what we have done. We must also look in the mirror and be realistic. Many things we do are detrimental to furthering our country and the world's economy. We need to change these to move forward. Our forefathers would have wanted us to.

Bureaucracy

We have levels of management here in America in our large bureaucratic organizations. The information age is flattening the structures,
enabling line workers to have a discussion with CEOs and CFOs,
but there's a lot more flattening to do. Our economic system is
plagued by technical failures, corruption, and plain old theft. Yet our
system still appears to be more efficient, profitable, and productive
than state-run economies. In China, a political official can force people off their land that they've been farming for decades in the quest
for new manufacturing plant of which he may have a part ownership.
In this country, this type of conflict of interest wouldn't survive the
barrage of e-mails and blogs by the time the next morning paper was
delivered.

However, the incentives in U.S. corporate management today
seem far divorced from a public purpose. Business leaders' lack of
interest in the issues of the day is disturbing. "I cannot recall a time
when there were so many daunting national challenges, with business
engagements are lacking," said Pete Peterson.[239] We may have taken
this self-interest a bit too far. It's essential that we lead by example.

Twenty-five years ago, the government dismantled "Ma Bell," AT&T.
The breakup set forth a surge of progress in communications as the
Baby Bells competed with one another. The airline industry was de-
regulated, which created a free-for-all in competition for $69 flights
to anywhere. Bureaucracy is a productivity killer and free markets
do work best to keep institutions lean and mean. Bureaucracies stifle
competition. A little competition never hurt anyone.

Crime

├─────┤

The United States has the highest crime rate in the developed world. The homicide rate, which is a direct consequence of the freedom to bear arms, has resulted in the most number of murders in the industrialized world. The homicide rate was nearly three times as high as in Canada and more than five times as high as in Germany.[240] There are other countries with higher crime rates, like Russia, Venezuela, Jamaica, and Columbia, but among the industrialized nations, we are unfortunately the leader.

We have a record 7 million people in prison, on probation, or on parole, with 2 million of them behind bars. China ranks second, with 1.5 million people. The United States has 5% of the world's population and 25% of the world's people in prison. Within federal prisons, over half of the inmates are serving time for drug offenses.[241] The U.S. is a rich society with disposable income, and drugs seem to be a part of the national fabric.

I don't have any quick solutions for our prison or drug problem. However, it is something that we must deal with to further our cause.

Debt

├─────┤

Debt has been ingrained in the American culture as a good thing. Leverage, through a system of ropes and pulleys, allows a man to lift an automobile. In the financial sense, it is when a small amount of capital can lift a large amount of assets, and capital invested can be quickly grown. Leverage is simply the amount of debt outstanding versus ownership equity. A one-to-one ratio would represent 50% of assets are funded with debt and 50% with equity. Many of us buy a house with something like 10% down. That's a leverage ratio of 10. No-money-down mortgages created sky-high leverage with ratios of 100 to one. Debt has gotten to excessive levels and now needs to be reduced. The largest challenge for this country is how to deal with its debt burden and pay off its obligations.

We have, as a civilization, become more comfortable with debt. Unfortunately the leverage ratios got too high, especially for financial companies: 20 to one, 30 to one, and higher. It was a very dry field where the subprime match was dropped that led to an economic forest fire. Leveraging the economy means increasing the potential for gains when asset prices rise. However, it also means asset prices can't fall too much before equity capital is wiped out. That's what happened. Too much of those assets were supported by debt. With declining asset prices, the equity was wiped out.

It pays to be an owner. Generally, equity owners will earn more than bond holders over time. Stock returns over the very long term, the last hundred years, have averaged around 10%. Bond returns over the same period have averaged about half that amount with inflation eating up the majority of that return. So adjusted for inflation over time, an equity holder's real return is 7% and a bond holder's return is, at best, 2%. Equity holders receive *triple* the "real" return of a bond holder, along with more risk. The risk of an equity holder is varied. Bankruptcy, margin calls, and banking panics are all risks that equity owners take on. Debt holders also take on the risk that their interest payments and principal won't be paid, but it is more controlled and measurable. It's not evil to be an owner of debt, just not prudent to be too much of one.

On the corporate side of things, risks in the world seemed to be diminishing and that was reflected in financial markets. Perceived risk, as evidenced by differences in interest rates, was falling. Leverage was welcomed as a way to capture better returns. Financial companies leveraged up to compensate from the lower returns available in this perceived lower-risk environment. Leverage ratios in banks moved from 10 and 20 to one all the way to 30 or 40 to one. Companies that were suffering under mismanagement, poor marketing, or simply bad product lines could easily be taken over and restructured with a large amount of debt and a small amount of capital. Many of these LBOs were created with optimistic projections of revenues and earnings that didn't pan out. Even though banks provide the lifeblood of financial transactions in our economy, they became more like leveraged hedge funds speculating on interest rate swaps, credit defaults, funding private capital, and trading foreign exchange. Banks are a necessary component of the modern economic machinery and should be thought of more as utilities rather than unregulated hedge funds. Reducing our leverage in the corporate side should be directed to separating financial companies from those that can fail and seek higher returns, and those that cannot fail and provide more stable but lower returns. Let banks be boring again!

Consumers in America have enjoyed a tremendous increase in net worth over long periods of time. Unfortunately, they also spent most of it. At a time when Americans were enjoying trillions of dollars

In additional net worth, we were spending this wealth faster than
we were accumulating it. It will take some time to de-leverage the
consumer side of the economy. The consumer balance sheet, though,
doesn't look as dire has the headlines in your local newspaper suggest.

According to J.P. Morgan, total assets of consumers were $67 tril-
lion versus total liabilities of $14 trillion. Certainly, that looks more
manageable. Americans have not been saving for quite a long time and
now have to. Home values were the piggy bank that people thought
would save them. Many houses were like ATM cards and home-equity
loans funded purchases. The primary asset that most U.S. households hold is their home and the values are still dropping, although
recently more slowly. Forces are still working against a strong recovery. There is a shadow inventory of foreclosed homes that would
send home values plummeting. Banks are reluctant to take the loss
from a sale.

There's no doubt that much of our growth of the past was fueled
by debt. With job losses in this recent recession, the worst of the
post-Depression era, the challenges to pay off debt are going to be
enormous. In an economy dependent upon consumer spending, how
can GDP rise when personal income from job losses is falling? It will
take a decade for households to reduce their debts to a more sustainable level. It has taken Japan longer. We have to be prepared for
a lower growth track.

The debt burden of our government is monstrous, with over a
$1.4 trillion deficit in the fiscal year 2009 and totals over $12 trillion.
A trillion is a thousand billion, so that would mean that even at 1%

interest, you would have to come up with $120 billion a year in interest costs, equivalent to about $400 million per business day. Then, you have to ask the question, "What's the money being used for?" If it is being used for productive investments that will result in income-producing enterprises in the future, that's an investment. Wisdom does not immediately translate into cash to make interest payments; we have to transform it into products and services. If the government's investments are increasing economic activity, the additional tax revenue generated could pay the interest. With a $1 trillion-investment, if you could move U.S. GDP from zero to positive 3%, you've just moved a $12-trillion economy to $12.4 trillion, or an increase of $400 billion. Taxed at only a 25% rate, it would amount to $100 billion in tax revenue or ten percent of the investment in the first year. That pays for a lot of interest costs. If, however, the stimulus is short-term and temporary, and doesn't result in long-term growth, the $1 trillion is not an investment; it is just postponing the inevitable. Like kicking the can up the road.

So we have to ask the question, "Is this new debt being used for investment that will increase productivity and future tax revenues?" The good news is that most of the debt increase of the last three decades has funded investment in the U.S. economy, which has generated impressive productivity gains of about 3% a year.[242] We should strive to make these investments even better. They shouldn't be made as earmarks that protect certain regions from voting out their elected officials. The deficits are going to be running so high that politically elected officials will need to do something different...and quick. "The empire is at risk," to use Nile Ferguson's historical comparison with other leading countries of the world economy in the past. We are in a new age of information and there are certainly ways to think our way through this.

Let's face it; without the government filling the void of markets, we would've collapsed even further in 2008. The tremendous surge in spending by the government was needed. However, we do need to spend wisely and for the future. When it is no longer needed, let's take it back. Reduce the size of government when we can, so it has more flexibility and power when it is needed. Let's invest in our intellectual capital. That is the only way we can grow our way out of our debt.

There is some fear in the public's mind that foreigners own too much of U.S. Treasury securities, over half of outstanding public U.S. Treasuries. Foreigners hold them to begin with because they're safe investments, predictable, and the most liquid in the world. We, as Americans, ironically, hold little of them through our institutions. Should these foreigners want to sell them, prices would go down, and interest rates could go up, and thus become more attractive for other investors. They hold these securities for a reason: investment. They shouldn't be able to dictate policies to our government. They are bond holders, not equity holders!

As measured as a percent of GDP, our debt ratio is one of the largest and in total is expected to reach $13 trillion soon or about equal to the size of our economy. Debt-servicing costs today are so minimal that the economy is not pulled down by an interest burden—yet! As interest rates rise, more of our annual budget will go to pay interest costs. There may be a point in time when the interest burden could become the largest item in the budget. Our flexibility as a government would be greatly diminished.

The largest portion of the U.S. government budget is funding entitlements. When the government calculates the debt and deficit, it does so on a cash basis. There is an estimated $60 trillion in **unfunded** liabilities in the future that the government is promising with policies today. We must change these existing policies to soften the blow of the future possible liabilities. The largest areas of these future liabilities lie in Social Security, Medicaid, and Medicare. Of the budget outlays in 2009, Social Security, Medicaid, and Medicare are 37% of the total. Entitlements are going to increase tremendously under a new health care program. Unless entitlements are cut or taxes are raised, you will never see another balanced budget. However, if the deficit is cut and the economy expands, there is a way to grow through the problem. Everything hinges on the assumptions about costs, demographics, and growth rates, which are very hard to pin down. The unprecedented and absolute scale of the U.S. debt could at some point destabilize markets, undermine the currency, or both.

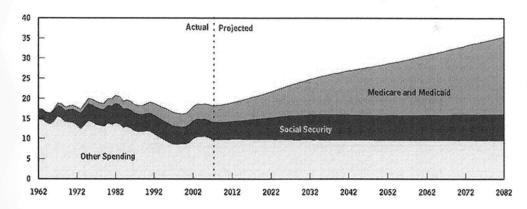

Projection of Government Spending as a Percent of GDP
(Source: January 2008 Budget and Economic Outlook,
Congressional Budget Office)

Now, if you asked the average baby boomer on the street what their chances were of seeing a Social Security check, they would tell you they have a better chance of seeing a UFO or being one of the first to land on Mars. You might find it amazing that people that make over $1 million a year from investments will still receive Social Security checks. If you wait until your full retirement age, there is no maximum income limit. With the average American earning something like $50,000 a year, it would make sense to begin to limit these benefits and completely eliminate them at certain income levels. Politically incorrect or not! Many people don't deserve Social Security; they have contributed to a social safety net that makes them safer and more comfortable walking down their street. They have already been paid back. In Medicaid and Medicare, there are those receiving benefits that haven't paid in. Then there are the estimated 10 to 20 million illegal immigrants who flood the system. The government bureaucracy of mismanagement adds another layer of confusion. We are an information economy and we should be able to get these things right, or at least better.

Our defense spending has funded the police force of the world. Why does Japan need our protection, let alone our meddling in Iraq and Afghanistan? We cannot afford to operate in the old world order any longer. It is now a new world. We need to embrace the multipolar world and push for a new contributory system where the beneficiaries pay up. So it's up to us to face this head-on and prove to be the leader of the world that we are. It may be destabilizing at first, but we have no choice. Our wealth is not limitless.

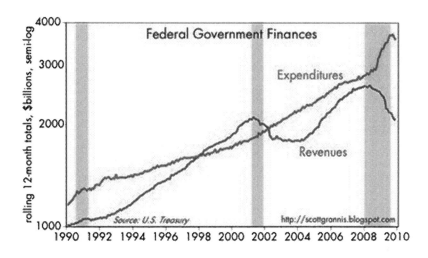

(Source: January 2008 Budget and Economic Outlook,
Congressional Budget Office)

∾ ∾ ∾

We need to start focusing the federal budget on federal issues. States, for the most part, have balanced budget amendments, which require them to be frugal with spending. Many state budgets therefore need to cut spending as tax revenues fall at the bottom of a recession. The federal government needs to be counter-cyclical. Yes, we did what we had to do in 2008, but the earmarks to particular politicians' districts have to end at the state line. Bring on the presidential line-item veto, which almost every governor of the fifty states has, but the president of the United States does not!

The federal government for federal issues! I think that's what the signers of the Declaration of Independence and the creators of our Constitution would have wanted. We have to see through the current debt crisis in America with solutions to cut spending. We need to find ways to eliminate government programs that don't work, are outdated, or poorly designed. "The nearest thing that we have to eternal life on this earth is a government program." [243] We need to focus the federal budget on federal or national issues.

Elementary Education

Whereas our higher education is an example for the world, our primary school system needs to be analyzed for its underperformance. In such a connected world, it's odd that our educational system is so decentralized and disconnected. If there's a school district, it's elected. Every little town has its own school district and its own school board with no real contact with an overall national directive or strategy. Providing education for everyone through programs like "No Child Left Behind" is outstanding. But it's no longer about whether Johnny can read; it's about whether he can succeed, and that's a skills-based argument. If we keep teaching to the lowest common denominator, everyone's going to lose. Children aren't as held back against barriers to learning as adults who are set in their ways and schedules; they can leap as high as the bar is set. They will study as hard as it takes to pass the test and if that exam is more difficult, they study harder. Children are also not confined to classrooms, either, as they pick up how to play a video game quickly without reading the direction manual.

The distinction that we have in elementary versus higher education is all about the market mechanism. Higher education is basically a capitalist system where you compete for teachers, you pay on performance, you compete for students, and the output is measured by what students can earn in the real world.[244] The recent movement to attain school vouchers that are exchangeable at many different types of institutions may be a movement to push the school system along a more market-based path. What about students voting for their best teachers and awarding bonuses accordingly? Today, teachers in elementary schools across the United States may earn the same amount, if they are good or bad. There are great schools in America that motivate young individuals to an extremely high level. Let's find them and bring their findings to the masses.

We can look overseas to find some good ideas in training people once they've chosen their field of work. Europe's answer may be vocational training and apprenticeships during elementary and primary schooling. This creates a workforce of intelligent laborers with needed and predictable salaries. If you want to become a painter in Europe, you decide that in high school. Before graduation, you know your track to enter a vocational school, where two years may be required. From there, many young workers are individually matched to experienced workers who serve as mentors for the young. The total program may last five years or more and by the time you're officially out on your own, you may have spent a decade in school or training. Government regulations and permits provide a barrier to entry to other painters. In Europe, the painting market is controlled by a regulating body that controls how many enter the business, the rates that can be charged, and the education and training required.

In America, the market makes these decisions. You leave high school and, finding no other opportunities, fall back on something you've done in the summers. You have had no formal training, but learn on the job. If you were a good painter, you will get referrals, but there is a lot of competition because there are no barriers to entry. Painting is a very decentralized business. If you've done a poor job somewhere, it's easy to pick up a job in another area. If bad reports come in to the Better Business Bureau, simply change the name of the business and move to another location. The market decides who wins. There may be some aspects of the vocational system that we can adopt here to our market system.

We, as a country, could further strengthen our community colleges, allowing them to offer more vocational skills and provide a viable way for more people to work their way into four-year colleges. We can prepare people to be better able to judge their own skills and place themselves onto a learning path toward individualized career opportunities. You are generally good at what you like to do, but primary schools in America do a poor job of evaluating what you're good at doing. Most school systems are focused on graduation rates and the percent that move on to college. The preponderance of undeclared majors at colleges and universities illustrates the general trend of no career path orientation. More than seventy percent of U.S. college students will change their major sometime during the course of their college career.[245] We could really do a better job of understanding people's strengths and weaknesses earlier on, and then scale schooling toward individual segments, rather than the general least common denominator.

Chances are you know a person, maybe your son or daughter, who has the ability to do five things at once: texting, watching TV, carrying on a conversation, all the while downloading music and uploading videos. The networking generation is changing how we communicate—and quickly. Multitasking is all part of the human species and makes us more efficient and productive. Informational flows prioritize job tasks and attention can be directed to those areas where it's most needed. This attention can also be diverted, as evidenced by the inexperienced multi-tasker, i.e., the teenager. We need to know how to sift through and use information, and be able to spot changes in patterns that require immediate analysis. Our schools should be teaching students how to multi-task, how to sort through information and recognize patterns in data and images, not teaching in the old segmented methods! English is first period, science is second..... How about we combine the two? The barrage of information is a challenge for everybody, especially some of the largest companies in the world! In the information age, the ability to analyze data will be crucial.

Energy

We are running out of oil and the United States is ill prepared for the transition to other sources of energy. This may be an understatement. Energy consumption per capita is the highest in the world. Our energy usage is 40% from petroleum oil, 23% from coal, 22% from natural gas and the remainder from nuclear and renewable energy sources.[246] Due to cheap oil, the United States has significantly scaled back many research initiatives in alternative energy substitutes over the past few decades. We do sit on vast resources of oil, natural gas, and other resources but continue to purchase foreign oil on the open market rather than explore on our own. As the result of the rather low tax on gasoline, Americans enjoy cheap energy to drive and that has resulted in poor decisions with mass transit and personal driving habits.

The evolution of the energy business also parallels that of the human race. As more sophisticated energy sources have been available, human civilization has progressed rapidly around these technological and innovative advances. History comes alive today by evaluating the fuel use by the world's different income groups. The lowest income groups in the world's poorer countries use wood and other biomass. The next income groups in the world use charcoal and coal. Kerosene and oil dominate the third group, with natural gas and electricity representative of the higher-income levels. The ordering of fuels on this ladder also corresponds to their efficiency and the cleanliness. As people's incomes rise, they tend to consume more energy and it costs less.[247]

The world is much closer to running out of oil than official estimates would project, especially with China and the emerging markets beginning to consume so much of it. Gaining support is the theory of peak oil, which states that discoveries of new oil fields have slowed substantially and that the oil fields already pumping are reaching their maximum efficiencies. This will lead to a decline in overall production.

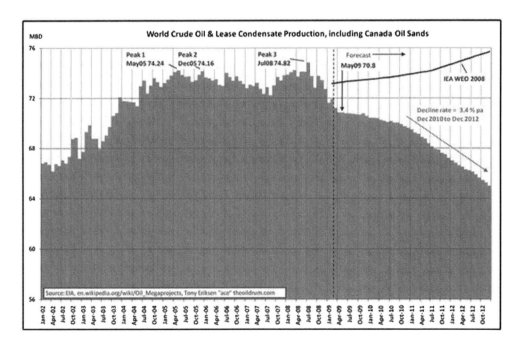

Production of Oil May Have Already Peaked
(Source: Energy Efficiency)

This is at a time when demand is at an all-time high and increasing rapidly. The current level of oil production is about 72 million barrels a day (as seen from the chart). In order to keep up with demand, it's estimated that oil supplies will be required at 80 to 90 million barrels a day. Those estimates continue to require technological advancements to recover previously unrecoverable oil and new methods of drilling to find previously un-drillable areas. The supply/demand scenario desperately needs alternative sources for energy.

With American policies over the years seeking to exploit oil resources, many countries have found a renewed vigor in their own nationalism. As a result, many countries now wish to control the development of their own energy resources, with state-owned companies exploring, producing, and refining oil. That has sent the energy industry into many decentralized and uncoordinated efforts. Information on research and drilling techniques is not as readily shared. The oil industry is progressing at a much slower pace because of it.

Mexico is a great example. Despite being one of the world's largest oil reserves and the world's seventh largest oil producer, forecasts have it becoming a net importer by 2017.[248] In 2008, Mexico produced some 2.6 million barrels of oil a day, but that was thirty percent down from its peak. Without any major new discoveries, Mexican reserves will last just another decade. Without the ability to tap innovation, Mexico seems lost. Taxes and royalties from Pemex, the state-owned oil monopoly, have accounted for over half of federal revenues in recent years. British Petroleum just found a huge field in the Gulf of Mexico, whereas Pemex has drilled ten deep-water wells, but found little oil. Pemex lacks the expertise, technology, and capital needed to further its own knowledge base. In the information age, these decentralized and "go it alone" policies are unsettling and could lead to problems with energy quickly.

The Chinese have gotten quite a foothold in many controversial areas of the world to obtain oil, including a massive resource grab in Africa. Including Nigeria, the Sudan, Iraq, and Iran, the Chinese will literally do business with anyone to gain access to oil rights or to development projects. With oil production of only about 4 million barrels per day, China is expected to need twice that to run its economy today.

The solution to the energy crisis has to be from the demand side, since the supply side is constrained. Most of the oil that we burn here in the United States is for automobiles and transportation. There are over 240 million cars in America. Despite the popularity of an electric car, we don't have the electric capacity to plug in even 10 million of them right now. The best long-term solution is the hybrid, a self-sustainable electric motor and combustion engine. This doesn't require any different supply structures, nor does it radically change any industry. It would be important to put a tax on gasoline in favor of hybrid research even if we have to initially lease Japanese technology. We could learn a lot by getting cars off the road in favor of public transportation, also utilizing fewer cars per family, and smaller, more efficient cars, like in Europe. The structure of our economy is going to change considerably if transportation costs soar. It's going to be much more important to locate operations close to the final markets. It is also going to severely curtail imports, as the cost of shipping will also rise. This new world of high-cost energy we are just entering lies immediately ahead. Costs to everyone are going to rise. It's simple supply and demand.

Financial Engineering

Securitization has provided a huge benefit to the average American. The local bank is able to put a mortgage in a security and then sell it on the open market. That allows them to reduce their own concentration risk in their community, and provide a more competitive interest rate and different payment options for the homeowner. They also make a profit. We got carried away with this: lenders, securities firms, banks, brokers, and, yes, borrowers. The industry was reckless and financial engineering itself has gotten a bad name.

There were so many flavors of interest and principal repayment schedules, it was numbing to the home buyer. The worst may be over, but there is more bad news to come. The majority of the so-called "option ARM" mortgages have yet to reset their interest rate. These were called "pick-a-payment" loans, where borrowers could literally pick a payment amount for them, even if it meant not paying monthly principal. Some even didn't fully pay the interest and the principal continued to grow. That is in the face of declining home values. Many of these loans have yet to reset from their "teaser" rates, especially in California.

When you look at the amount of subprime mortgages that have already reset their interest rate mostly on the left side of the chart below, we have been through only the first part of the storm. That could be called wave one. In the second wave, on the right hand side of the chart, many option arm mortgages are going to reset to higher interest rates. That is yet to come. It is difficult to imagine more homes coming on the market from the distressed situation and the already slow sales pace that we have today. Many of these home mortgages that reset their interest rates upward will find the home value below the mortgage amount. We are in the middle of these two waves, the so called eye of the hurricane. There is a difficult period ahead for those states that issued these, mostly in California, Nevada, Arizona and Florida.

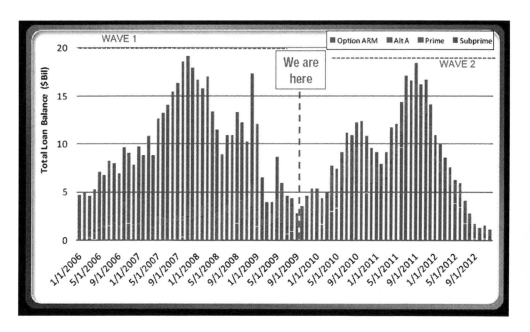

The Year 2010 Could Be the Eye of the Hurricane in the Amount of Mortgages That Will Reset Interest Rates
(Source: Dr. Housing Bubble)

However, let's not forget what got us here in the first place. The lessons are learned and let's hope the next generation of consumer financial products will be simpler to understand and easier to ascertain the risks inherent in them. And before we throw financial innovation into the junk heap, we must understand that it can help the world's poorest countries.

Micro-finance has been one of the world's best innovative gifts. Muhammad Yunus received the Nobel Prize for Peace in 2006 for his pioneering work on micro-finance. His Grameen Bank, founded in 1976, provided small loans, sometimes as little as twenty dollars, to the rural poor in Bangladesh. Today the bank runs over two dozen related ventures to combat poverty. The Grameen Foundation operates in over forty-three countries and the majority of its clients are women.[249] Micro-finance not only helps those people climb out of poverty, but can also lift whole communities into more productive contributors to society. Financial engineering also affects innovation as new ideas can be funded through these new arrangements.

The center of financial engineering is in derivatives and within that are credit default swaps. Called swaps because they would avoid insurance regulation, these are essentially default insurance against a creditor going bankrupt. Investors would purchase these if they also own the bonds to protect them in case of a bankruptcy. However, many also purchase the bonds to force bankruptcy, triggering a payment on their swaps. These are traded "over-the-counter," meaning not in a major exchange where the security can be standardized and evaluated, versus others like it. An over-the-counter security is simply a written arrangement between two parties and many of these agreements had unique qualities that were specific to it. It's not that these securities are bad, either; it's how they're used that creates large systematic risks. By purchasing the credit default swap on AIG for 300 basis points, it would equate to three percent or a $3 million-investment. That could pay you $1 billion in a debt default. That's leverage!

These large systematic risks were not followed closely by the authorities. Within the financial crisis, the government spent hundreds of billions of taxpayer money to make good on these investments. Oddly enough, many of the holders of these CDS did not expect to be made whole. As in most bankruptcies, holders of debt expect to get some amount less, in some cases just cents on the dollar. The government paid out because of the risks that a Wall Street failure would create a downward spiral from which we couldn't recover. It's odd that fully a year after the meltdown, there is still no definitive clearinghouse for these swap securities.

With consumer finance, we have to get our act together, too. The regulators have been asleep at the switch and products were engineered without any hope of the actual investor understanding them. The regulatory agency's first priority is to make sure that lenders are financially sound with sufficient capital to survive if loans go bad. This crisis revealed a tendency among regulators to forget about consumers, but that's why they exist in the first place, to protect them. Almost half of the lower-income buyers of homes could not describe the basic feature of their mortgages.[250] "Some mortgage options presented to buyers during the housing boom were mind-numbingly complex, even an economist adept at spreadsheets would have trouble calculating future payments on an interest only or an option arm loan."[251] Borrowing and investing today is extraordinarily complex and Americans don't understand finance as well as they should. There needs to be some regulation here.

In some industries, regulations protect everything from trees and landscapes to drug testing in animals, but in the financial area, we can't even protect common citizens. The rule for a financial product should be: If you can't understand it, don't buy it, or if it's too good to be true, it probably isn't.

Foreign Policy

The United States has been a leader of the world for over a century but we need to face the reality that the world is a much smaller and flatter planet today. Our leadership is going to be challenged from this point forward. We are "a" leader, not "the" leader, of the world. Part of the problem is America's astonishing ignorance. Americans need to face the truth about themselves and where our place is in the world, no matter how unpleasant it may be. We are highly self-critical and judge ourselves by a high standard. Americans are always examining whether they could've done something better.

In his book *The White House Years*, Henry Kissinger says that America has no permanent friends or enemies, only "interests." The American people have asked the government to act on their behalf against their adversaries, but at times this select group of military leaders has seemed to reach over the line to pursue their own self-interests and personal vendettas. Although we pride ourselves on being a moral nation in pursuing freedom, at times individual instances of misconduct are appalling and almost unbelievable. Alas, we are only human.

"Critics of U.S. foreign policy judge us by a standard applied to no one else," says the Heritage Foundation.[252] Twice in the 20th century, the United States helped save the world, first from the Axis threat and then from Soviet totalitarianism. After helping destroy Europe, America then proceeded to rebuild many nations, including Germany, through the Marshall Plan. After having bombed Japan at the end of World War II, the United States proceeded to help rebuild that nation and, today, we are close allies. We are involved deeply in the Middle

East, first in Kuwait, then Iraq, and more recently in Afghanistan. While the successes are hard to judge at this point in time, no one can question the path toward freer societies and democratic elections that is opening up for the people of these countries.

Healthcare Delivery

The United States spends more money on health care than any other country. In fact, we far outspend any other nation measured in both per capita spending and in percentage of GDP. The World Health Organization ranks our health care system as first in responsiveness, but 37th in overall performance.[253] Comparisons are hard to make with America versus other countries because over 15% of the population or almost 50 million Americans are uninsured. This is about 5 million more people than were uninsured in the year 2001. In 2006, Massachusetts became the first state to mandate universal health insurance. Their experiment seems to be working. With the passage of the health care bill we will have to evaluate how we progress.

Overall life expectancy has dropped from eleventh to forty-second in the world in the last two decades. Infant mortality rates of 6.37 per thousand people places the United States at forty-second of 221 countries and behind all of Western Europe. Our adolescent pregnancy rate is nearly four times what it is in Europe. Obesity is an epidemic with approximately one-third of the adult population listed as obese and an additional third as overweight. Obesity-related type 2 diabetes is spiraling out of control. There are some real problems in our health and health care delivery system that need to be addressed quickly.

Have you been to a doctor's office lately? Have you been asked to fill out forms of health history, other specialists that you see and a list of your current medications? The most typical method of obtaining this information is simply filling out forms by hand. Doesn't that lead to errors of input, remembering what and when you had a procedure, dosages, allergies and adverse reactions? Wouldn't it be better for everyone if you kept that information on a standardized memory device that could be utilized by a physician in a few keystrokes? The cocktail party chatter will never be the same. "You're a doctor? Did you bring your card reader? I have been having a pain right here. Here's my medical history" Health care is an information business.

There are some bright spots, though. The research and development in chemical-based and biomedical research has created many new innovative drugs and techniques. The medical device industry is one of the world's largest. U.S. cancer survival rates are the highest in the world. The U.S. life expectancy of 77 years at birth is only three to four years lower than that of the leaders: Norway, Switzerland, and Canada. The surgeons and specialists that we have here in America are among the best and brightest in the world.

Manufacturing

The manufacturing sector of the United States has been in decline for many decades. Employing over 18 million people as recently as 1990, today the sector employs less than 12 million Americans. America no longer makes many of the things that it uses, such as consumer electronics, general-purpose goods or manufactured goods, and automobiles. However, these things are extremely important for our economy to continue to produce. Our value-added, high-end manufacturing sector is a world leader. In recent years, there has been a historic supply shift in which imports of manufactured goods have replaced domestically produced goods both massively and quickly. This trend has been magnified by U.S. producers moving production offshore.

It is extremely important that a healthy portion of the automobile industry remain under American company ownership. A large number of manufacturing jobs are from that industry. Manufacturing is important in our future as assemblers of value-added products. Most governments around the world assist their own manufacturing sectors and we shouldn't leave ours out in the cold to global market forces. This is especially true if other countries are not playing by the same rules. It is a measure of national security. The decline of the U.S. dollar in recent years and in future years should help our competitive position in manufactured goods.

The National Association of Manufacturers (NAM) released studies in 2003 and 2006 on the structural costs of manufacturing in the United States compared with its trading partners. They found that U.S. manufacturers pay over 30% more in non-production costs relative to its nine largest trading partners. Much of the difference is accounted for in higher tax and regulatory compliance costs, health and retirement benefits, and litigation. Businesses with these higher costs will still be able to compete, but must remain more flexible, entrepreneurial, and dynamic, responding to the needs of the marketplace in order to demand higher prices. Many of the global competitors in the world today do not regard profit as the overwhelming goal of an enterprise. Revenues are more important to exporters in order to grow their business. As a result, many products can be sold here in the United States below the cost of production because the companies are attempting to expand volume and not profits. Many socialist-directed economies, including China and Japan, have an extraordinary focus on sales rather than profit.

Much of America's manufacturing output is destined for emerging markets, from bricks and bulldozers to automobiles and aircraft. Emerging economies are likely to grow faster than America for years to come, which should help our export position. Conversely, the domestic economy will have a high level of unemployment, resulting from a reduction of consumption. Manufacturers are increasingly looking to the federal government for help. Both the "cash for clunkers" car-trading scheme and the homebuyer credit were temporary measures to help boost manufacturing production. There was even cash for your old toaster! The government is also focusing on infrastructure and has appointed a "manufacturing tsar" to help direct stimulus money to domestic manufacturers. These are all needed initiatives.

Poverty

For such a rich country, a lot of people go hungry in America. Over 10% of Americans are below the poverty line and an astounding 58% spend at least one year in poverty between the ages of 25 and 75.[254] In 2007, approximately 30 million Americans lived in poverty, which is about $10,000 a year in income for an individual and about $20,000 a year for a family. A 2007 UNICEF study of children's well-being in 21 industrialized nations ranked the United States next to last. Where the American welfare state does well in reducing poverty among the elderly, it seems the children received little assistance. Wealth concentration and income inequality is the primary cause of this poor ranking. The top one percent of the richest Americans possesses

33% of the country's net worth. We are top-heavy. The top 10% possesses 70% of the country's household wealth. The 2008 recession hit real median household income as it fell to $50,303, the lowest level since 1997. Executive compensation has hit a record. The rich and poor are becoming farther apart. Something has got to be done. Higher taxes for excessive income, those over $1 million per year, are appropriate. Most Americans would agree.

With more than a billion hungry people around the world, we have to get our own house in order before we can help them but, as a leader, we **have** to do this and quickly. With an additional 2 billion people who are somewhat malnourished, half the population of the world needs food. We have not only wealth but knowledge of agricultural technology that can help raise per capita food production, which in some places is declining. To the richest Americans, if you ask them, they would help.

Regulation

The United States leads the world in labor productivity but no longer leads in productivity per hour, as it did from the 1950s to the 1990s. One factor could be how the economy has evolved and how regulations have increased the cost of doing business. There are regulations and regulatory agencies that are "asleep at the switch." With all the lawyers that we have in the country, you would think we'd be good at regulating. We need to not only evaluate existing regulations for their effectiveness, but abolish those that get in the way of doing business.

"America has too many laws, and the laws we do have are tedious, overly complex and sometimes not only impossible to understand, but impossible to comply with," says Fox News.[255] Politicians pass laws in response to the latest scare headlines with little regard about whom they will affect, let alone the cost of complying. The federal criminal code spans some 1,400 pages, and that's the abbreviated version. The Federal Registry, which covers all the regulations that the federal government imposes, exceeds 75,000 pages. "The Office of Management and Budget estimates that merely complying with these regulations—that is, paying lawyers to keep educated on them, interpret them and implement them—costs U.S. business another $500 to $600 billion per year."[256] And to top it off, the health care legislation was rumored to be 2,000 pages. If you read one page a minute, it would take you thirty-three hours without sleep or breaks. I wonder how many earmarks were included?

Today's financial regulatory system was developed piecemeal and was created for a world that is barely noticeable from today's complex, interrelated world. The Securities and Exchange Commission recently estimated that derivative paper securities are worth ten times the total value of economic activity throughout the world in one year. Studies at the Bank for International Settlements in Basel, Switzerland, have recently estimated that could be twice that much—yes, $1.2 quadrillion! There is a word that we haven't heard, but get used to it: quadrillion.[257]

The insurance company AIG was regulated by insurance, investment, and banking agencies all from different areas, states, and levels of government. There was no one overall regulator to ensure that AIG knew what was going on in total, and, alas, no one really did! In a global network, cross-border banking provides tougher challenges as well. Interconnectedness can prove to be a virus should one company get sick. In such an interlocking world, we need to rethink some of our institutions that are "too big to fail" because they are so vital to the world. In a market economy, no one participant should be so important.

In financial reform, we need to create a financial oversight council to monitor risk across the financial system. This council should be composed of many private sector members with advanced market knowledge that are paid for their input. The Federal Reserve is the best supervisory authority to house this regulatory body since it is independent of politics. We need to eliminate some offices that were created in past eras and streamline the structure to make it a high-profile and important position for former employees of other firms than just Goldman Sachs. We should definitely regulate over-the-counter derivatives since they now total such an overwhelming amount. Finally, we need to seek to deter lenders from making bad loans and then passing them off in securities by keeping a certain percentage stake investment in each underwritten security. That part we have gotten, but, of course, the financial companies pushed against it. Additionally, to the area of compensation packages for chief executives, we should let the shareholders vote annually on approving such compensation, as is done within some companies in Europe.

Saving

The U.S. population has a savings problem; we don't save enough and have to encourage other countries to save here to provide our capital. For the purposes of illustration, listed below are the amounts of savings per age group in the U.S. Look at the age breakdown from the Employee benefit Research Institute:[258] This does not include pension, retirement or profit sharing plans.

Age < 35:	**$ 6,306**
35 – 44:	**$22,460**
45 – 54:	**$43,797**
55 – 64:	**$69,127**
65 – 75:	**$56,212**

We have a problem if everyone is expecting Social Security to pay them in retirement. Someone better start telling us the truth or people will never prepare.

Special Interests

Our economy is led sometimes by the smallest number of its people. The growth in campaign spending has been one of the strongest growth areas in our economy. The amount of money that a politician has to raise to get elected is growing exponentially. Barack Obama spent more money than any other presidential candidate in winning the 2008 presidential race. His campaign raised $650 million by Election Day 2008, an increase of 150 percent from George Bush's campaign contributions in 2004. In 2004, George Bush spent 170 percent more than he did in 2000. And what is that money doing to further our country economically?

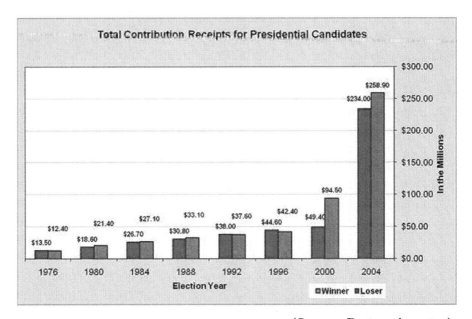

(Source: Project America)

∾ ∾ ∾

When you wonder why we got in such a big financial mess, you'll find that the largest single contributor to political campaigns is financial businesses. The second largest is health care. Total lobbying in Washington, D.C., in the year 2009 is estimated to be close to $3 billion.[259] When legislation is being drawn up, you can bet there is a lot of money flowing around. On the list of top donors from 1989 to 2009, AT&T is number one, with $44 million in contributions over the two-decade span, and Goldman Sachs is number four, with $31 million. Citigroup is number thirteen with $26 million in contributions.

What is best for the economy and general public doesn't seem to be the goals of our leaders in Washington. In his book *The Rise and Decline of Nations*, Mancur Olson observes that as nations prosper, special interest groups seek control and attention. They favor policies that distribute money their way. Since the economy is so large and successful, many people do not notice. As time goes on, this narrow distribution of income contributes to a decline in overall economic growth.[260] As the monies illustrate, financial institutions that got money from TARP were major contributors to politicians in the first half of 2007. Politicians did fear that their funding might be substantially reduced, as was experienced in the first half of 2009. The incentives of political maneuvering may not have been fully to preserve the system, but to preserve the funding to stay in office.

Political donations from TARP recipients

	1st half 09	1st half 07	GOT FROM TARP
Citigroup	$228,100.00	$245,800.00	50 billion
Morgan Stanley	($3,000.00)	$250,000.00	10 billion
JP Morgan	$26,000.00	$361,265.00	25 billion
Wells Fargo	($3,500.00)	$215,700.00	25 billion
PNC	$11,650.00	$19,725.00	7.6 billion
Goldman Sachs	$23,000.00	$236,000.00	10 billion
Bank of America	$126,000.00	$244,500.00	45 billion
US Bancorp	$117,000.00	$76,500.00	6.6 billion
BB&T	$34,350.00	$39,500.00	3.1 billion
Key Bank	$18,000.00	$18,500.00	2.5 billion
Capital One	$164,140.00	$236,100.00	3.57 billion
American Express	$38,500.00	$11,500.00	3.4 billion
Regions	$18,500.00	$40,500.00	3.5 billion
State Street	$0.00	$3,000.00	2 billion
Comerica	$14,800.00	$114,000.00	2.3 billion
TOTAL IN TARP	$413,550.00	$898,725.00	
TOTAL OUT OF TARP	$399,990.00	$1,213,865.00	

(Source: Washington Independent)

Just when you think you understand, there's more. Politicians collect money for their own campaigns, but many of them also raise a separate pot of money called a political action committee to help out other politicians. They can use this pot of money to gain clout among their colleagues and boost their bid for political leadership in campaigns, committees, or higher office. Some use these PACs to hire staff, and others for dining at fancy restaurants. It is a money machine. The political system looks unresponsive to the average American because it is monopolized by a few powerful industry groups to control campaign contributions.[261]

Individuals are limited to $2,400 as a campaign contribution to each candidate, or $30,000 to a national party committee annually. Rules also limit $10,000 to state, district, and local party committees per year, and $5,000 to any other political committee. These seem like reasonable limits. Why aren't limits like these made for corporations? The Supreme Court recently made a ruling favoring unlimited corporate commercials for political candidates under our right to free speech. We haven't yet seen the effect from this action, but be prepared for even more political commercials and paid advertisement mini-movies.

It seems that whenever campaign reform becomes a campaign issue, the resultant legislation is like the wolves guarding the henhouse. There needs to be an independent public/private partnership to review campaign reform and the amount of money involved. If we follow the money and determine, after analysis, how votes are bought, that's not the type of system that represents all Americans and will not work for the long term. With the amount and level of challenges that we face, with the increasing speed with which everything happens, we have to make some progress in campaign contributions.

Taxes

Americans pay a huge tax burden to live in this country. As recently as 1948, only two percent of the average wage went to federal tax.

Today, taxes of all shapes and sizes have made the effective tax rate somewhere near 50% or half of the family gross income. Tax rates can vary from state to state, but combined with federal taxes can be as high as 42% and as low as 35% in those states with low or no tax. Even a 35% corporate rate places America at a disadvantage to countries with lower tax rates, like France, Italy, Spain, Australia, and the United Kingdom. For those companies seeking a competitive advantage, check out Ireland, with a 12 corporate tax rate, or Hungary, Turkey, Poland, and Iceland, with about a 20% rate. Switzerland has a 21% rate, while Austria and the Netherlands come in at 25%. The U.S. **federal tax code** today covers 17,000 pages and has over 700 different taxpayer forms. The IRS estimates Americans spend 5.1 billion hours annually merely preparing their taxes.[262]

Over the last decade, almost every member of the European Union has **cut** its corporate tax rates.[263] In the meantime, America's top federal corporate tax rate has not been cut in over a decade. However, the top federal corporate tax rate is rarely paid. Surveying the Fortune 500 companies that made a profit each year from 2001 to 2003, the vast majority pays considerably less than the 35% top rate. About half of the companies, 275 of them, paid less than half that rate and 82 paid zero or less in federal income taxes in at least one year. How do they do that? Through accounting methods such as accelerated depreciation, accounting for tax credits, or offshore tax sheltering, U.S. companies are experts at avoiding tax. Using the effective U.S. corporate tax rate of about 25%, that rate is less than Germany, Japan, and Canada.

It would be difficult to think of reducing taxes at a time when federal budget deficits are so large. However, taxes are a large cost of doing business and can be an incentive for certain businesses or industries to relocate, or continue to be located here.

Trash

Every year, the U.S. creates more trash than anyplace else on earth. However, the Green Revolution might have woken up the slumbering giant. According to BioCycle, an environmental website, in their annual "State of Garbage in America," an estimated total of 400,000,000 tons of garbage was generated in 2008. That represents about a ton of garbage per person and is an increase of about 25 million tons since the survey in 2006.[264] Of this amount, 28% is now recycled and composted, with 7% used in waste to energy plants. The remaining 65% was land-filled. There are almost 2,000 landfills in the United States, whereas there were only 103 waste-to-energy plants, but they are on the increase.

Waste management in the United States is in a state of disarray with no effective federal plan to maximize recycling and energy usage while minimizing waste. Many states do not report the number of landfills or usage, so in order to define the problem, experts work with incomplete statistics. Many waste disposal services are private and utilize off-site or unpermitted landfills and incinerators. However, the tide is turning, and recycling is up! Accounting for only 8% of total municipal waste in 1990, recycling was measured to be 33% of municipal waste or more in 2005.[265]

Recycling helps prevent greenhouse gas emissions and saves energy. Since resources are limited in the world, we must address the problem of resource overconsumption. It is clear that the world cannot live as Americans do today. We must go back to the drawing board and redesign our products so that they are either consumable or recyclable. It is not only a matter of saving the environment, but a matter of business. America is running to catch up to the Green Revolution.

Yes, even great countries don't do everything great, and the U.S. is no exception. We have to come up with ways to think and do better!

13. Directions

"The greatest challenge facing mankind is the challenge of distinguishing reality from fantasy, truth from propaganda. Perceiving the truth has always been a challenge to mankind, but in the information age it takes on a special urgency and importance."

—Michael Crichton, Author, Commonwealth Club, September 2003

We have quite a challenge ahead of us. The future of the world depends on it, certainly the future of human civilization. The fact that there is no hard evidence of life outside of our earth may mean that the future of intelligent living beings also depends on it. That is a lot of pressure.

We are entering the information era of human civilization. Innovation across all industries will grow exponentially. Predictions and projections will be less reliable in such a fast moving world. We are moving faster than we ever have before. It will be crucial to change with the times. It will difficult for non-market based societies to keep up. Humans make mistakes. Little ones are better than big ones. Our societies should be set up to minimize the effect that one human error can cause by allowing more people in on the decision-making. In the United States there are 300 million people making important market decisions every day. Decision making is quite dispersed. Markets make trial and error decisions every day, adjusting to new information. In socialist societies, several select people determine the direction of the masses in an ivory tower. Even the madness of the crowd will most likely be better than a mad man at the helm.

It's easy to suggest things to do, but it's much harder to actually do them. Granted, trend lines are generally not straight. There tend to be wiggles around the general trend that sometimes create an uncertainty as to whether that trend will continue. It is important to recognize the forces that will perpetuate the trend. The long-term trend of globalization and increasing wealth will not be challenged, but it is difficult sometimes to see that through the battles of an economic downturn. The huge debt that we've taken on in this country and Americans' appetite for borrowing is the largest issue of the day and will determine how we will recover from the Great Recession. However, it's simply stupid to think that the short-term trend lines of the last few years will continue forever. A market economy adjusts, and so will we.

In 2008, the market economy was lying on the floor, having just experienced a total knockout. Markets were frozen. By whom? Well, there have been some scapegoats, but mostly they're free and living on easy street today. Profiteers made money, lots of money! And it will be a long time before the rest of us sort out the whole mess. But we do know where it began; it began with subprime mortgages: the lack of regulation, the aggressiveness of lenders, the mortgage originators, the securitization companies, and, finally, the investors who were duped by flashy salespeople. There was this faith in market systems that came at us from the very top. From the Fed to the committees of market regulators, this freedom and nirvana came from blindly following free markets. Hopefully that era is over.

How do we rebuild faith in markets systems and restore confidence and trust among people and participants? The Fed has done its job in stepping in as private enterprise was stepping out. We have definitely averted a bigger failure and something far worse than imaginable. What have we done to prevent another market failure? The next crisis of confidence will be in the governments that have taken on too much debt. This challenge is already upon us. Remember, there is ten times the amount of derivatives in the world than in world annual economic growth. Ten times. With this amount in financial derivates we have created a system that is more leveraged. This structure is based more on the status quo continuing than for unexpected, random, material events. Black swans are more likely. We have built more risk in the system and it has been evidenced by large failures every five years. The crash of 1987, the Asian contagion, the Long Term Capital crisis, the tech boom, the housing bubble and now the sovereign debt problem. We have been having hundred year floods every few years. It will continue. The world is not getting less complicated.

If confidence is lost, the market based economy falls apart quickly. Trust is based on not only who you are trading with but with the rules and regulations that will guide your transaction. Not all regulation is good, but good regulation is needed. Dynamic thinking is required. There need to be circuit breakers that prevent the whole system from collapsing. Companies need to be able to fail. It's part of the market system. We cannot just stand around and wait for bubbles to form and then just pick up the pieces. We need to be able to focus our financial radar on risk taking and speculation to be able to let the air out of bubbles more slowly. Knowing "where" to look is a start. Knowing "how" to look is what we need to work on. Markets do have this tendency to swing from positive to negative, and rarely stay right in the middle, but markets work better than governments. It's that simple.

Without the Fed's rapid movements, the money supply would have contracted, trust would have quickly deteriorated further, and banks would have failed. The weekend that Lehman failed, Merrill Lynch was bought by Bank of America, and AIG needed government assistance was the point in time of **no return**. If the Fed allowed them all to fail, who knows where we would be today? A whole lot worse off. There was an interconnectivity to everything that was not anticipated. In fact, the real world was much more chaotic than the mathematical equations predicted. Yes, the system was saved, but at what price? We survived and live to see another day, but need to analyze what has happened in order to prevent something like it in the future. Have we learned a lesson from this experience, or has anything really changed?

So, who is paying the cost? Well, of course, you and me! By bailing out the banks and investment houses, the Federal Reserve has also flooded the system with money and lowered interest rates to historical levels. How does zero percent interest feel? Yes, the investors of short-term money market funds, especially those that invest in high-quality, safe investments, have bore the brunt of the crisis. At zero percent, inflation is eating away at your purchasing power. Knowing that retirees typically invest the majority of their money in fixed income investments, it is the senior citizen who is feeling the pain the most. So the banks and brokers are free and easy, and our grandmothers and grandfathers are feeling the pinch. That's simply not fair. Something's got to change! The political system today is far too unsophisticated to understand these complex financial matters and too dependent on financial company contributions to keep an open mind and draw a hard line.

Speculation is part of human emotion. It can be called greed when one individual seeks profits only for themselves, or for those they represent, at the cost of others. Rampant speculation without any regulatory guiderails is damaging because there are no repercussions. Hedge funds controlled assets equal to the value of all the stocks in the U.S. market at the end of 2008. Now, wouldn't it be nice to know where this risk is concentrated? If you were running the United States, wouldn't you want to know where that money was? Some regulatory body needs to understand where the risk is, where the bets are being placed, and how big the bets are.

Financial innovation is not the enemy; in fact, it is a lot of what made America great and made the world grow, and will continue to do so in the future. It must be understood, though. The government's role in financial innovation is to shepherd resources, and encourage or discourage certain types of speculation and plot direction. When it came to people owning homes, securitization was good. However, it was brought to an unimaginable level. People who shouldn't have owned homes were talked into the American dream. Their incomes did not justify these purchases. They were simply based on ever-rising home values, nothing more. That ended the music and everyone had to find a chair in which to sit.

The shadow banking system is injured but not broken. The institutions that securitize mortgages, credit card debt, automobile loans and other liabilities are operating at minimal volume levels. Those that used to buy such securities, banks and pension plans, are now quite skeptical of these investments, and can you blame them? Confidence and trust among buyers and sellers has to return before these markets return to health. Reform will go a long way to restoring confidence. Securitization is going to be helpful in dissipating the risks of single-credit borrowers and providing liquidity to the mortgage market. The volatility of financial institutions should be decreased by making them look more like banks and less like hedge funds.

Picking up the pieces from this mess is a challenge. There is a monster that we have created: the debt incurred in the cleanup. The debt could become an anchor against future growth. In addition to the borrowing that's already in existence, there are the enormous entitlement obligations that this country will face in the future. This president or the next needs to be a financial analyst, do the math, and figure out ways to reduce this debt and entitlement burden.

The government could learn a lot from Wal-Mart and FedEx. After 9/11, we found out that our fire, police, emergency, and state authorities are not connected as well as they should be. This one's a no-brainer! When Katrina hit the city of New Orleans, we also found that top officials had not dealt effectively, efficiently, or immediately with the problem. No one at the top realized the magnitude of the situation. Our economy should be interconnected from our defense systems, medical facilities, and our schools. It is government's responsibility to respond to "tale events," those infrequent occurrences of large magnitude, both good and bad. It is an informational problem to determine if an event is large enough in magnitude from the norm. We should be an expert at determining bubbles before an impending crisis hits, and have the ability to act quickly when one is identified.

The United States is the leader in freedom. Innovation begins with an idea and a discussion of that thought. Without the freedom to assemble and discuss, innovation is lost. The smartest man in the world would be little benefit to society if he couldn't express his opinions. With our open and networked society, we will have access to the best ideas from most far-off places in the world. With immigrants from just about every country to the U.S. learning of our products and services, and keeping their ties back home, we will be inter-connected to the world.

The government should identify areas needing improvement and encourage activity and innovation with targeted tax breaks and research and development grants. Our research and development focus is part of our economy's fabric. A market-based system requires an obsession with what is sold. Profitability drives what is made. The federal government does have the ability to incentivize the private sector to spend on innovation. Expenses for research and development should be rewarded. It is a long-term investment._

The world is in a long upswing that is technology-driven and spills over into many, if not all, industries. A characteristic of a long wave upturn is that expansions tend to be long and strong, and recessions are short and mild. Surprises tend to be on the upside. The aftermath of the financial crisis of 2008 has brought on fears of a depression, or at least a double dip recession. Information is simply traveling faster than it ever has before, and the world will adjust much more quickly than experts and economists believe. Comparisons with the 1930s are almost irrelevant. The size and speed of issues today are unprecedented. We need to be alert, insightful, and adept with problems of the day. Adjustment is the key. There is nobody in the world today that really knows what is going to happen. If you think that they know, you are just kidding yourself. We really are in uncharted waters and every day new data will emerge that will guide us.

The problems that we face have very few similar reference points in history. The issues of today are the largest the world has ever seen. There are massive forces colliding with one another and it is difficult to see which side will eventually overwhelm the other.

Market versus Socialism

We have made the case that market systems work better. They will, in the course of evolution, make mistakes that are usually corrected quickly. Socialist systems have no market system displaying prices as information. There is no feedback loop telling the producers what to produce. In history, socialist systems work well, until they don't. Usually the mistakes are catastrophic. Like an earthquake that has been building up pressure for many years without release, socialist systems end up taking longer to correct imbalances and making big mistakes. Prediction - Market systems will be the predominant economic system in the world but will be influenced by socialist and national policies in market failures, social direction and overall resource management.

Poor versus Rich

We must bring everyone with us. Demographic trends point to a rapidly increasing poor population. The developed world is shrinking. The U.S. will benefit greatly from world growth and must pull along the impoverished. Simple things like improved food and water will help the poorer half of the world population. Education and information flows will further assist them in a better life. Their future also has endless possibilities. As newcomers to the world economy they will gravitate to American products. There will be an enormous benefit to our country if world growth continues upward. We have a vested interest in it. Prediction – The poorer areas of the world will benefit greatly from simple improvements in water delivery, health care and agriculture bringing a more vibrant and civilized society to most parts of the world. The middle class will continue to grow rapidly favoring global trade.

Debt versus Innovation

The debt that we have incurred is enormous but not crippling. American citizens will take a long time re-positioning themselves from the housing crisis. We are over the worst of the fallout, but there are several more years of housing inventory that has not yet hit the market for sale. Banks are reluctant to put properties for sale at big mark downs. Additionally, many more mortgages will reset and fall under water. With the high unemployment rate, the commercial real estate market may not recover quickly either. The government has taken on a lot of debt that will alter the flow of resources. Tax rates will rise, not a good thing economically speaking. Fortunately, non-financial corporations are in good shape. Due to the uncertainty in the past decade, corporations have hoarded cash and pulled back on capital spending. Interest rates are low which makes possible projects more viable. Prediction - Innovation will continue its rapidly upward pace from lean and cash rich corporations as consumers retrench and the government figures out future payment plans for its obligations.

Money Flows

The Asian economies will continue to accumulate reserves. China will take its slow and steady path to increase the value and convertibility of the Yuan over time. China's exchange rate policy has led to strong export production at the cost of other countries. There is excess production capacity in the world and some of these other countries may retaliate. Recent shocks to the Euro and Yen have once again favored the Dollar as the currency to invest in. The amount of debt outstanding by the developed economies will pressure officials to create inflation. Investors will continue to seek other investments for capital preservation. Prediction – The US dollar will continue its long downward decline as the world currency after several years of sideways movement after the shocks of 2008. It will take years if not decades to bring the Yuan into world acceptance.

Economics

The mathematicians have been sent back to school. Behavioral scientists are the new world economists. The Austrian school of economics which questions the predictability of human behavior becomes more main stream. The world view of economics will incorporate both math and chaos. Securitization will not be so dependent on models and allow for more variation in human behavior. We are unpredictable, spontaneous and non-linear in our thinking and behavior. Prediction - The economics profession is more respected even though it is less reliable in forecasting.

Energy

Energy is our biggest challenge to economic development. There is a lack of energy resources in the world that needs to be address quickly. Oil is the primary means to transportation and is in short supply. We must create more hybrid, natural gas and ethanol vehicles to slow the rapid consumption of what oil is left in the world. Switching to alternatives will not be easy. Nuclear power electricity is the best answer but requires long lead times and large budgets. Wind, solar and geo-thermal are advancing and growing but will not be able to met new additional demand. There are other forms and structures that we must push further up the road to providing fuel. Prediction – Oil remains the predominant means for transportation and only high and sustainable prices bring new solutions for energy usage.

Government

The business of government is about budgets and entitlements and they need to be negotiated down. The developed world needs to understand this or else face the prospect of default, where all obligations are subject to change without warning. Politicians must change their thinking of today and make changes that will affect this country tomorrow. Financial expertise will become more important in elections. Prediction – The entitlement war is just beginning and will last long into the next generation as new employees are not given such generous retirement and health benefits.

Education

We are the "information economy." Anything having to do with information flow, data crunching, and interconnectivity, we should lead. Public schools should be multidisciplined and have several learning tracks, not just "college bound". We excel at obtaining, distributing, and analyzing information, and it should show at the primary school level. Multi-tasking, statistics and finance should be taught at middle school. We are currently educating students for jobs that don't yet exist, without any job description that we can comprehend in today's world. A student today by the eighth grade has probably been exposed to more information than a college student just a decade ago. A college student today has more information at their fingertips than world leaders did. The information age is connecting and educating more people every day. Prediction – Our higher level education breaks new ground in innovation, collaboration and management and requires elementary education to better prepare students for the information age.

Worldviews

Our two views of the world, of mathematical equations in relativity theory and the chaos of particle physics, will become more intertwined. Although not an elegant elaborate predictable model of how the universe works, it is our view of reality for now. "The mistake of science is to pretend everything is a clock when the world is more like a cloud" [266] We have become experts on the left side of the brain, processing information in a linear, predictable manner. What we need to work on is the creative side. The brain works well because it is a combination of the two. It is how we should construct our social systems, based on mathematical models but with the ability to recognize and respond to random but material events. Prediction – The world view of scientists will incorporate the two present conflicting paradigms as one, both math and chaos co-existing.

Globalization

There's a struggle in world trade against the forces of openness and interconnectedness. America's interests lie in opening the world economy more from a strong, rules-based multinational trading system. America's leadership is more important today because of the large role of information flow in this increasingly interconnected planet. Information is our business. The retrieval, analysis, evaluation, and decision-making of information are how market systems work in America and beyond. With more connections in the world economy, the complexity of our economic systems becomes more difficult to manage from the top. As capital is free to move to wherever conditions are the most favorable, it is an advantage to America's economy. Prediction - America is in the best position of any country in the world to take advantage of information-based, market systems.

The United States has led the way for decades promoting free trade and globalization. It is important that we don't take a step back and create barriers to entry and heightened tariffs. Trade and innovation are connected at the hip, as ideas move freely back and forth across borders, a circle of feedback loops is created. Free trade is the path to world growth and America's position as the leader in trade will continue to make our country the place where discovery and innovation happen. Not only will the world economy perform better and grow more quickly through globalization, but countries tend to be more stable when there is a liberal, open, international economy. Globalization is about the free exchange of information and countries that limit this interaction will suffer.

In Darwinian theory, the justification for a mutation is that it may be more capable of survival in the future. The same is true for societies and cultures, forms that are in constant evolution due to new ideas, with democracies being more responsive to change. The notion of a better human future is not a guarantee. It is seldom known which change in direction will eventually result in better outcomes. Remaining attached to the present or past is not the way to progress. It will not give someone the ability to dream of the possibilities of the future. Whether it is certain (remaining attached to what is real and what has happened,) or if it is about hope (some positive expectation of the future), Americans must choose every day which way to think.

It's up to us! In a sense, no other country has been a leader like we have. Americans have a tremendous responsibility to lead the world by example and by actions. We cannot be so focused on ourselves; we need to be more understanding of other viewpoints and welcome people into our melting pot. Immigration will grow this country stronger and keep our dynamic quilt work of human ingenuity going. Just like the molecular particles of life itself, we need to be aware of all that is going on around us and make sure we do our part. The future of the world depends on it.

The resources of the world are constrained now and, with additional population growth, will become even more so. Our world is not limitless. However, those alive today are experiencing the largest parabolic shift upward in innovation and knowledge that the world has ever seen. What will it bring? Our collective imagination is the only barrier. A hundred years from now, our society will look as primitive as barbarians look today. Two hundred years? Let's hope we have the fortitude to manage the world through this innovative era and resource dependency.

Investors need to understand these changes and challenges in the world and be prepared for failure as well as success. This is a new world and the old styles of solving investment problems will not be as effective. The S&P500 was your father's index. Your index is the MSCI All Country World with a healthy dose of alternatives and absolute return strategies. For a world in so much disarray, a good investment advisor and network of specialists in insurance, taxes, estate planning and overall household management is a necessity. Long term relationships are the key to good communication. Do not think you can go it alone.

The world is in the most unpredictable state it has ever been. The massive amount of debt and savings flowing around the world is becoming increasingly complex. History books are a good guide for human behavior but are of little help for the modern day, fast paced investor. We must keep an open mind to accept new ideas from multiple sources. We must push ourselves to listen to the other viewpoints to verify the strength or weakness of our own position. It will be a difficult time to just rely on the "status quo".

More than anything, the future is uncertain. It is not pre-ordained. Massive shifts in demographics, politics, religions, technology, money and power are all upon us. It is the most uncertain time to invest in, but most likely one of tremendous opportunity. There are changes coming that only science fiction writers can dream about today. You will want to understand as much as you can about these developments when they arise. A healthy dose of weekly reading is required for the investor.

It is the nature of humans to confront decisions and challenges with a trial-and-error process. That means mistakes will happen until a successful solution is found. Correcting these mistakes is often difficult and admitting that you are wrong goes against human nature. Little mistakes are better than big ones. We are human. We will make mistakes. The problems that we will confront in this generation and next are going to come at us with a size and speed that is unprecedented in human history. It will be vital to have an economic and social system that responds to change and adjusts to errors quickly. A constant feedback loop is needed that can take ideas and nurture them into productive actions.

We are at the point of "lift-off" from the physical world to the mental, from building things to designing them where information, calculation and analysis will be highly valued. Modern life is all about information and communication. Innovation is a social process of communicating ideas, refining them through discourse and improving them through discovery. It is not the leadership of one person or even one nation that will propel the world to new heights, but the wisdom of the crowd with each participant being an expert in their own field of endeavor, contributing to the whole. A market-based system. The innovation wave will continue at a rapidly increasing pace, which will create disparities around us. Overall, it will be an exciting time to experience and learn.

Understand the world in which you live and be *up on America*!

Appendix

Global Macro Investment Trends
Secular Themes
Ideas that Are Long-Term, Predictable, and Investable
(Three-to-Five-Year Target)

Emerging Markets

- Emerging markets are growing faster than the developed markets.
- The world's middle class is growing and demanding non-essential consumer goods.
- Democracy is spreading around the world, which brings freedom and open markets.

Broadband

- Global explosion of data traffic networks and linking of global consumers
- Retail sales on the Internet will continue to increase and change trends.
- Personalization using advertising technology to identify buying instincts
- Smart phones are becoming portable computers and are empowering people.

Biotech

- There is a revolution occurring in drug discovery from chemicals to bio-genomics.
- Biotech is 20% of total US. drug sales. In 5-10 years, that could climb to 30-40%

- Nano-technology and robotics are also revolutions occurring to further health care.

Energy

- There is a lack of fossil fuel in the world to power the world's future growth.
- The U.S. sits on an enormous amount of natural gas that could be utilized better
- Government incentives will be increased to producers of clean forms of energy.
- The next energy sources must be discovered rapidly in nuclear, wind, solar, and waves.

Global Savings

- Developed economies will continue to seek capital from developing ones
- Large unregulated, international investment pools are searching for good investments.
- Savings flows can distort market movements and reinforce trends.
- Technical analysis can help identify where money is flowing.

Demographics

- Large population growth in the poorest countries and religions with less flexibility
- Smaller working populations in more developed countries without immigration
- Cities in emerging markets don't have sufficient services to support them.

Agriculture

- Demographic trends will mean large population growth in poorer countries.
- The growing middle class of the world is demanding higher-level food products.
- Climate change may have adverse repercussions for feeding the world.

Infrastructure

- The U.S. will be reinvesting in roads, bridges, tunnels, and public transport.
- The emerging economies will be building out their own infrastructure.

Innovation

- The world is in the most inventive period in its history with change accelerating.
- Countries and companies that are able to change will prosper.

Currency

- U.S. dollar leadership will give way to a basket of currencies and commodity approach.
- The world will be in a state of adjustment as the yuan rises to become more market-based

Debt

- De-leveraging will continue for many years as debt was extended without credit or value

For more information,
contact:

uponamerica@aol.com

Famous Last Words

"This 'telephone' has too many shortcomings to be seriously considered as a means of communication. The device is inherently of no value to us."
—Western Union internal memo, 1876

"Heavier than air flying machines are impossible."
—Lord Kelvin, president of the Royal Society, 1895

"Everything that can be invented has been invented."
—Charles H. Duell, director of the U.S. Patent Office, 1899

"That the automobile has practically reached the limit of its development is suggested by the fact that during the past year no improvements of a radical nature have been introduced."
—Scientific American, 1909

"Who the hell wants to hear actors talk?"
—Harry M. Warner, Warner Bros. Pictures, 1927

"Stocks have reached what looks like a permanently high plateau."
—Irving Fisher, professor of economics at Yale University, 1929

"There is not the slightest indication that [nuclear energy] will ever be obtainable. It would mean that the atom would have to be shattered at will."
—Albert Einstein, 1932

"I think there is a world market for maybe five computers."
—Thomas Watson, chairman of IBM, 1943

"Video won't be able to hold on to any market it captures after the first six months. People will soon get tired of staring at a plywood box every night."
—Daryl F. Zanuck, 20th Century Fox, 1946

"We don't like their sound, and guitar music is on the way out."
—Decca Recording Co. rejecting the Beatles, 1962

Additional Sources of Information

BCA Research	Economic data	www.bcaresearch.com
Brookings Institution	Public policy	www.brookings.edu
Cato Institute	Public policy	www.cato.org
Chart of the Day	Economic charts	www.chartoftheday.com
CIA Fact Book		www.cia.gov/library/publications /the-world-factbook
Don Tapscott	Capitalism and Technology	www.dontapscott.com
Economagic	Economic data	www.economagic.com
Heritage Foundation	Public policy	www.heritage.org
International Monetary Fund	Global government	www.imf.org
Lemelson Foundation	Innovation	www.lemelson.org
Peter G. Peterson Foundation	Fiscal responsibility	www.pgpf.org
PIMCO	Investment Commentary	www.pimco.com
Ray Kurzweil	Future and lifestyle	kurzweilai.net
Real Clear Markets	Investment News	www.realclearmarket.com
Stratfor	Global forecasts	www.stratfor.com
Thoughts from the Frontline	Commentary	www.frontlinethoughts.com
White House	Government	www.whitehouse.gov
Up with America	American spirit	www.upwithamerica.org
US Debt Clock	U.S. fiscal position	www.usdebtclock.org
Visualizing Economics	Data	www.visualizingeconomics. com/category/bls

Other News sources: The Economist, The Wall Street Journal, Forbes, Fortune, The New York Times, The Financial Times, Business Week

About the Author

Richard Catts has been immersed in the investment management business for over thirty years. He is a friend and partner to some of the largest and most successful financial advisors in the investment community.

Throughout his career, Rick has been involved in all aspects of the investment process, from the actual management of portfolios to trading, security analysis, sales, and client service. Most recently, he was a senior portfolio manager at Alliance Bernstein, where he participated on several large investment committees. He began his career as a portfolio manager at a Philadelphia-based trust company at the age of twenty-five. He became an adjunct professor in the MBA program at St. Joseph's University and education chair of the Financial Analysts of Philadelphia. He rose to become one of the most respected representatives of an investment firm within the advisor community.

Rick has spoken at national conferences, appeared on TV and radio, and has conducted thousands of seminars and client meetings. He is an industry veteran and pioneer within the separately managed account business, in which portfolios are individually managed for both families and institutions.

Rick holds a bachelor's of science in economics from the University of Delaware, and a master's of science in finance from Temple

University. He holds the Chartered Financial Analyst designation, the highest degree attainable in investment management. He is also a member of the Investment Management Consultants Association.

Rick lives with his wife, Ann, and their two daughters, Melanie and Madeline, in Valley Forge, Pennsylvania.

Footnotes

[1] Throughout this book, I use the term "Americans." The standard way to refer to a citizen of the United States is as an "American." North America includes Canada and Mexico. They are part of the fabric of the United States of America. They are technically Americans as well, and share in our aspirations, growth, and ideals. For the purposes of this book, "Americans" will refer to the people of the United States.

[2] "Who Were History's Greatest Leaders?, *Time*, July 15, 19974, Jules Masserman, an American psychoanalyst, quoted on the website, www.time.com/time/magazine/article/0,9171,879377-3,00.html

[3] William F. Baker, Ph.D., and Michael O'Malley, Ph.D., *Leading with Kindness, How Good People Consistently Get Good Results*, Amacon, 2008

[4] The Global 2000, *Forbes*, April 2009, Royal Dutch Shell ranking, www.forbes.com

[5] "Americans Turn More Isolationist", *Philadelphia Inquirer*, December, 4, 2009, citing Pew Research study, www.philly.com/inquirer/world_us/78497922.html

[6] Pew Research study, Pew Research Center, www.pewresearch.org/pubs/1428/america-seen-less-important-china-more-powerful-isolationist-sentiment-surges (December 3, 2009)

[7] Arnold Schwarzenegger's speech to the Republican National Convention at Madison Square Garden, August 31, 2004, www.gov.ca.gov/speech/2889

[8] Hoover Institution, Facts on Policy, Homeownership Rates, www.hoover.org/research/factsonpolicy/facts/26963064.html, (September, 2009)

[9] From a study by Income Mobility in the U.S. from 1996 to 2005, Report of the Department of the Treasury, November 13, 2007, www.americanthinker.com, (September, 2009)

10   The American Dream, www.wikipedia.org/wiki/american_dream, (October 2009)

11   Oprah Winfrey, www.Wikipedia.org/wiki/oprah_winfrey, (October 2009)

12   Mchael Jordan, www.Wikipedia.org/wiki/michael_jordan, (October 2009)

13   Henry Kissinger, www.wikipedia.org/wiki/henry_kissinger, (October 2009)

14   Barack Obama, www.wikipedia.org/wiki/barack_obama, (October 2009)

15   Sergey Brin,www.wikipedia.org/wiki/sergey_brin, (October 2009)

16   Sergey Brin,www.wikipedia.org/wiki/sergey_brin, (October 2009)

17   Thomas J. Stanley, Ph.D., and William D. Danko, Ph.D., *The Millionaire Next Door: The Surprising Secrets of American's Wealthy*, MJF Books, September, 2003

18   U.S. Bureau of Economic Analysis, National Income and Product Accounts Table, Gross Domestic Product, December 22, 2009, www.bea.gov

19   The United States, trade, www.globaltenders.com/economy-united-states.htm, (October, 2009)

20   U.S. Bureau of Economic Analysis, National Income and Product Accounts Table, Gross Domestic Product, www.bea.gov, December 22, 2009

21   World Fact Book of the United Nations,*www.cia.gov/library/.../the-**world-factbook***

22   United States, www.wikipedia.org/wiki/united_states

23   Federal Highway Administration, *Our Nation's Highways*, Rough Guides travel book series, www. wiki.answers.com

24   Ranking of countries' armed forces and infrastructure, www.globalfirepower.com

25   U.S. Bureau of Economic Analysis, National Income and Product Accounts, 2008, www.bea.gov

26   United States, www.wikipedia.org/wiki/united_states

27   United States, www.wikipedia.org/wiki/united_states

28   Market values as of September 2009, www.Yahoo/finance.com

29   United States, www.wikipedia.org/wiki/united_states

30   United States, www.wikipedia.org/wiki/united_states

31   United States, www.wikipedia.org/wiki/united_states

32   World Population Policies 2005, United Nations, Department of Economic and
      Social Affairs, March 2006, www.un.org

33   "A Ponzi Scheme that Works," *The Economist*, December 19, 2009

34   United States, www.wikipedia.org/wiki/united_states

35   CIA World Factbook, List of Country GDP, www.cia.gov/library/publications/
      the-world-factbook/fields/2195.html?countryName=&countryCode=&region
      Code=%3E, (April, 2010)

36   Trade and Investment Opportunities in China, Asean Co-operationwww.asean-
      cooperation.com/trade-and-investment...in-china/286/ - (September, 2009)

37   Huang Zhe, "In Depth, China Business," *Businessweek*, November 2, 2009

38   "Chimerica" is a term coined by Niall Ferguson and Moritz Schularick describ-
      ing the symbiotic relationship between China and the United States, www.
      en.wikipedia.org/wiki/Chimerica

39   Big Mac Index, *Businessweek*

40   James Miles, "China and the West, A Time for Muscle Flexing," *The Economist*,
      March 19, 2009

41   Niall Ferguson, "The Trillion-Dollar Question: China or America?", www.tele-
      graph.co.uk, June 1, 2009

42   Macquarie Research Commodities, "China to act as the key driver of the com-
      modities market for the next year," www.im-mining.com

43   China Briefing, "China Overtakes Japan as World's Second-largest Oil Importer,"
      www.china-briefing.com/news/2008/06/26/china-overtakes-japan-as-worlds-
      second-largest-oil-importer.html

44   Hugh Hendry, *Investment Outlook*, November 2009

45   "Land of the Setting Sun, Japan as Number One," *The Economist*, November 14,
      2009

46   Richard Koo, Leslie P. Norton, "A Japanese Rx for the West: Keep Spending,"
      Barron's, January 4, 2010

47   Jerzy Linderski, "Imperium sine fine: T. Robert S. Broughton and the Roman
      Republic", Steiner, 1996

⁴⁸ Cullen Murphy, "Are We Rome? The fall of an empire and the fate of America" Houghton Mifflin Harcourt (May 10, 2007)

⁴⁹ Robert Reich, *Super-Capitalism*, (Vintage Books, 2007)

⁵⁰ The Manufacturing Institute, "The Facts about Modern Manufacturing," www.nam.org/~/media/AboutUs/ManufacturingInstitute/ FactsAboutModernManufacturingVer8.ashx

⁵¹ The Manufacturing Institute, "The Facts about Modern Manufacturing", www.nam.org/~/media/0F91A0FBEA1847D087E719EAAB4D4AD8.ashx

⁵² "Iceland nationalizes Glitnir bank," BBC News, www.news.bbc.co.uk

⁵³ "A New Pecking Order," G20 summit in April, www.indianexpress.com/news

⁵⁴ From a summary on India, www.ers.usda.gov/Briefing/India

⁵⁵ An un-named Bush official told Ron Suskind, www.thenation.com/doc/ 20050509/alterman

⁵⁶ Conference on innovation, Chicago 2007

⁵⁷ Lou Gestner, Conference on innovation, Chicago 2007

⁵⁸ *Encyclopedia Britannica*, definition of "economics," 2007

⁵⁹ Mark Thoma, "The 21st century will be the century of inductive economics," April 30, 2009, www.roubini.com/globalmacro-monitor

⁶⁰ The Audacious Epigone, Wednesday, March 12, 2008, www.anepigone. blogspot.com

⁶¹ Dr. David Kelly CFA, managing director, chief market strategist, J.P. Morgan funds, investing without precedent, September 8, 2009

⁶² Fareed Zakaria, "The Sky Isn't Falling," *Newsweek*, May 20, 2009

⁶³ John Maynard Keynes in his general theory of employment, 1936

⁶⁴ Tax rates of the U.S., 1930-40, www.bea.gov

⁶⁵ Christina Romer, chairwoman of Council of Economic Advisors, Economic Focus, The Lessons of 1937, June 20, 2009

⁶⁶ Ben Bernanke, talk to guests at celebration of Milton Freidman's birthday

⁶⁷ Jacob Marschak, "What Went Wrong with Economics", *The Economist*, July 16, 2009

[68] John Maynard Keynes, in his General Theory of Employment, Interest and Money, (CreateSpace, 2009) originally published in 1936

[69] Paul McCulley, Central Bank Focus, PIMCO, "The Shadow Banking System and Hyman Minsky's Economic Journey", May 2009

[70] Michael Lewis, "The Man Who Crashed the World," *Vanity Fair*, August 2009

[71] Michael Lewis, "The Man Who Crashed the World," *Vanity Fair*

[72] Quote by Charles O. Prince, Chairman of Citigroup, www.dealbook.blogs. nytimes.com/2007/07/10/citi-chief-on-buyout-loans-were-still-dancing/

[73] Mohamed El-Erian, PIMCO, Secular Outlook, May 2009, www.pimco.com

[74] Richard Koo, chief economist at Nomura Research Institute, as quoted by Prieur du Plessis, Investment Postcards from Cape Town, October 1, 2009, www.investmentpostcards.com

[75] Alan Greenspan at a congressional conference in 2008, blogs.worldbank.org/ publicsphere/category/tags/governance

[76] Niall Ferguson, *The Ascent Of Money*, (Penguin, 2007)

[77] Edmund Phelps, "Uncertainty doubles the best system," *The Financial Times, Ltd.*, April 14, 2009,

[78] Barry Eichengren in his book "The Last Temptation of Risk", (The National Interest, May , 2009)

[79] Beniot Mandelbrot and Nassim Nicholas Taleb, call of "wild randomness", www. math.yale.edu/mandelbrot/web_pdfs/mildvswild.pdf

[80] Sprout Asset Management, from Bloomberg, Bank Equity Leverage Calculations

[81] Harry Markowitz, "Modern Portfolio Theory, Financial Engineering and their Roles in Financial Crisis," CFA Institute, December 2009

[82] C.S. Venkatakrishnan, JP Morgan, "The Impact of the Financial Crisis on Asset Classes"

[83] Paul Krugman, "The Big Zero," *The New York Times*, December 28, 2009

[84] JP Morgan Guide to the Markets, 1Q, 2010

[85] Niall Ferguson, telegraph.co.uk, "The Trillion-Dollar Question: China or America?" June 1, 2009

86   James Burke, *The Day the Universe Changed*, (St. Martin's Press, 1985)

87   "The state of economics," *The Economist*, July 18, 2009, page 69

88   Paul McCulley, PIMCO

89   "The global economy," *The Economist*, September 22, 2007

90   "The totalitarian state against man," Count Coudenhove-Kalergi, 1935

91   Ichiro Hatoyama, "My political philosophy, the banner of party politician,"
     September 2009, www.scribd.com/doc/21587303/My-Political-Phylosophy-
     Essay-of-Yukio-Hatoyama

92   Michael Caine, www.ain'titcool news.com

93   Sidney Homer and Richard Sylla in *History of Interest Rates* by, fourth edition,
     (Wiley, 2005)

94   history of currency trading, October 2009, www.historyof.net

95   The dollar crisis and why, www.realtruth.org,

96   foreign exchange market, Wikipedia.com

97   Floyd Noris, "Weak dollar? Not so much in China," *New York Times*, October
     16, 2009

98   "A special report on the world economy," *The Economist*, October 3, 2009,
     page 24

99   David Kay, "The economic impact of changing demographics," *Investments and
     Wealth Monitor*, January/ February 2009, page 33

100 U.S. census, 2006

101 Percentage of Americans who were born or had one parent born in a foreign
     country, www.nytimes.com/2002/02/07/us/foreign-born-in-us-at-record-high.
     html?pagewanted=1

102 Twelve million may be the most popular number cited for illegal immigrants in
     the U.S. at present, but some estimates have it over 20 million, www.ohmygov.
     com/blogs/1265.aspx

103 Education in the U.S., Wikipedia.com

104 The State of Small Business, Report to the President, executive summary, 2009
     edition

[105] Jonathan R. Laing, "Is the sun setting on Japan?" *Barrons*, September 28, 2009

[106] Population of countries, www.overpopulation.org/culture.html

[107] United Nations Population estimates

[108] *The Economist*, July 25, 2009

[109] P. Malaney, Demographic change and poverty reduction, DHAKA conference, April 1999

[110] Allen L. Hammond , *Which World? Scenarios for the 21st Century*, (Island Press, 1998)

[111] Leo Buscalia, *Personhood, the art of being fully human*, (Charles B. Slack, Inc., 1978)

[112] Basic Religious origin and worldview from www.religionfacts.com

[113] Mahabharata, an epic of Indian history and part of the Hindu history

[114] Confucianism, www.wikipedia.com

[115] William Kashatus, *Philadelphia Inquirer* editorial, "Framers Envisioned Separation," December 3, 2009

[116] Christianity, www.wikipedia.com

[117] Pew Research Study – Religious Composition of the United States, 2007, www. religions.pewforum.org/pdf/affiliations-all-traditions.pdf

[118] A quote from Edgar Cayce, www.edgarcayce.org

[119] Muslim, www.wikipedia.com

[120] Abu Bakar Baasyir, founder of the Indonesian Mujahdeen, as quoted in article by Mark Bowden, "Struggle for the Soul of Islam: Inside Indonesia: In Indonesian Tug of War, Radical Islam Thrives on Democracy and Despair", April 19, 2007 *New York Times*, April 19, 2007

[121] Ali Allawi, *The Crisis of Islamic Civilization*, Yale University Press

[122] "Industrial design: Can governments help revive innovation and trade?" *The Economist*, October 3, 2009

[123] "The Innovator's DNA," *Harvard Business Review*, December 2009, www.hbr. org

[124] "Inside Innovation," *Businessweek* , October 5, 2009

[125]   Tim Brown, *Change by Design*, (Harper Business Publishing, 2009)

[126]   Tim Brown, "Change by Design," *Businessweek*, October 5, 2009

[127]   *Harvard Business Journal*, working paper on research, www.hbswk.hbs.edu/item/5441.html

[128]   Ray Kurzweil, *The Singularity Is Near*, (Penguin Books, 2005)

[129]   A quote attributed to Bill Gates, www.thinkexist.com

[130]   Dr. David Pensak with Elizabeth Licorish, *Innovation for Underdogs, How to Make the Leap From What If to What Now*, Career Press, October 2008

[131]   "Building a social network that pays," *Businessweek*, July 13, 2009

[132]   Nick Murray

[133]   Gary Brinson, UBS, Dow Jones asset management, The changing face of asset allocation, June 1999

[134]   Nassim Nicholas Taleb, *The Black Swan: The Impact of the Highly Improbable*, (Random House, 2007)

[135]   Andrew Bary, "Big Squeeze on Ivy League Endowments", *Barron's*, June 29, 2090

[136]   Citi investment research as of November 21, 2008

[137]   Alan Greenspan, *The Age of Turbulence*,(Penguin Press, 2007)

[138]   Dalbar, www.dalbar.com

[139]   Plan sponsor network and AllianceBernstein study of top-quartile managers, versus the S&P 500, in July 1998 through June 2008

[140]   All Country World Index, MSCI

[141]   Standard and Poors

[142]   R. David Ranson, Ph.D., and Penny M. Russell, "Six ironclad tenets for market-based forecasting," *Investments and Wealth Monitor*, January/February 2009

[143]   Cathie Wood, CIO, Strategic Research and Global Research Growth, AllianceBernstein

[144]   Greg Porter, Principal, Flippin, Bruce and Porter

[145]   United States Department of Agriculture, Reading Rooms, wheat, trade, October 27, 2009

[146]   United States agriculture, www.Wikipedia.com

[147] Josette Sheeran, Executive Director of the United Nations World Food Program, in a quote within an obituary, Washington Examiner, September, 14, 2009

[148] *Philadelphia Inquirer*, obituary, September 12, 2009

[149] Interbrand, "World's Best Global Brands"

[150] Bond Market, www.wikipedia.com

[151] Derivatives, www.wikipedia.com

[152] Stock market, November 2009, www.wikipedia.com

[153] Foreign exchange market, www.wikipedia.com

[154] Dollar, www.wikipedia.com

[155] Essential2business, November 2009, www.Americanchemistry.com

[156] American Chemistry Council, industry fact sheet, June 2009, www. Americanchemistry.com,

[157] Generating wealth of innovation, November 2009, www.Americanchemistry. com

[158] Deloitte, world's top 250 consumer product companies, www.deloite.com, press releases, November 13, 2009

[159] Wal-Mart, November 12, 2009, www.wikipedia.com

[160] Forbes, January 30, 2007

[161] Economic Report of the President, 2008

[162] Military Bases, www.wikipedia.com

[163] United States military strength, October 19, 2009, www.Global firepower.com

[164] *60 Minutes*, www.CBS news.com, August 16, 2009

[165] "Overkill: China is piling up more weapons than it appears to need, a special report on China and America," *The Economist*, October 24, 2009

[166] Alliance Bernstein estimates

[167] Fareed Zakaria, "The Post-American World," (W.W. Norton and Company, 2007), page 190

[168] Times higher education, world university rankings, November 2009, www.wiki-pedia.com

169 "The case for optimism," *Businessweek*, August 24, 2009

170 "On shaky foundations: Germany's mediocre universities," *The Economist*, June 27, 2009

171 "Education and the Arab world, Liger trying to catch up," *The Economist*, October 17, 2009

172 "Pakistan sees a big growth in private schools," *Philadelphia Inquirer*, November 8, 2009

173 United States, popular media, www.wikipedia.com

174 Justin Lahart, "Has the financial industry's heyday come and gone?" *Wall Street Journal*, April 20, 2008

175 Industry employment, Monthly Labor Review, November 2001

176 "Market fatigue, the Anglo-Saxon model has taken a knock, special report on the world economy," *The Economist*, October 3, 2009

177 In Pursuit of Happiness Research. Is It Reliable? What Does It Imply for Policy? The Cato institute. April 11, 2007

178 *Freedom in the World*, (Freedom House, 2007)

179 "Eastern Europe's media woes, shut up or be sued," *The Economist*, October 24, 2009.

180 "Italy and the Free Press, mostly in the messengers," *The Economist*, October 3, 2009

181 *Guinness Book of World Records*

182 Population Estimates on www.Internetworldstats.com

183 Commentary on www.Levitt Brothers.com blog, October 7, 2009

184 Insurance premiums in the world, www.ifsl.org.uk/upload/Insurance_2009.pdf, PDF page 2

185 American Lawyers Association for 2007

186 Brazil's Lawyer Regulation Organization, OAB

187 Nathalie Martin, *The Role of History and Culture Developing Bankruptcy and Insolvency Systems: the Perils of Legal Transplantation*, Social Science Research Network, www.papers.ssrn.com/sol3/papers.cfm?abstract_id=1444531

[188] Megan McArdle, "Sink and Swim, Bankruptcy helps the undeserving—and that's the way it should be," *The Atlantic*, June 2009

[189] Generating wealth through innovation, November 2009, www.American chemistry.com

[190] United States, language, www.wikipedia.com

[191] History of English language, www.anglik.net/englishlanguagehistory.htm

[192] English, The International Language of the Internet?, www.als-alexander.org/languageInternet1.htm

[193] Data on airport activity, www.airports.org/cda/

[194] Federal Express 2008 annual report, message from the chairman, page 11

[195] Dr. Angelo Hullman, "The economic development of nanotechnology—and indicators-based analysis," European commission, DG research, November 28, 2006

[196] Zakaria, "The Post-American world"

[197] U.S. Chamber of Commerce, nanotechnology, summary of the issue, November 4, 2009

[198] Richard Reeves, *Businessweek*, June 2009

[199] Corriere della Sera, Father Gieussani, *Traces*, volume 5, number 3, pages 39-40

[200] Michael E. Scheier and Charles S. Carver, "This positional optimism and physical well-being: The influence of generalized outcomes expectancies on health," *Journal of Personality*, 55

[201] "That irrepressible American optimism," *Forbes*, February 27, 2009

[202] Dan Ariely, "The curious paradox of optimism bias," *Businessweek*, August 24, 2009

[203] Development aid rose in 2009 and most donors will meet 2010 aid targets, www.OEDC.org

[204] Report on Global Philanthropy and Remittances from the Hudson Institute

[205] Ted Turner, November 13, 2009, www.wikipedia.com

[206] World Economic Forum in Davos, Switzerland, Bill Gates

[207] Global R&D funding forecast 2009, R&D Magazine, December 2008, www. RDMAG.com

[208] Global R&D funding forecast 2009

[209] Global R&D funding forecast 2009

[210] Hart Rudman commission on national security, 2001

[211] Statistics on small businesses, SBA.gov/advo

[212] Small-business at a glance, various sources, www.entrepreneur.com

[213] Office of Advocacy, U.S. government, 1979 Task Force on Small Business and Innovation

[214] NASA, statistics, www.nasa.org, and other countries, space programs, www. wikipedia.com

[215] David Baker, Inventions from Outer Space, (Random house, May, 2000)

[216] Space travelers, www.cbsnews.com/network/news/space/democurrent.html

[217] NASA web site, www.nasa.org

[218] Futron Corp. every year collects, analyzes, and ranks statistics for space-faring nations and measures them in space competitiveness.

[219] Boeing website, www.boeing.com

[220] Golf's impact on U.S. economy, www. PGA Tour.com

[221] Golden Book of the Olympics

[222] "Finishing the job, mobile phone access will soon be universal, a special report on telecoms in emerging markets," The Economist, September 26, 2009

[223] Nick Murray

[224] Redwood Neuroscience Institute, www.rni.org

[225] Task force on the future of American innovation, www.futureofinnovation.org

[226] IBM marketing

[227] ,speech, American leadership in the world, Supachai Panitchpakdi, Www. WTO.org

[228] Cordell Hull, www.WTO.org

[229] Jude Hayes, University of Illinois professor, "U.S., other free-trade leaders, now among most vulnerable to backlash," www.news.Illinois.edu

230 Venture impact, Economic importance of venture capital-backed companies in the U.S. economy, National Venture Capital Association, www.nvca.org

231 Dow Jones, top destinations for venture capital, second-quarter 2009, www.DowJones.com

232 Venture impact, Economic importance of venture capital-backed companies into the U.S. economy

233 Venture impact, Economic importance of venture capital-backed companies into the U.S. history

234 Rightsizing U.S. venture capital industry, Kauffman Foundation, www.Kauffman.org, Social Science Research Network, papers, www.papers.ssrn.com/sol3/papers.cfm?abstract_id=1456431

235 "The United States of Entrepreneurs: Report on entrepreneurship," *The Economist*, March 14, 2009

236 "The United States of Entrepreneurs," *The Economist*

237 Rightsizing the U.S. venture capital industry, Kauffman Foundation

238 Katherine Rampell, "Women still not half of workforce," *New York Times*, December 10, 2009

239 Peter G. Peterson, "Businesses missing in action," *Businessweek*, November 16, 2009

240 Homicide rate in 2004, crime in United States, www.wikipedia.com

241 crime in the United States, www.wikipedia.com

242 Joe Carson, Alliance Bernstein fixed income, U.S. economic update

243 Entitlements, www.UpwithAmerica.org

244 Conference on innovation, Chicago 2007

245 Choosing a College Major: The Stigma of the Undeclared Label , www.| http://colleges.suite101.com/article.cfm/choosing_a_college_major

246 United States, www.wikipedia.com

247 Studies by Hosier and Dowd, 1987; Analysis by Ready and Ready, 1994

248 "How many Mexicans does it take to drill an oil well?" *The Economist*, October 3, 2009

249 Rob Katz, "Micro-finance plan received Nobel prize," World Resources Institute, October 13, 2006

250 Mark Zandi, "Economy.com, an FDA for consumers of financial products," *Philadelphia Inquirer*, November 8, 2009

251 Mark Zandi, excerpt from an article. "How to Prevent the Next Crisis, Recession Wire, June, 29, 2009, www. http://www.recessionwire.com/2009/06/29/mark-zandi-book-excerpt/?281f3420

252 What's great about America, www.Heritage.org/research/political philosophy

253 World Health Organization, 2000

254 United States, poverty, www.wikipedia.com

255 Radley Balko, "America Mired in Morass of Laws and Regulations," Foxnews.com

256 Radley Balko, "America Mired in Morass of Laws and Regulations,"

257 Hernando DeSoto, "A global meltdown rule number one, do the math," *Los Angeles Times*, opinion, April 12, 2009

258 Employee Benefit Research Institute, www.EBRI.org (2007 figures adjusted to 2009)

259 Lobby estimates for various industries, www.Open secrets.org

260 Market commentary, Ed Yardeni on policy, David Kojak, chairman and chief executive officer, Cumberland Advisors, October 8, 2009

261 Paul Craig Roberts, "The rich have stolen the economy," www.counterpunch.org, October 16, 2005

262 Radley Balko, "America Mired in Morass of Laws and Regulations,"

263 Ambassador Terry Miller and Anthony B. Kim, "High corporate taxes undermine U.S. global competitiveness," The Heritage Foundation, www.heritage.org/research

264 "Biocycle, the State of Garbage in America," December 2008, volume 29, number 12, page 22, www.jgpress.com/archives/_free/000848.html

265 Waste and recycling data maps and graphs, www.ZerowasteAmerica.org

266 Quote from Karl Popper in article by Jonah Lehrer, "Lost in the Details, How breaking everything down to particles blinds scientists to the big picture", *Wired*, May 2010

Made in the USA
Charleston, SC
20 July 2010